PAULA DEEN
& Friends

Family Favorite Recipes

PAULA DEEN
&Friends

Family Favorite Recipes

Living
It Up
Southern
Style!

PAULA DEEN WITH MARTHA NESBIT

RODALE

This exclusive direct mail edition, published by Rodale Inc. in 2012 under license from Simon & Schuster,
includes text and photos from *Paula Deen & Friends: Living It Up, Southern Style* and *Paula Deen Celebrates!:
Best Dishes and Best Wishes for the Best Times of Your Life.*

Printed in the United States of America

Rodale Inc. makes every effort to use acid-free ♾, recycled paper ♻.

Book design by Carol Angstadt

Library of Congress Cataloging-in-Publication Data is on file with the publisher.

ISBN 978–1–60961–923–7

2   4   6   8   10   9   7   5   3   hardcover

We inspire and enable people to improve their lives and the world around them.

For more of our products, visit rodalestore.com or call 800-848-4735.

Contents

Introduction

Hey, y'all! The way I look at it, life's all about your family and your friends—after all, what's more important than the people we love? And for me, the best way to show them how much they mean to me is by heading to the kitchen and cooking up a storm. When you think about it, what's a birthday celebration or a cookout or even Sunday-night supper but a chance to do something special for the people who mean so much to us? Food has always been a big part of our family celebrations, but one thing I've learned is that you don't really need a special occasion to bake a cake or whip up some fried chicken. Having a great home-cooked dish with your family and friends is totally underrated.

I've been so blessed in so many ways—my wonderful husband, Michael; my sons, Jamie and Bobby, and my stepchildren, Michelle and Anthony; my brother, Bubba; and dozens of amazing friends who've been there for me through thick and thin. I've got a ton of people to be thankful for—and a never-ending list of reasons to celebrate! When we're all together, grateful for each other and enjoying each other's company, it's just natural—and fun—to eat together. And nothing makes me happier than fixin' something delicious!

I feel so fortunate every single day, and I bet you do, too. You have incredible people in your life, too—maybe a sister who shares your sense of humor or a friend who shares her chocolate-chip cookies, children who surprise you with special gifts or their funny homemade valentines, or a spouse who loves you even when you're itchin' for a fight. I'm pretty sure you've got a lot to celebrate, just like I do.

So I'd like to share with y'all this exclusive edition of *Paula Deen & Friends: Family Favorite Recipes*. It's chockful of dishes from me and my friends that I just know you're gonna love, too. With my good friend Martha Nesbit, food editor of *Savannah Magazine*, we spent hours thinking about how our friends like to cook and entertain—and we put together a long list of events they'd hosted, from christening parties to tailgates to Saturday-evening barbecues. Then we set out to find the recipes that went with each party, going to some of the best southern cooks we know and begging them for their favorite recipes. We threw in some of our own favorites, too, and as I do on my show, I tried to provide tips whenever I could to help you whip up these recipes just right.

You'll find easy, down-home recipes for everything from soup to nuts, appetizers to desserts. And along the way you'll read lots of stories and get to know my friends and family who contributed recipes—or who just like to eat! And at the end of every section, I think you'll like the menu suggestions—I don't know about y'all, but even though I love to cook, planning a menu always throws me into a tizzy!

There is nothing that makes my heart sing like the joy of loving friends and devoted family members. And there is nothing in the world that I love more than spending time with these wonderful people, laughing, talking—and, yes, eating! I have to tell ya, I've met Oprah, and I've cooked for President Jimmy Carter, and I've had my own cooking show on TV—heck, I've even been to Hollywood! But nothing compares to the delight of just sitting down at my kitchen table and sharing a cup of coffee and some homemade buttermilk pound cake with Michael and the kids.

My life has been an amazing journey, and when I think about it, what comes to mind is always the wonderful people and the good food. It's my wish for all of you that these recipes will mean as much to you on your journey as they have to me on mine. Having good friends and family to share your cooking with is the best blessing any of us can have. I feel so blessed every day. I hope you do, too.

It's all about family and friends, food and fun. So enjoy! As always, y'all, I send you best dishes and love from my kitchen to yours.

BREAKFAST & BRUNCH

Spinach and Bacon Quiche

6 eggs, beaten

1½ cups milk

Salt and pepper

2 cups chopped fresh baby spinach, packed

1 pound cooked bacon, crumbled

1½ cups shredded Swiss cheese

One 9-inch refrigerated piecrust, fitted into a 9-inch glass pie plate

1. Preheat the oven to 375°F.

2. Combine the eggs, milk, and salt and pepper to taste in a food processor or blender. Layer the spinach, bacon, and cheese in the bottom of the piecrust, then pour the egg mixture on top.

3. Bake for 35 to 45 minutes, until the egg mixture is set. Cut into 8 wedges.

Serves 8

Sausage Balls

Put these out in a pretty basket and let the kids grab one or two while they are waiting on the real meal!

One 1-pound package ground sausage

3 cups Bisquick baking mix

4 cups grated sharp Cheddar cheese

⅛ teaspoon pepper, or more if desired

1. Preheat the oven to 375°F. Spray a 15-by-10-by-1-inch baking sheet with vegetable oil cooking spray.

2. Combine all of the ingredients in a large glass bowl; mix well with your fingers. The mixture will be very crumbly. Form into 1-inch balls, squeezing the mixture so it holds together, then rolling it between the palms of your hands to form balls. Then place the balls on the prepared baking sheet.

3. Bake for 18 to 20 minutes, until golden brown. To prevent sticking, move the sausage balls with a spatula halfway through cooking. Cool, then remove from the cookie sheet.

Makes 5 dozen

Mushroom and Sausage Quiche

This makes a huge, rich quiche. Leave out the sausage and you have a basic mushroom quiche.

One 9-inch refrigerated piecrust, fitted into a 9-inch glass pie plate

One 1-pound package ground sausage

1 tablespoon butter

½ pound fresh mushrooms, sliced

½ large Vidalia onion, chopped

4 eggs

1 cup sour cream

1 cup cottage cheese, 2% or 4% milkfat

3 tablespoons all-purpose flour

3 tablespoons freshly grated Parmesan cheese

1 teaspoon hot sauce

One 8-ounce package shredded sharp Cheddar cheese

1. Preheat the oven to 350°F. Crimp the edges of the crust.

2. In a large skillet, cook and drain the sausage, and set aside. Wipe out the pan, and in the same pan, melt the butter over medium-high heat. Add the mushrooms and onion, and sauté for 5 minutes, or until tender.

3. Place the eggs, sour cream, cottage cheese, flour, Parmesan cheese, and hot sauce in a food processor and process until smooth, stopping to scrape down the sides of the bowl.

4. Stir together the crumbled sausage, mushroom mixture, egg mixture, and Cheddar cheese, and spoon into the piecrust. Cover the edges of the piecrust with aluminum foil to prevent the crust from burning.

5. Bake for 50 to 60 minutes, until golden brown and the center is set. Cool for 10 minutes and cut into 8 wedges.

Serves 8

Breakfast Casserole

You surely don't want to be up cooking bacon and eggs after a sleepless night. Preheat the oven, pop this in, and the whole house will wake up to the smell of something yummy. As a matter of fact, you have to make this savory casserole the night before the party so the bread soaks up all the seasoned egg mixture.

5 slices thick-sliced white bread, crust and all, buttered and cubed

1 pound mild sausage, cooked, crumbled, and drained

3 cups grated extra-sharp Cheddar cheese

4 eggs

2 cups milk

1 teaspoon dry mustard

1 teaspoon salt

1 teaspoon hot sauce

1. Spray a 1½-quart casserole dish with vegetable oil cooking spray. Place the bread cubes in the casserole. Evenly distribute the sausage over the bread cubes. Sprinkle evenly with the cheese. Combine the eggs, milk, mustard, salt, and hot sauce and mix well. Pour the egg mixture over the bread. Cover with plastic wrap and refrigerate overnight.

2. The next morning, remove the casserole from the refrigerator and allow it to sit on the counter for 15 minutes while you preheat the oven to 350°F. Remove the plastic wrap, place the casserole in the oven, and bake for 1 hour.

Serves 6 to 8

Hash Brown Casserole

Well, you know how I love meat and potatoes, so I've used both sausage and prepared hash browns to make this eggy casserole an extra-hearty dish. I love that you have to make this ahead of time: at least eight hours or up to a day in advance.

I'd serve this for Sunday brunch anytime, with biscuits and a fresh fruit salad.

3 tablespoons butter

1 small yellow onion, chopped

4 cups frozen shredded hash browns

8 cups cubed French or Italian bread, crusts removed

1 pound bulk sausage, mild, hot, or sage

2 cups (½ pound) grated Gruyère cheese

2 cups (½ pound) freshly grated Romano cheese

2¼ cups whole milk

8 large eggs

1 teaspoon salt

¼ teaspoon pepper

¼ teaspoon freshly grated nutmeg

2 tablespoons Dijon mustard

1. Spray a deep 13-by-9-inch casserole with vegetable oil cooking spray. Melt the butter in a large frying pan. Add the onion and sauté over medium-low heat until soft, about 5 minutes. Add the hash browns and break apart. Sauté until soft, about 5 minutes. Place the bread cubes in the bottom of the casserole. Spread the onion and hash browns evenly over the bread cubes.

2. Sauté the sausage in the same pan as the potatoes, breaking apart large clumps. When the sausage is cooked through, remove it with a slotted spoon and distribute it evenly over the hash browns. Distribute the grated cheeses evenly over the sausage.

3. In a large mixing bowl, combine the milk, eggs, salt, pepper, nutmeg, and mustard, whisking briskly to blend. Pour over the cheese. Cover with plastic wrap and chill overnight or at least 8 hours.

4. Remove the casserole from the refrigerator 30 minutes before baking. Preheat the oven to 350°F. Bake the casserole, uncovered, for 45 to 50 minutes, until puffed and golden brown.

Serves 8 to 10

Crab and Spinach Casserole

This is a perfect dish if you love the combination of spinach and crabmeat, which I do.

Two 10-ounce packages frozen leaf spinach

½ cup (1 stick) butter

1 clove garlic, minced

2 tablespoons grated yellow onion

⅓ cup all-purpose flour

3 cups whole milk (not 1% or 2%)

1 cup (¼ pound) grated Swiss cheese

1 cup half-and-half

2 teaspoons fresh lemon juice

Pinch of garlic powder

Dash of freshly grated nutmeg

1 teaspoon salt

¼ teaspoon cayenne pepper

2 pounds fresh crabmeat, picked through twice for shells

1 cup fresh bread crumbs

1. Preheat the broiler. Butter a shallow 2-quart baking dish or eight ovenproof individual ramekins or scallop shells.

2. Thaw the spinach in its package in the refrigerator overnight or defrost in the microwave following the package directions. Remove the packaging and sauté the spinach in 2 tablespoons of the butter in a 12-inch skillet over medium heat with the garlic and onion for 3 minutes. Drain the spinach mixture and chop finely. Transfer the spinach to the baking dish.

3. Melt 4 tablespoons of the butter in a 2-quart saucepan. Stir in the flour and whisk until smooth. Over low heat, gradually add the milk, stirring constantly with a spoon until smooth and thickened, 8 to 10 minutes. When the sauce has thickened, add the cheese, half-and-half, lemon juice, garlic powder, nutmeg, salt, and cayenne. Cook over low heat until thickened again, about 10 minutes. Remove the sauce from the heat and carefully fold in the crabmeat.

4. Pour the mixture over the spinach. Sprinkle with the bread crumbs and dot with the remaining 2 tablespoons of butter. (You may need more bread crumbs and butter if you are preparing individual ramekins.)

5. Broil about 5 minutes, until browned.

Serves 8

Note: This dish can be prepared ahead and refrigerated covered. When ready to cook, preheat the oven to 350°F and bake for about 30 minutes, until bubbly. Change the oven setting to broil and broil the top for about 5 minutes.

Beason Breakfast Burritos

Carole Beason, a landscape designer in Savannah, created this recipe when camping with her husband, Fred, and sons, Ben and Thomas. Not only delicious for camping, these packets can be prepared and frozen for a tasty breakfast at the ready.

1 egg per person

1 tablespoon butter per person

Salt and pepper

1 corn or flour tortilla per person

1 tablespoon cooked, crumbled bulk sausage per person

1 tablespoon grated Monterey Jack cheese per person

Sour cream

Salsa

1. Scramble the eggs in the butter and add salt and pepper to taste.

2. Lay each tortilla on a large square of heavy-duty aluminum foil. Spoon a scoop of eggs on each tortilla. Add a tablespoon each of sausage and cheese. Wrap the tortilla around the filling and wrap tightly in the foil, rolling the ends to completely seal the package. Freeze. Place the packages in your cooler for the camping trip.

3. Cook the packages over hot coals for 5 to 6 minutes, until heated through. (The tortillas will burn on the bottom if you leave them on the grill grates too long). Serve with sour cream and salsa.

Note: To prepare on the stovetop, warm the tortillas in the oven. Prepare the eggs as above. Spoon a scoop of eggs on each tortilla. Add a tablespoon each of sausage and cheese. Wrap the tortilla around the filling and serve.

Sausage Swirls

Two ingredients? We're not kidding! You can't believe how easy and delicious these little numbers are. You can also bake them in advance. Reheat them in a warm oven and they'll taste like you just made them.

Two 8-ounce cans refrigerated crescent dinner rolls

1 pound ground sausage, mild for kids, hot for adults, or sage if you prefer

1. Separate 1 can of dough and form into 4 rectangles. Firmly press the perforations to seal. Take the uncooked sausage and cut it into 8 chunks. Using 4 chunks of the sausage, spread each of the rectangles with a thin layer (about ⅛ inch thick). Starting at the short end, roll each rectangle tightly into a cylinder. Repeat with the other can of dough and remaining sausage. Place on a plate, cover with plastic wrap, and chill until firm, about 30 minutes, then cut each roll into 4 slices.

2. When ready to bake, preheat the oven to 375°F. Place the sausage swirls ½ inch apart on ungreased baking sheets. Bake for 18 to 20 minutes, until golden brown and the sausage is thoroughly cooked.

Makes 32 swirls

Baked Tomatoes

The topping is nice and spicy, the perfect contrast to the rich crabmeat. This recipe makes even winter tomatoes taste delicious.

4 ripe tomatoes

½ cup (1 stick) butter

2 cups fresh bread crumbs

¼ cup freshly grated Parmesan cheese

1 teaspoon Worcestershire sauce

1 teaspoon salt

½ teaspoon pepper

1 teaspoon dried thyme

¼ teaspoon hot sauce (I like Texas Pete)

1. Preheat the oven to 350°F.

2. Slice the stem ends off the tomatoes. Cut the tomatoes in half and place cut side up in a 13-by-9-inch baking dish.

3. In a 10-inch skillet over low heat, melt the butter. Stir in the bread crumbs, cheese, Worcestershire sauce, salt, pepper, thyme, and hot sauce. Place 2 tablespoons of the mixture over each tomato half.

4. Bake for 30 minutes, until the topping is browned.

Serves 8

Broiled Parmesan Tomatoes

A recipe like this, which is quick and easy and delicious, makes it easy on the hostesses. Tomatoes always taste so good with brunch food.

Tomatoes are canned by weight, which means that one 14½-ounce can might have eight small tomatoes in it, and the next one might have six. Count on each can having six tomatoes; better to have leftovers! Each guest would have one tomato.

Three 14½-ounce cans whole tomatoes, drained, any variety, including Italian plum

Salt and pepper

½ cup (1 stick) butter

1½ cups freshly grated Parmesan cheese

Place the tomatoes in a 13-by-9-inch casserole dish. Sprinkle with salt and pepper to taste and top each with a pat of butter. Generously sprinkle the cheese over the tomatoes and broil for 10 to 15 minutes, until the tomatoes are heated through and the cheese is bubbly.

Serves 16

Praline French Toast Casserole

Everyone will love this! It's very rich, so it goes a long way.

8 eggs

1½ cups half-and-half

⅓ cup maple syrup

⅓ cup packed light brown sugar

10 to 12 slices soft bread, 1 inch thick

Topping

½ cup (1 stick) butter

½ cup packed light brown sugar

⅔ cup maple syrup

2 cups chopped pecans

1. Generously butter a 13-by-9-inch casserole dish.

2. Mix the eggs, half-and-half, maple syrup, and sugar in a large bowl. Place the bread slices in the prepared casserole dish and cover with the egg mixture. Cover with plastic wrap and let soak overnight in the refrigerator.

3. Preheat the oven to 350°F. Remove the casserole from the refrigerator.

4. Make the topping: Melt the butter in a saucepan. Add the sugar and maple syrup and cook for 1 to 2 minutes. Stir in the pecans. Pour the mixture over the bread and bake for 45 to 55 minutes. Allow to sit for 10 minutes before serving.

Serves 8

Sweet Noodle Kugel

Everybody's favorite! Robbie Hollander created this recipe with a little of this and a little of that from several recipes that she liked.

1 pound wide egg noodles, cooked and drained

1 cup (2 sticks) butter, melted

1 pound cottage cheese

2 cups regular or reduced-fat (2% or 4%) sour cream

1 teaspoon ground cinnamon

1 cup sugar

2 teaspoons vanilla extract

6 eggs, beaten

½ cup raisins (optional)

One 8-ounce can crushed pineapple, drained (optional)

1. Preheat the oven to 350°F. Grease a 13-by-9-inch baking dish.

2. Combine the warm noodles and butter in a large glass bowl. Add the cottage cheese, sour cream, cinnamon, sugar, and vanilla and stir gently. Add the eggs and mix gently but thoroughly. Add the raisins and pineapple, if using. Pour into the prepared baking dish and bake for 1 hour.

Serves 12

Baked Cheese Grits

A Southern favorite. This goes well with seafood, too.

6 cups chicken broth
  (canned is fine)

1 teaspoon salt

¼ teaspoon pepper

2 cups regular grits

  One 16-ounce package
  cheese food, cut up

½ cup milk

4 eggs, beaten

½ cup (1 stick) butter

1 cup grated sharp Cheddar
  cheese

1. Preheat the oven to 350°F. Grease a 4-quart casserole dish.

2. Bring the broth, salt, and pepper to a boil in a 2-quart saucepan. Stir in the grits and whisk until completely combined. Reduce the heat to low and simmer until the grits are thick, about 8 minutes. Add the cheese and milk and stir. Gradually stir in the eggs and butter, stirring until all are combined. Pour the mixture into the prepared casserole dish. Sprinkle with the Cheddar cheese and bake for 45 minutes, or until set.

Serves 12

Kentucky Spoon Bread

Spoon bread should be crusty and brown around the edges, and creamy in the center. This recipe goes a long way, as guests generally take just a tablespoonful.

3 cups whole milk

1¼ cups white cornmeal

2 tablespoons butter, melted

3 eggs, well beaten

2 teaspoons baking powder

1 teaspoon salt

1. Bring the milk to a boil in a medium saucepan. Add the cornmeal and stir rapidly with a whisk until smooth. Reduce the heat to very low and continue to cook, stirring occasionally, for 3 to 5 minutes, until the mixture becomes very thick. Remove from the heat and let cool.

2. Preheat the oven to 375°F. Grease a 2-quart casserole dish.

3. Place the cooled mixture in a large mixing bowl; add the butter, eggs, baking powder, and salt. Mix with an electric mixer until combined and free from lumps, about 5 minutes. Pour into the prepared casserole dish and bake for 30 minutes. Serve hot with plenty of butter on the side.

Serves 12

Vidalia Onion Corn Bread

Vidalia, Georgia, is the home of the best onion ever created—the Vidalia sweet onion. Vidalia onions get sweeter when they are cooked, so this is sort of a sweet-savory corn bread. If you can't get Vidalias, you can use any sweet onion that your market sells.

¼ cup (½ stick) butter

1 large Vidalia or other sweet onion, chopped

One 8-ounce package corn bread mix

1 egg, beaten

⅓ cup whole milk

1 cup sour cream

1 cup grated sharp Cheddar cheese

¼ teaspoon salt

¼ teaspoon dried dill weed

1. Preheat the oven to 450°F. Spray an 8-inch square baking pan with vegetable oil cooking spray.

2. In a medium saucepan, melt the butter and sauté the onion until tender but not brown, about 3 minutes. Remove the pan from the heat and add the muffin mix, egg, milk, sour cream, ½ cup of the cheese, the salt, and dill weed. Stir to combine. Pour into the prepared pan and top with the remaining ½ cup cheese. Bake for 30 minutes, until set and a toothpick inserted into the center of the corn bread comes out clean. Allow to cool slightly before cutting into squares.

Makes about 16 squares

Lace Hoecake Corn Bread

2 cups plain enriched white cornmeal, sifted

1 teaspoon salt

Vegetable oil

1. Combine the cornmeal, salt, and 2½ cups water and allow the mixture to sit for a few minutes.

2. Spray a flat hoe skillet with vegetable oil cooking spray and drizzle with approximately 1½ tablespoons of oil. Heat the skillet over medium heat. Pour about three 2-ounce ladlefuls of the batter onto the skillet. The batter will sizzle and have a lacy appearance. If the batter gets too thick, add a bit of water. When the edges are slightly brown, place a wet glass plate over the hoecake. With a pot holder, grab the handle of the pan and flip the plate and pan so the hoecake falls onto the plate. Slide the hoecake off the plate back into the pan to cook the other side, and cook until golden brown.

3. Stir the batter and add additional oil to the pan before making your next hoecake.

Makes 8 to 10 large hoecakes, or 24 to 36 small hoecakes

Note: If you do not have a hoe skillet, make small (2- to 3-inch) hoecakes in a flat, cast-iron skillet.

Buttermilk Corn Bread

Here's your basic buttermilk corn bread. Southerners like theirs with butter and jelly (Bubbles served mayhaw jelly) or syrup. Mayhaw jelly is made from the tart red berries of the mayhaw trees that grow only in southwest Georgia; try the Internet for mail-order sources. It's worth the search!

1 cup yellow cornmeal
⅓ cup all-purpose flour
1 teaspoon baking powder
½ teaspoon salt
¼ teaspoon baking soda
1 egg, beaten
1 cup buttermilk

1. Preheat the oven to 400°F. Grease well a 9-inch square pan or two nonstick 12-cup miniature muffin tins.

2. Combine all of the dry ingredients in a small mixing bowl. Add the egg and buttermilk. Stir with a fork until just blended. Pour the batter into the prepared pan. Bake for 20 minutes for a square pan, or 15 minutes for miniature muffins. Serve with butter and mayhaw jelly. (Some guests asked for maple syrup with their corn bread muffins, but they were flat out of luck.)

Makes 16 small squares or 24 miniature muffins

Green Chili Corn Muffins

These little muffins are so beautiful. Put them in a big basket and let guests help themselves.

1¼ cups stone-ground cornmeal

½ teaspoon salt

2 teaspoons baking powder

1 cup shredded sharp Cheddar cheese

One 8-ounce can cream-style corn

1 cup sour cream

One 4-ounce can chopped green chilies

½ cup canola oil

2 eggs, lightly beaten

1. Preheat the oven to 400°F. Spray miniature muffin tins with vegetable oil cooking spray.

2. In a small mixing bowl, combine the cornmeal, salt, and baking powder, stirring with a metal spoon. Add the cheese, corn, sour cream, and chilies. Stir until lightly combined. Add the oil and eggs and stir until everything is just combined; do not overmix. The batter will be very stiff.

3. Place about ½ tablespoon of batter into each muffin cup. Bake for 18 to 20 minutes. Serve warm.

Makes 48 miniature muffins

Sandee's Challah

Challah is the braided egg bread eaten on the Sabbath and many holidays. This recipe comes from Sandee Eichholz.

1 teaspoon salt

⅓ cup sugar

3¾ cups flour (half bread flour and half all-purpose flour)

One ¼-ounce envelope active dry yeast

2 eggs, beaten, plus 1 egg for glaze

¼ cup vegetable oil, plus more for greasing bowl

Sesame or poppy seeds

Butter for glazing

1. In a food processor, pulse the salt, sugar, and flour to combine.

2. Soak the yeast for 10 minutes in 1 cup water that is warm to the wrist but not hot enough to kill the yeast (between 105° and 115°F). Add the yeast to the food processor, then add the eggs and oil. Process until the mixture forms a ball on the steel processor blade. (If the weather is humid, you may have to add more flour, 1 tablespoon at a time.) Place the dough in an oiled bowl and turn to coat all sides. Cover with a towel and let rise in a warm place for about 1½ hours, or until doubled in size.

3. Divide the dough into 3 pieces. Roll each into a long skinny log. Braid the dough, tucking in the ends. Place the braided dough on a cookie sheet and let rise, covered, for 1 hour.

4. Preheat the oven to 350°F.

5. Brush the risen loaf with beaten egg and sprinkle with sesame or poppy seeds. Bake for 30 minutes, or until golden. While the bread is hot, rub with a stick of butter to glaze it.

Serves 10 to 12

Bob's Dutch-Oven Bread

Imagine serving this hot baked bread to hungry Scouts at the end of a long day. I suspect this would earn you some Brownie points! This is prepared over a charcoal fire. We do not recommend wood, as different woods burn at different temperatures, and you are trying to "bake" the bread at a consistent temperature. Robert English, of Savannah, makes a tripod with sticks and hangs his Dutch oven in the center.

One ¼-ounce envelope active dry yeast

2¼ cups Bisquick baking mix

½ cup milk

Butter

1. Spray a cast-iron Dutch oven with vegetable oil cooking spray and heat over the coals.

2. Place the yeast and Bisquick in a large resealable plastic bag and shake to combine. Add the milk and knead through the bag until you have a stiff, smooth dough. Shape into a rounded loaf and place in the bottom of the Dutch oven.

3. Place the Dutch oven over about 12 coals; cover with the lid and place about 12 coals on top. Check in about 10 minutes to make sure the top and bottom of the bread are browning but not burning. Remove or add coals if necessary. Bread should cook for 25 to 30 minutes. Remove from the Dutch oven, slice the bread, and serve warm with butter.

Note: To prepare in the oven, preheat the oven to 350°F. Spray a 9-inch baking pan with vegetable oil cooking spray. Combine the yeast and Bisquick in a large bowl. Add the milk and mix to form soft dough. Turn the dough out onto a surface lightly dusted with Bisquick. Knead gently for 3 minutes; let dough rest for 15 minutes. Place the dough in the prepared pan and bake for 22 to 25 minutes.

Garlic Cheese Biscuits

These are almost better the day after than when you first make them. It's the garlic butter that makes them so tasty. Leftovers (if there are any!) can be refrigerated. When ready to serve, split and reheat biscuits in a toaster oven for about 3 minutes at 300°F.

1¼ cups Bisquick baking mix

½ cup grated sharp Cheddar cheese

¼ cup (½ stick) butter, melted

¼ teaspoon garlic powder

¼ teaspoon salt

⅛ teaspoon dried parsley flakes

1. Preheat the oven to 400°F. Line a baking sheet with parchment paper.

2. Combine the Bisquick and cheese in a small bowl. Add ⅓ cup water and stir just until combined. The dough will be slightly moist. Drop the dough by tablespoonfuls onto the prepared baking sheet. Bake for about 10 minutes, until firm and beginning to brown.

3. While the biscuits are baking, make the garlic butter. In a small bowl, combine the butter, garlic powder, salt, and parsley flakes. Mix well.

4. As soon as you bring the biscuits from the oven, brush them with garlic butter, using a pastry brush.

Makes 12 small biscuits

Southern Biscuits

Jane Wells got this basic biscuit recipe from an old cookbook. She bakes the biscuits well in advance and freezes them.

2 cups all-purpose flour, plus more for dusting work surface

1 tablespoon baking powder

1 teaspoon salt

1 tablespoon sugar

⅓ cup vegetable shortening

⅔ cup whole milk

1. Preheat the oven to 450°F. Spray a cookie sheet with vegetable oil cooking spray.

2. Place the flour, baking powder, salt, and sugar in a food processor. Pulse four times to combine the dry ingredients. Add the shortening and process until the shortening is completely incorporated. Add ⅓ cup of the milk and pulse four times. Add 1 tablespoon more milk and pulse four times. If the dough holds together, stop adding milk. If you need more, add a little more.

3. When the dough holds together, turn it out onto a floured board. Roll or pat out about ¼ inch thick. Cut out biscuits with a 1½- or 2-inch cutter. Place the biscuits on the prepared cookie sheet and bake for 8 minutes. Let cool on wire racks. Freeze on cookie sheets. When frozen, place in resealable plastic bags.

4. When ready to serve, preheat the oven to 375°F. Remove the biscuits from the freezer and place on cookie sheets. Allow to thaw at room temperature. Bake for about 5 minutes. Let cool. Serve with country ham.

Makes about 30 small biscuits

Butterhorns

These yeasty, buttery light rolls are gorgeous to look at and easy to eat.

1 package (1 scant
   tablespoon) active dry
   yeast
½ cup plus 1 teaspoon sugar
½ cup (1 stick) butter, melted
3 eggs, beaten
4 cups all-purpose flour
1 teaspoon salt
   Butter, softened

1. In a small glass dish, add the yeast and 1 teaspoon of the sugar to 1 cup lukewarm water. Allow the mixture to sit until the yeast begins to bubble, about 10 minutes.

2. In a medium mixing bowl, combine the butter, the remaining ½ cup sugar, and the eggs. Add the yeast mixture and stir well. Sift together the flour and salt. Add the flour to the yeast mixture and stir well. Place the dough into a large greased bowl and turn the dough to grease all sides. Cover with plastic wrap and refrigerate the dough overnight.

3. Punch the dough down and divide in half with a sharp knife. On a heavily floured surface, roll out half the dough into a large circle about ¼ inch thick. Using a pizza cutter, cut the dough into 16 wedges. Roll up each wedge from wide end to the tip, making a crescent. Repeat with the other half of the dough. Place each roll onto a baking sheet lined with parchment paper and cover with a clean, lightweight tea towel. Allow to rise in a warm place for about 1 hour, until doubled in size.

4. Preheat the oven to 375°F.

5. Bake the rolls for 10 to 12 minutes, until lightly browned.

6. Rub the tops of the rolls with softened butter immediately after they come out of the oven. Serve warm.

Makes 32 rolls

Note: The rolls may also be underbaked (tops will just begin to brown), allowed to cool completely, then stored in the freezer in resealable plastic bags. When ready to serve, thaw for about 30 minutes at room temperature. Reheat for 3 minutes at 350°F.

Sourdough Garlic Herb Bread

Alice J. Giddens, Martha Nesbit's mother, makes her own sourdough bread, which she often takes to shut-ins and dialysis patients; it's also a hit at Keen-ager luncheons (see page 76). You can buy sourdough loaves from any good supermarket bakery. Slice it yourself, or buy it already sliced.

Sourdough bread—at least 1 slice per person

Olive oil

Garlic salt

Fines herbes (equal parts dried parsley, chervil, chives, and tarragon, mixed well)

1. Preheat the oven to 350°F.

2. Place the bread slices on baking sheets. With a pastry brush, brush each slice of bread with olive oil. Sprinkle with garlic salt and a smattering of fines herbes. Bake for about 10 minutes, until the bread just begins to brown.

3. Serve in large baskets in the center of each table.

Blueberry Gems

These tender little muffins taste like dessert! The flavor of sweet fresh blueberries is just perfect with the Crab and Spinach Casserole (page 6) and Baked Tomatoes (page 9). I don't have to tell ya just how important a colorful table is to me—and with the creamy white-and-green crab and spinach casserole, the bright red baked tomatoes, and these brown-and-blue blueberry muffins, I'm a happy girl.

  2 cups self-rising flour

1½ cups sugar

  2 eggs, lightly beaten

  1 teaspoon vanilla extract

  ½ cup vegetable oil

  ½ cup whole milk

  1 cup blueberries (preferably fresh, but frozen will work)

1. Preheat the oven to 375°F. Line 18 muffin tin cups with paper liners.

2. Combine the flour and sugar in a large bowl. In a smaller bowl, combine the eggs, vanilla, oil, and milk. Whisk together until well combined. Make a well in the center of the flour mixture. Pour in the liquid. Mix with a spoon until the flour is moistened. Gently fold in the blueberries.

3. Spoon the batter into the prepared muffin cups, filling about half to two-thirds full.

4. Bake for 23 to 25 minutes, until nicely browned and puffed.

Makes 18 muffins

Pecan Pie Muffins

What could be better than pecan pie? How about pecan pie muffins! These are great on any brunch table, and I like to bring them along on picnics, too.

½ cup (1 stick) butter, softened

¾ cup packed light brown sugar

2 eggs, beaten

½ cup all-purpose flour

¾ cup chopped pecans

1. Preheat the oven to 350°F. Grease and flour 8 muffin tin cups or use paper liners.

2. In a medium bowl, cream the butter and sugar. Add the eggs and mix well. Add the flour and stir until just combined. Stir in the pecans.

3. Spoon the batter into the prepared muffin cups, filling about two-thirds full.

4. Bake for 25 minutes. Serve warm with more butter!

Makes 8 muffins

Almond Danish Swirls

Crescent rolls again? Yes! This time they're rich and sweet with cream cheese, almonds, and almond glaze. Wez Childers modified a recipe from the thirty-fifth Pillsbury Bake-Off contest cookbook to make individual Danish swirls. The original recipe was one large Danish. Wez has served hundreds of these to church groups and kids. These can be made the day before and stored in a plastic bag in the refrigerator. Bring to room temperature before serving.

6 ounces cream cheese, softened

1 teaspoon almond extract

½ cup confectioners' sugar

4 ounces slivered almonds, chopped fine

Two 8-ounce cans refrigerated crescent dinner rolls

1 egg white

Glaze

⅔ cup confectioners' sugar

4 teaspoons milk

½ teaspoon almond extract

1. In a small bowl, beat the cream cheese, almond extract, and sugar until fluffy. Fold half of the chopped almonds into the cream cheese mixture.

2. Separate 1 can of dough and assemble into 4 rectangles. Firmly press the perforations to seal. Press or roll each piece of dough to form a 7-by-4-inch rectangle, and spread each with about 2 tablespoons of the cream cheese filling to within ¼ inch of the edges. Starting at the short end, roll each rectangle tightly into a cylinder. Repeat with the other can of dough and remaining filling. Place on a plate, cover with plastic wrap, and chill until firm, about 30 minutes.

3. Preheat the oven to 350°F while the rolls are chilling. Remove from the refrigerator and cut each roll into 4 slices. Place ½ inch apart on ungreased baking sheets.

4. In a small bowl, combine the egg white with 1 teaspoon water. Brush over the swirls. Sprinkle with the remaining chopped almonds.

5. Bake for 18 to 20 minutes, until light brown.

6. While the swirls are baking, combine the glaze ingredients in a small bowl. Cool the swirls for 3 minutes on wire racks placed over a sheet of waxed paper. Drizzle the icing over the warm swirls.

Makes 32 swirls

Puttin' It All Together

New Year's Eve Brunch

New Year's Eve is probably my least favorite time to go out. What I really like is to spend the night at home—mine or someone else's. I want to be around old friends, not new people.

Billy and Kathy Lamas's house is the one stop we make—they live close by and we're usually home by midnight. Billy cooks the *best* standing rib roast on the grill and he serves the meat right off the grill just for me! Everyone brings a dish (usually the same one every year), and we have the most wonderful special foods that we all just look forward to digging into—shrimp dip, crab stew, steamed shrimp, and that dried beef and cream cheese dip that men just adore.

Rather than a heavy meal, I think hors d'oeuvres are nice for New Year's. Or, you can take it the other way as we have here, and have a late-night breakfast. Start the party after midnight, and your friends can make it their last stop on the way home. I always take our tree down before New Year's Eve, even though I keep up the rest of the decorations, like Christmas greenery and flowers. It's just an old superstition—my Granddaddy Paul wouldn't allow that tree to be in the house going into a New Year.

Menu

CRAB AND SPINACH CASSEROLE
6

BAKED TOMATOES
9

HASH BROWN CASSEROLE
5

BLUEBERRY GEMS
24

PECAN PIE MUFFINS
25

HUMMINGBIRD CAKE
214

IRISH COFFEE
111

MIMOSAS

CHAMPAGNE AND SPARKLING CIDER

A Christening Brunch

I f there is anything southerners enjoy, it's a christening or baptism, followed by a brunch for family and special friends. Whether the event takes place in a small church or a large cathedral, there is nothing any sweeter than a baby in a christening gown. Of course, no telling how long it has taken the frazzled mom and dad to get the little one dressed and ready for the big day! Although you can always go to a club for a brunch, it's much nicer to do this at home, and if you're organized and have a simple make-ahead meal, I just know you can do it!

It's important to think about who is coming to the party, as you are likely to have children running around as well as grandparents who need a quieter setting. So perhaps you could set up an "adult" area, and have some smaller tables set outside with a teenage babysitter for the children.

Much of this menu comes from Katie Borges, who is in charge of menus and meal preparation at the Isle of Hope United Methodist Church in Savannah. Church members often call upon Katie to prepare the food for their baby's baptismal day. There's no perfect menu, she says. Some people want egg casseroles, others want quiches, and still others want cold salads—chicken, pasta, green, and fruit. (Katie chose a salad lunch after the baptism of her son, Jonathan.) Whatever you choose, Katie recommends that it be a substantial meal. Remember, it's been a long morning!

Menu

Praline French Toast Casserole
10

Baked Cheese Grits
12

Broiled Parmesan Tomatoes
9

Mushroom and Sausage Quiche
3

Spinach and Bacon Quiche
2

Sausage Balls
2

Watermelon Fruit Basket
with Ginger–Poppy Seed Fruit Dressing
270

Animal-Shaped Sugar Cookies
252

A Teenager's Slumber Party

Wez Childers, a preschool teacher and director, has been on dozens of overnight church retreats with elementary- and middle-school kids, and has planned a half-dozen slumber birthday parties for her daughter, Paige. She really knows how to plan a party to please teenage girls, which is something that this mother of two sons never had to do!

Here's Wez's formula for a successful slumber party:

1. Good food.

2. Fun activities that are optional if the kids aren't interested.

3. More good food.

"What you decide to do depends on the mix of personalities you wind up with," Wez says. "I always have plenty of stuff planned, but sometimes you have a group that is happy just watching a movie and eating popcorn."

For groups that need more, Wez organizes activities like:

- A design-your-own-flip-flop party. Buy cheap flip-flops for each guest, and with colorful yarn, paste-on jewels, and artificial flowers, let the girls create their own beach looks.

- A design-your-own-pocketbook party. You provide the jewels and basic pocketbook and let the girls do the rest.

- A T-shirt party—guests add designs and autographs with fabric paint.

- And don't forget the old standby: the hair, makeup, and manicure party. You provide the beauty supplies and let the girls get gorgeous.

- A decorate-your-own-cake party. The individual cakes are a morning-after activity. After the girls have breakfast, they can decorate the cakes and take them home to enjoy later.

You'll notice that all of our recipes serve six. That's because that's all the teenage girls we think each party mom or dad can handle! You can certainly double the recipes if you dare to spend the night with twelve squealing females!

Menu

Nighttime Food

MEXICAN PIZZA
36

OR

CHILI IN A BISCUIT BOWL
59

MOM'S BANANA DESSERT
262

INDIVIDUAL BIRTHDAY CAKES
(FOR THE MORNING AFTER)
207

Morning Food

BREAKFAST CASSEROLE
4

SAUSAGE SWIRLS
8

ALMOND DANISH SWIRLS
26

FRUIT KEBABS
269

LUNCHES & LITE BITES

Mexican Pizza

Save yourself some time and trouble: buy ready-made pizza crusts or use frozen cheese pizzas as the base for your Mexican toppings. Either way, the addition of salsa and Mexican cheese makes this pizza taste "totally awesome." Patty Ronning, of Savannah, provided this recipe.

1 tablespoon vegetable oil

¾ cup sliced fresh mushrooms

¾ cup chopped green bell pepper

Two 12-inch pizza crusts or two 12-inch frozen cheese pizzas

1 cup chopped cooked ham

One 2¼-ounce can sliced black olives, drained

Two 16-ounce jars chunky salsa

Two 8-ounce packages shredded Mexican cheese (Monterey Jack, Cheddar, and other mild cheeses combined; available in most supermarkets in the dairy/cheese section)

Shredded lettuce

Sour cream

1. Position the oven rack at the lowest level. If you have a pizza stone, place it in the oven on the rack. Preheat the oven to 425°F.

2. Heat the oil in a small saucepan and cook the mushrooms and green pepper over medium heat until crisp-tender, about 2 minutes. Distribute the vegetables evenly over the crusts. Distribute the ham and olives evenly over the crusts. Reserve 1 cup of the salsa and spoon the remaining salsa evenly over the 2 pizzas. If you don't have a pizza stone, place the pizzas on a baking sheet. They won't be as crisp as they would be if you had placed them directly on the rack, but this is a lot less messy.

3. Bake the pizzas for 10 to 12 minutes, then sprinkle with the cheese. Bake for 7 minutes more. Serve pizza slices topped with the reserved salsa, shredded lettuce, and sour cream.

Two 12-inch pizzas

Pesto and Feta Pizza

This is a sophisticated pizza for those who don't care for tomato sauce.

½ recipe **Basic Pizza Dough (page 38)**

Cornmeal, for dusting

½ cup **basil pesto, homemade or store-bought**

6 **sun-dried tomatoes, sliced in ribbons**

One 6-ounce jar **marinated artichoke hearts, drained and chopped**

½ cup (2 ounces) **crumbled feta cheese**

½ cup **diced fresh tomato, about 1 small Roma or ½ a beefsteak**

2 cups (½ pound) **shredded mozzarella cheese**

Olive oil

1 teaspoon **freshly grated Parmesan cheese**

1. Preheat the oven to 450°F.

2. Roll out the pizza dough into a 12-inch circle. Place on a cornmeal-dusted pizza stone, pizza pan, or cookie sheet. Roll up the edge slightly to create a ridge around the pizza. Spread the pesto over the crust. Evenly distribute the sun-dried tomatoes, artichoke hearts, feta cheese, and fresh tomato over the dough. Top with the mozzarella cheese. Brush the edge of the pizza with a pastry brush dipped in olive oil and sprinkle Parmesan cheese around the rim.

3. Bake for 16 to 18 minutes, until the cheese is bubbly and the crust is light brown.

Makes 8 slices

Basic Pizza Dough

This is really easy to make and soooo much better than a bought pizza crust.

One ¼-ounce package
active dry yeast, regular or
RapidRise

2 teaspoons salt

4½ to 5 cups bread flour

3 tablespoons olive oil

1. Measure out 1¾ cups warm water (it should be pleasantly warm on your wrist). Sprinkle the yeast on top of the water and allow it to activate, about 10 minutes.

2. Put the salt and 2 cups of the flour into a food processor. Pulse five times to blend. Pour in the yeast and water and pulse five times. Add the olive oil. Add the remaining flour 1 cup at a time, pulsing and scraping the sides of the bowl until well blended. As soon as the mixture is combined, dump it out onto a well-floured board and knead for fifteen turns, until the dough is smooth and elastic.

3. Place the dough in a greased bowl and turn to coat all sides. Cover with plastic wrap or a tea towel. Allow the dough to rise in a warm place for about 45 minutes, until doubled in size, then punch it down. Divide it in half; each half will make one 12-inch pizza. You can make two pizzas, or freeze half the dough for another time. Freeze the dough in a resealable freezer bag. To thaw, remove the bag from the freezer and place in the refrigerator for 24 hours. Roll the dough out while cold, then allow it to come to room temperature before adding toppings.

Makes enough dough for two 12-inch pizzas

Tomato Pie

Everybody fell in love with the tomato pie I made on my cooking show. Well, the following recipe is just a little different from mine. Either recipe you decide to make is sure to be a big hit. This particular recipe was created by caterer Sarah Gaede, who moved from Savannah to become an Episcopal priest. The smell while this is baking is just terrific! Serve it for breakfast, lunch, or dinner.

One 9-inch refrigerated piecrust, fitted into a 9-inch glass pie plate

¾ **pound grated Monterey Jack cheese**

2 **ripe tomatoes, halved lengthwise and cut into thin wedges**

1 **teaspoon dried basil**

1 **teaspoon dried oregano**

½ **teaspoon salt**

⅛ **teaspoon pepper**

2 **green onions, thinly sliced, white and green parts**

2 **tablespoons fresh bread crumbs**

2 **tablespoons butter, melted**

1. Preheat the oven to 425°F.

2. Crimp the edges of the piecrust and prick all over with a fork. Bake for 12 to 15 minutes, until just set and lightly browned. Let cool on a wire rack.

3. Sprinkle the cheese evenly over the crust. Top with overlapping tomato wedges in a circular pattern around the edge of the pie. Sprinkle the basil, oregano, salt, and pepper evenly over the tomatoes. Place the green onions in the center. Sprinkle with the bread crumbs and drizzle the butter over the pie. Bake for 20 minutes. Allow to sit at least 10 minutes before cutting into wedges.

Serves 8 as an appetizer or 4 as a main course

Jamie's Cheeseburger Pies

My son Jamie made these on my Food Network Thanksgiving special. They are oh so good!

1 pound lean ground beef

½ cup finely diced Vidalia onion or other sweet onion

1 teaspoon Montreal Steak Seasoning

1 tablespoon Dale's Steak Seasoning Sauce (available from www.dalesseasoning.com)

5 slices cheese, American, Swiss, or sharp Cheddar

1 sheet frozen puff pastry dough, allowed to sit at room temperature for about 20 minutes

1 egg yolk

1. Preheat the oven to 375°F. Prepare the grill.

2. Mix the ground beef, onion, steak seasoning, and seasoning sauce together (using your hands is the most efficient way to do this). Form into 5 small flat patties. Grill the hamburgers to medium-well. (You may also panfry the patties.) Remove from the grill and top each burger with a slice of cheese.

3. Roll the puff pastry sheet to flatten slightly. Eyeball the sheet and cut it into 5 relatively even rectangles. They don't have to be exact.

4. Cover each burger with a piece of puff pastry and wrap it around the bottom, pinching all of the edges to seal. Place on an ungreased baking sheet, pinched side down.

5. Whisk together the egg yolk and 1 teaspoon water to make an egg wash. Brush each wrapped pastry with the egg wash. Bake for about 15 minutes, until the puff pastry is nice and brown.

Serves 5

Tomato Sandwiches

There is almost nothing a southerner likes better than a tomato sandwich. You'd think these were easy and cheap, but they're neither! Good tomatoes cost an arm and a leg, and you need a whole loaf of bread for just ten sandwiches. There is an art to a perfect tomato sandwich: vine-ripened tomatoes that have been peeled and sliced and drained overnight on paper towels; day-old white bread (your store brand is fine!); and mayonnaise seasoned with seasoned salt. If you don't have ripe tomatoes, don't serve these!

This recipe makes ten large sandwiches, which serves five guests. Make as many as you need for your party. The bread will go farther if the tomatoes are smaller, like Romas, as you can get two rounds out of one slice of bread.

2 vine-ripe or Roma tomatoes, peeled and sliced into about 5 slices

1 loaf day-old thin-sliced white bread

½ cup mayonnaise

1 teaspoon seasoned salt

1. Place the tomato slices on cookie sheets lined with paper towels. Allow to drain for several hours or overnight in the refrigerator.

2. Cut bread rounds with a biscuit cutter the size of the largest tomato slices. Stir together the mayonnaise and seasoned salt.

3. An hour before serving, slather some mayonnaise on a bread round, top with a tomato slice, and cover with another bread round, also slathered with seasoned mayonnaise.

Cucumber Sandwiches

I like to use thin-skinned English cucumbers (also called hothouse cucumbers) for these because they have fewer seeds and a sweeter flavor than the regular supermarket variety. Mix white and pumpernickel breads for interest, if you wish.

1 English cucumber, at least 8 inches long

1 cup mayonnaise

6 tablespoons sour cream

1 tablespoon grated yellow onion

½ teaspoon seasoned salt

Two 1-pound loaves thin-sliced bread, white or pumpernickel or 1 of each

1. Wash the cucumber. Take a fork and score the peel from top to bottom. Trim the ends and slice the cucumber ¼ inch thick; you should have about 25 slices. Place the slices on paper towels to drain.

2. In a small bowl, combine the mayonnaise, sour cream, onion, and seasoned salt. Using a small biscuit cutter or juice glass, cut the bread into rounds the size of the cucumber slices. Spread a bread round with the mayonnaise mixture and place a cucumber on top. Top with a second bread round.

Makes about 25 sandwiches

Cheese Sandwiches

Cheese, pecans, and pepper? It's delicious, I promise!

2 cups (½ pound) grated Cheddar cheese

½ cup finely chopped pecans

½ cup mayonnaise, plus extra for spreading on the bread

1 tablespoon grated yellow onion

¼ teaspoon black pepper

⅛ teaspoon cayenne pepper

One 1-pound loaf thin-sliced white bread (store brand or Pepperidge Farm)

In a medium bowl, combine the cheese, pecans, mayonnaise, onion, black pepper, and cayenne pepper. Mix well. Spread some mayonnaise on one side of each slice of the bread, then spread with the cheese mixture and top with a second slice. Trim the crusts, if desired, and cut into triangles or fingers.

Makes 12 to 15 sandwiches, enough for 24 to 30 triangles or 36 to 45 fingers

Ginger-Nut Sandwiches

This was one of the most unusual sandwich spreads and one of the best!

1 cup chopped pecans

One 8-ounce package cream cheese, softened

1 cup golden raisins, left whole

2 tablespoons diced crystallized ginger

Orange juice to moisten, about 1 teaspoon

One 1-pound loaf thin-sliced white bread (store brand or Pepperidge Farm)

1. Combine the pecans, cream cheese, raisins, and crystallized ginger in a small bowl, adding just enough orange juice to make the mixture a spreadable consistency. Cover and refrigerate until ready to use.

2. Spread the cheese mixture on a slice of bread and top with another slice. The filling can be made ahead, but the sandwiches are best made no more than 30 minutes before serving. Trim the crusts, if desired, and cut into triangles or fingers.

Makes 12 to 15 sandwiches, enough for 24 to 30 triangles or 36 to 45 fingers

Ham Salad

I have never baked a ham and not had leftovers. Choose some kind soul who doesn't cook but likes to help to pick all of the fat and gristle from the meat and remove the ham from the bone for you. Store the meat in a resealable plastic bag until you have time to make this wonderful ham salad. Serve it in sandwiches, or all by itself with good crackers. I just love dill pickles in cold salads.

  3 cups ground cooked ham

  1 teaspoon Dijon mustard

¼ cup mayonnaise

  2 tablespoons chopped
     sweet pickle

  2 tablespoons chopped dill
     pickle

  2 hard-boiled eggs, peeled
     and grated

     Salt and pepper

Combine all of the ingredients gently but thoroughly. Store in a covered container in the refrigerator for up to 3 days.

Makes about 3½ cups

Fried Peanut Butter and Banana Sandwich

I wouldn't serve this as a part of my Elvis meal, but I wanted to share this recipe because it was one of Elvis's favorites! If you've got kids in the house, this would be a real treat on a Saturday morning.

  2 slices white bread

  2 tablespoons creamy
     peanut butter

  1 small ripe banana

  2 tablespoons (¼ stick)
     butter

Spread 1 slice of the bread with the peanut butter. Slice the banana evenly over the peanut butter. Top with the second slice of bread. Spread the outside of the bread with the butter. Fry the sandwich in a small skillet over medium heat until the bread is browned on both sides.

Serves 1

Cuban Sandwiches

Let's think about lunches for a second. I highly recommend the Smoked Turkey Wraps on page 46 or these Cuban sandwiches, which are different and tasty. The recipe came from Maria Oxnard, of Savannah, who served them along with jalapeño-spiked potato salad on a sunset cruise on the Intracoastal Waterway.

1 loaf French bread

Mayonnaise

Dijon mustard

½ pound thinly sliced ham, your favorite brand

4 slices Swiss cheese

Sliced kosher dill pickles

Butter

1. Slice the bread in half lengthwise. Spread one half with mayonnaise and the other with mustard. Layer the ham and Swiss cheese on one half of the bread. Layer pickle slices over the cheese. Top with the other bread half.

2. In a large skillet or on a flat-bottomed griddle over medium-high heat, heat enough butter to coat the cooking surface. (You may need to cut the loaf in half so it fits in the pan.) Place the sandwich in the pan and press down with another heavy pan or a brick wrapped in foil and grill until the cheese is melted. Cut the loaf to make 4 sandwiches.

Serves 4

Smoked Turkey Wraps

When Alison and Danny Mahfet, of Savannah, originally submitted their menu (on page 72), we felt it needed one more thing: a good sandwich. So we turned to James Roszkowiak, who is famous for his green and red wraps served up on card tables set up in the parking lot prior to Savannah Christian Preparatory School Red Raider football games. These wraps are perfect for a tailgate, as they need to be made early in the day and wrapped in plastic to "mold" them into shape. Of course, you can do your own thing—we've made a roast beef wrap with horseradish/sour cream spread, and a vegetarian wrap made with artichoke hearts, roasted red peppers, and feta cheese. All of them are yummy, but these are the best.

6 sun-dried tomato–basil or spinach-herb 10-inch tortilla wraps

One 7-ounce container roasted red pepper or other flavor hummus

¾ pound very thinly sliced smoked, cracked-pepper, Salsalito, or other spicy turkey

Boston or Bibb lettuce leaves, washed and dried

¼ red onion, slivered

2 tomatoes, thinly sliced

12 slices bacon, cooked crisp (optional)

Salt and pepper (optional)

1. Heat each wrap for about 10 seconds in a hot skillet or in the microwave.

2. Spread each wrap with hummus, spreading to within 1 inch of the edge all around. In the center of each wrap, place some smoked turkey, a lettuce leaf, 2 or 3 onion slivers, and 2 tomato slices. Top with 2 slices of bacon, if using, and sprinkle with salt and pepper, if desired. Fold in each side of the wrap, then roll tightly from the bottom. Wrap each tightly in plastic wrap.

3. To serve, cut each wrap into halves or thirds, depending on how many other items you have on the menu.

Makes 6 wraps

Curry Chicken Salad

This is a recipe from Dottie Courington, a Savannah lawyer, who was served the salad by her aunt Myrtle Donaldson, of Statesboro. When Aunt Myrtle died, this recipe passed to Dottie. Serve this over lettuce or as a sandwich filling.

1 **large roasted or rotisserie chicken (3 to 3½ pounds), cut into 1-inch cubes**

1 **cup chopped celery**

One 8-ounce can sliced or chopped water chestnuts, drained

2 **cups seedless red grapes, halved**

One 2-ounce package slivered almonds

Dressing

1 **cup mayonnaise**

1 **teaspoon soy sauce**

1 **tablespoon fresh lemon juice**

1½ **teaspoons curry powder**

1 **tablespoon prepared chutney, like Major Grey's**

Salt

1. Gently combine the chicken, celery, water chestnuts, grapes, and almonds in a large glass bowl.

2. In a separate bowl, combine the dressing ingredients and mix well. Add to the chicken mixture and stir gently to combine. Taste, and add salt if desired.

Serves 6 to 8

Grilled Chicken Pita

Don't let the long list of ingredients keep you from trying this delicious sandwich.

3 boneless, skinless chicken breasts (about 1½ pounds)

3 tablespoons plus 2 teaspoons fresh lemon juice

3 tablespoons soy sauce

1 clove garlic, minced

2 teaspoons dried oregano

2 small tomatoes, finely chopped

1 cup (¼ pound) crumbled feta cheese

¼ cup olive oil

1 large Vidalia or purple onion, cut into thin rings

6 pita breads

½ head romaine lettuce, finely chopped

One 10.6-ounce jar kalamata olives, drained, halved, and pitted, or other black olives

12 slices bacon, fried crisp

Alfalfa sprouts

Salt and pepper

1. Rinse the chicken breasts and pat dry. Combine 3 tablespoons of the lemon juice, the soy sauce, garlic, and 1 teaspoon of the oregano in a glass dish. Add the chicken, turn to coat, and cover with plastic wrap. Allow the chicken breasts to marinate for 30 minutes at room temperature or overnight in the refrigerator.

2. Combine the tomatoes and feta cheese in a small glass dish. Add the remaining 2 teaspoons lemon juice, the olive oil, and the remaining 1 teaspoon oregano, and stir to combine. Allow to sit at room temperature for 30 minutes.

3. Make the yogurt sauce: In a small bowl, whisk together the yogurt, garlic, walnuts, and olive oil. Cover and refrigerate until ready to use.

4. Prepare the grill. Spray a grill basket with olive oil. Grill the chicken breasts over medium heat for 8 to 10 minutes, until no longer pink in the thickest portion of each breast. Spread the onion rings over the surface of the basket and grill while the chicken is cooking. Turn the basket frequently. The onion rings will blacken as they cook; this will also take 8 to 10 minutes.

Yogurt Sauce

- 8 ounces (1 cup) unflavored yogurt
- 1 clove garlic, minced
- ¼ cup finely chopped walnuts
- 1 tablespoon olive oil

5. When the chicken and onion rings are cooked, place the pita breads on the grill for about 2 minutes per side, until grill marks show. Slice the chicken into very thin pieces.

6. At serving time, put out all of the ingredients and allow each person to assemble sandwiches: Slit each pita. Place several slices of grilled chicken, 3 or 4 slivers of grilled onion, a tablespoon of tomato-feta mixture, lettuce, olives, and 1 or 2 slices of bacon into each pita. Top with yogurt sauce and a wad of alfalfa sprouts. Add salt and pepper to taste. Fold up the sides of the pita and enjoy!

Serves 6

Note: If serving sandwiches on the go, store each ingredient in a separate plastic bag or covered container and place in a cooler.

Hot Chicken Salad

This hot chicken casserole is perfectly seasoned. Lots of celery and almonds give it a nice crunch. You may be inclined to leave off the potato-chip topping, but believe me, it won't be the same without it!

2 cups cooked chicken breast meat, cubed (You may use leftover rotisserie chicken—delicious!)

1½ cups diced celery

½ cup slivered or sliced almonds

½ teaspoon salt

½ teaspoon grated onion

¼ teaspoon pepper

2 tablespoons fresh lemon juice

1 cup mayonnaise

½ cup grated sharp Cheddar cheese

⅔ cup crushed potato chips

1. Preheat the oven to 375°F. Spray a 13-by-9-inch baking dish with vegetable oil cooking spray.

2. In a large mixing bowl, combine the chicken, celery, almonds, salt, onion, pepper, lemon juice, mayonnaise, and cheese. Place the mixture in the prepared baking dish. Spread the crushed potato chips on top. Bake for 20 minutes, or until bubbly.

Serves 8 to 10, depending on the appetites of your guests and the number of menu items

Salmon Salad

I made this on my show. It's a great summer dish and even better if you have salmon left over from the night before. Serve this over lettuce or as a sandwich filling.

2 cups cooked, flaked salmon

2 hard-boiled eggs, mashed

1 red or green bell pepper, diced

1 cucumber, peeled, seeded, and diced

½ cup chopped onion

4 to 5 tablespoons mayonnaise, or enough to moisten

¼ teaspoon cayenne pepper (optional)

Salt and pepper

Juice of ½ lemon

1. Gently toss together the salmon and hard-boiled eggs in a large glass bowl.

2. In a separate bowl, combine the bell pepper, cucumber, onion, and mayonnaise. Add the cayenne, if using, and salt and pepper to taste, and stir to combine. Pour the mixture over the salmon, add the lemon juice, and toss lightly to combine.

Serves 4 to 6

Artichoke Rice Salad with Shrimp

You can serve this cold as a salad or hot as a casserole; it's delicious either way. The colors are so beautiful—yellow curried rice, green pepper, onions, olives with pimiento, and pretty pink shrimp.

One 6.9-ounce package Rice-A-Roni, chicken flavor

One 6-ounce jar marinated artichoke hearts

½ cup mayonnaise

½ green bell pepper, chopped

3 to 4 green onions, chopped, white and green parts

12 to 14 pimiento-stuffed green olives, sliced

1 teaspoon curry powder

Salt and pepper

1 pound small or medium shrimp, peeled and deveined (see Note for cooking directions)

1. In a skillet sprayed with vegetable oil cooking spray, brown the Rice-A-Roni. (Do not add the butter or oil that the package directions suggest.) Add the water the package requires and the seasoning packet and prepare according to package directions.

2. Drain the artichoke hearts and reserve the marinade. In a small bowl, whisk the marinade and the mayonnaise to combine. Add the green pepper, green onions, olives, curry powder, salt and pepper to taste, and mix together. Add this mixture to the rice.

3. Gently stir in the cooked shrimp. If serving as a salad, chill. If serving as a casserole, place in a 2½-quart casserole dish and bake in a 350°F oven for 20 minutes, until heated through.

Serves 6 to 8

Note: If you are going to serve this recipe as a cold salad, cook the shrimp in a small amount of salted water for about 3 to 4 minutes, until firm and cooked through. Test a shrimp to see if it is the texture you like. If you are going to serve this as a hot casserole, just plunge the shrimp into boiling water for 2 to 3 minutes and drain, as they will continue cooking during the baking of the casserole. You do not want them to be overcooked. Larger shrimp will need to cook a little longer than small shrimp. Taste as you go!

Taco Salad

Martha's sister-in-law, Linda Giddens, made this famous. It's always a hit, particularly when you can get good tomatoes. The Giddens family has been serving this recipe for thirty years, long before Tex-Mex was the rage. The prepared ingredients can be stored separately in plastic bags in the refrigerator until you're ready to assemble the salad.

2 ripe tomatoes, diced

½ pound diced sharp
   Cheddar cheese

1 large onion, chopped

1 head iceberg lettuce,
   washed, drained, and
   chopped

1 pound lean ground beef,
   browned, crumbled, and
   drained

   One 16-ounce bottle
   Catalina salad dressing

   One 7-ounce bag taco-
   flavored corn chips,
   crushed

   One 8-ounce bottle hot or
   mild taco sauce

Combine the tomatoes, cheese, onion, lettuce, and ground beef in a large bowl. Add the entire bottle of salad dressing and mix well. Just before serving, add the taco chips, tossing to combine with the other ingredients. Top each serving with taco sauce. Serve with garlic bread.

Serves 6 to 8

Wild Rice Salad

The colors of this salad are fantastic—brown, red, green, and white. And what a great dressing! You'll have enough dressing for two recipes of the salad, or you can use it to dress any green salad.

Dressing

1⅓ cups canola oil

½ cup white vinegar

¼ cup freshly grated Parmesan cheese

1 tablespoon sugar

1 teaspoon salt

1 teaspoon celery seed

½ teaspoon ground white pepper

½ teaspoon dry mustard

¼ teaspoon paprika

1 clove garlic, minced

½ teaspoon salt

1 cup wild rice (Don't cheat—use the real stuff!)

One 6-ounce jar marinated artichoke hearts, drained and halved, marinade reserved

One 6-ounce can LeSueur early June peas, well drained, or any 6-ounce can green peas

⅓ cup coarsely chopped green bell pepper

3 green onions, chopped, white and green parts

1 cup cherry or grape tomatoes, halved

¼ cup slivered almonds, toasted

1. Combine all the dressing ingredients in a jar with a tight-fitting lid and shake well. Refrigerate until ready to use.

2. In a 1-quart pot with a lid, bring 2 cups water and the salt to a boil. Add the rice and stir well. Reduce the heat to low, cover, and simmer for 45 minutes. Drain excess liquid from the rice.

3. In a large bowl, combine the rice, artichoke hearts, peas, green pepper, green onions, tomatoes, reserved marinade, and half of the dressing. Toss well. Cover and chill. Just before serving, toss again and taste. Add some of the remaining dressing, if desired. Sprinkle with the almonds and serve.

Serves 8

Rene's Coleslaw

The colors of this coleslaw are beautiful next to the wild rice salad, and the dressing is tangy/sweet. The leftovers are terrific the next day. You can take the easy way out: buy the cabbage already shredded in the produce department. Do not buy angel hair shredded cabbage, however, as it becomes too limp when dressing is added.

5 cups shredded cabbage

½ cup almonds, toasted

1½ cups dried cranberries

½ cup diced celery

½ cup chopped green onions, white and green parts

½ cup chopped green bell pepper

Dressing

½ cup mayonnaise

1 tablespoon sweet pickle relish

1 tablespoon honey mustard

1 tablespoon honey

Salt and pepper

1. Combine the cabbage, almonds, cranberries, celery, green onions, and green pepper in a large plastic bowl with a snap-on lid.

2. Combine all of the dressing ingredients, adding salt and pepper to taste, and refrigerate until ready to serve. Pour the dressing on just before serving. Stir well.

Serves 10 to 12

Hot Slaw

This colorful side is a great alternative to a salad or traditional coleslaw made with mayonnaise. It makes a large quantity, and if you have leftovers, use it as a topping for a barbecue or grilled chicken breast sandwich. Delicious!

6 slices bacon

1 large yellow onion, chopped

1 medium green bell pepper, chopped

1 medium (3 pounds) head green cabbage, quartered, cored, and shredded

¼ cup chili powder

Kosher salt

One 14.5-ounce can diced tomatoes and green chilies

1. In a 12-inch skillet, cook the bacon until crisp. Remove the bacon to paper towels to drain, but leave the grease in the skillet. Crumble the bacon and set aside.

2. In the reserved bacon grease, cook the onion and green pepper until limp, about 5 minutes. Add the cabbage and cook until limp but not soft, 3 to 5 minutes. Add the chili powder and salt to taste. Add the tomatoes and simmer until just heated through. The slaw should be slightly crisp. Adjust seasoning and sprinkle the crumbled bacon over the top.

Serves 10 to 12

Corn, Avocado, and Tomato Salad

One night my brother, Bubba, had a small group of us over for dinner for his fabulous chickens that he cooks on the grill. My niece, Corrie, Bubba's daughter, is twenty-three years old and is turning into a real good cook. As we were getting the meal all put together, Corrie pulled out of the refrigerator a dish that I had not seen before. I said, "What's this?" Corrie said, "Oh, it's a delicious corn salad recipe that I got out of that wonderful magazine *Real Simple*." I took one bite of it and I was in love! It was so, so good. Naturally, I asked Corrie for the recipe and she gladly shared it with me. Corrie uses fresh hot corn: she cuts the corn off the cob, and mixes the salad together while it's still hot. The avocado almost turns into a paste. I loved it that way!

Here is the recipe as it appeared in *Real Simple*, or you can make it Corrie's way.

I highly recommend using fresh corn; my second choice would be frozen niblets.

2 cups cooked corn, fresh or frozen

1 avocado, diced into ½-inch pieces

1 pint cherry tomatoes, halved

½ cup finely diced red onion

Dressing

2 tablespoons olive oil

1 tablespoon fresh lime juice

½ teaspoon grated lime zest

¼ cup chopped cilantro

¼ teaspoon salt

⅛ teaspoon pepper

1. Combine the corn, avocado, tomatoes, and onion in a large glass bowl.

2. Whisk together the dressing ingredients in a glass bowl or measuring cup. Pour over the salad and toss gently to mix.

Serves 4 to 6

Cranberry-Pineapple Gelatin Salad

You can't have a luncheon without serving a gelatin salad. This one is particularly pretty on the plate. Alice Jo Giddens often prepares sugar-free gelatins and puddings, as so many older adults have diabetes.

Two 3-ounce packages raspberry gelatin, regular or sugar free

½ **envelope (1½ teaspoons) unflavored gelatin**

One 8-ounce can crushed pineapple, packed in its own juice

One 15-ounce can whole-berry cranberry sauce

¼ **cup finely chopped walnuts**

1. Spray a 4-cup gelatin mold or a 9-inch square pan with vegetable oil cooking spray. Make sure to spray all of the surfaces, especially any decorative indentations.

2. In a medium glass mixing bowl, combine the raspberry gelatin and unflavored gelatin. Add 1 cup boiling water and stir with a metal spoon continuously for 2 minutes, until the gelatin is completely dissolved. Stir in ½ cup cold water. Add the pineapple and juice, cranberry sauce, and walnuts. Stir with a metal spoon until all of the ingredients are completely incorporated. Pour the mixture into the prepared mold, cover with plastic wrap, and refrigerate until firm.

3. About an hour before serving, invert the mold onto a serving platter and allow to sit at room temperature; the salad will release itself and come cleanly from the mold. If you are in a hurry, fill the sink with about an inch of hot water and place the bottom of the mold into the hot water for about a minute, then invert the salad onto a serving platter. Slice the salad into 16 pieces. If using a square pan, cut the salad into 16 servings and carefully remove each one with a small spatula to a serving platter.

Serves 16

Chili in a Biscuit Bowl

The biscuit bowls are very cute. Eat the bowl along with the chili! The recipe calls for Mexican-style stewed tomatoes, but you can use any kind you like. This is yet another of Patty Ronning's recipes.

2 cups Bisquick baking mix

⅔ cup whole milk

½ teaspoon cayenne pepper

Flour for dusting the work surface

1 pound ground chuck

1 medium onion, chopped

1 medium green bell pepper, chopped

Two 14-ounce cans Mexican-style stewed tomatoes

One 15-ounce can kidney beans, drained and rinsed

2 tablespoons chili powder

1 teaspoon salt

Toppings: grated sharp Cheddar cheese, sour cream, sliced green onions (white and green parts), and corn chips

1. Preheat the oven to 450°F. Invert a 6-cup muffin tin and spray the underside with vegetable oil cooking spray.

2. Stir together the biscuit mix, milk, and cayenne. Shape into a ball. Turn out onto a floured surface and knead three or four times. Divide the ball into 6 pieces. Roll each piece into a 6-inch circle.

3. Place 1 dough circle over each muffin cup. Press around the cup to form a bowl shape. Bake for 10 to 12 minutes, until lightly browned. Let cool slightly. Remove the biscuit bowls and reserve.

4. Brown the ground chuck over medium heat in a Dutch oven. Add the onion and green pepper and continue to cook until the meat is completely browned and the vegetables are tender. Drain off any fat and discard. Stir in the tomatoes, beans, chili powder, and salt. Bring the mixture to a boil, cover, and reduce the heat to low. Simmer for 35 minutes.

5. When ready to serve, spoon hot chili into the biscuit bowls. Garnish with shredded Cheddar cheese, sour cream, sliced green onions, and corn chips.

Serves 6

Quick Crab Stew

When Patty Ronning sent in this recipe, I really didn't think it could possibly taste as good as made-from-scratch stew. Wrong! This is so easy and so good! The creamed canned soups give the stew the perfect texture without the fuss of starting with a cream sauce.

When you bring containers of this stew to your friend, label them with the following directions: If refrigerated, vent container. Microwave on 50 percent power until crab stew is hot, about 3 minutes. If frozen, vent container. Reheat on 30 percent power until thawed, about 10 minutes. Then reheat at 50 percent power until hot, about 2 minutes.

2 tablespoons butter

1 small onion, chopped

One 10¾-ounce can condensed cream of potato soup

One 10¾-ounce can condensed cream of celery soup

1 soup can milk

1 soup can half-and-half

1 pound claw crabmeat, picked through for shell

¼ cup dry sherry

Salt and pepper

In a large saucepan, melt the butter and sauté the onion until translucent, 3 to 4 minutes. Add the soups, milk, and half-and-half. Add the crabmeat and bring just to a boil. Add the sherry, and salt and pepper to taste. Serve hot immediately. Or allow to cool to room temperature, then refrigerate or freeze immediately in plastic microwavable reusable containers with lids.

Serves 4 to 6

Gumbo

This has a delicious flavor. If you use bone-in breasts, cook the chicken until it falls apart, then remove the bones before serving. Or you can buy boneless breasts and cut each breast into thirds after sautéing. Serve this over white rice with corn bread on the side.

3 large chicken breasts (about 2 pounds), halved and skinned

Salt and pepper

¼ cup vegetable oil

1 pound smoked sausage, cut into 1/4-inch slices

½ cup all-purpose flour

5 tablespoons margarine

1 large onion, chopped

1 green bell pepper, chopped

3 stalks celery, chopped

8 cloves garlic, minced

¼ bunch flat-leaf parsley, stems and leaves

¼ cup Worcestershire sauce

5 beef bouillon cubes

One 14-ounce can stewed tomatoes, with juice

½ pound small shrimp, peeled

2 cups fresh or frozen sliced okra

4 green onions, sliced, white and green parts

¼ cup chopped fresh parsley

1. Sprinkle the chicken with salt and pepper. Heat the oil in a heavy-bottomed Dutch oven. Cook the chicken until browned on both sides and remove. Add the sausage and cook until browned; remove. Sprinkle the flour over the oil; add 2 tablespoons of the margarine and cook over medium heat, stirring constantly, until brown, about 10 minutes. Do not let the roux burn or you will have to start over. Let the roux cool.

2. Return the Dutch oven to low heat and melt the remaining 3 tablespoons margarine. Add the onion and sauté for 10 minutes. Add the green pepper, celery, garlic, flat-leaf parsley, and Worcestershire sauce. Cook, stirring frequently, for 10 minutes. Add 4 cups hot water, whisking constantly. Add the chicken and sausage and cover. Bring to a boil, then reduce the heat and simmer for 45 minutes. Add the bouillon cubes, tomatoes, shrimp, and okra. Cover and simmer for 1 hour. Just before serving, add the green onions and chopped parsley.

Serves 8 to 10

Potato Soup with Shrimp

Potato soup is an unsung hero of the soup world; there is just nothing more belly-pleasing. As the potatoes cook, the soup thickens, leaving behind some chunks of potato. Cook the shrimp separately and add them at the last minute. They add great flavor and color, but if you don't have any shrimp on hand, the soup is still terrific without them.

¼ cup (½ stick) butter

1 small onion, diced

2 medium carrots, diced about the same size as the onion

2 tablespoons all-purpose flour

8 medium russet potatoes, peeled and cubed

4 cups milk, whole, reduced fat (2%), or low fat (1%)

2 chicken bouillon cubes, dissolved in ½ cup hot milk

1 cup half-and-half

1 teaspoon salt

¼ teaspoon pepper

1 pound medium shrimp

Crumbled bacon bits, for garnish

Grated sharp Cheddar cheese, for garnish

1. In a 4-quart saucepan, melt the butter and sauté the onion and carrots until both are slightly tender, about 5 minutes. Whisk in the flour and cook for 1 minute. Add the potatoes, milk, and dissolved bouillon cubes. Cook over medium heat for 15 minutes, until the potatoes are very soft and some of them have begun to dissolve into mush. Add the half-and-half, salt, and pepper. Let cool, then refrigerate until party time.

2. In a small saucepan, bring 2 cups lightly salted water to a boil. Add the shrimp all at once and stir well. Watch the shrimp closely; as soon as they all turn pink, turn off the heat and drain. The shrimp should be slightly undercooked. When they are cool, peel them, chop roughly into big chunks, and place them in a plastic bag. Refrigerate until party time.

3. Reheat the soup over very low heat (it will stick to the bottom of the pot if you heat it too quickly) about 45 minutes before the party. When the soup is hot, add the shrimp and stir well. Encourage your guests to sprinkle the soup with bacon bits and grated Cheddar cheese. They won't be sorry they did!

Serves 6 to 8

Minnesota Wild Rice Soup

This soup will change texture as it sits overnight, as the rice will continue to absorb the broth and thicken the soup. The flavors are delicious, and the almonds add an unexpected crunch.

¼ cup wild rice

2 tablespoons butter

2 medium stalks celery, diced small

1 medium carrot, diced small

1 medium onion, diced small

3 tablespoons all-purpose flour

Two 14-ounce cans chicken broth

1 cup half-and-half

⅓ cup dry sherry

1 teaspoon salt

½ teaspoon pepper

⅓ cup slivered almonds, lightly toasted

¼ cup chopped fresh parsley

1. Cook the wild rice in lightly salted water, according to instructions on the package, until almost done, about 45 minutes.

2. In a 4-quart saucepan, heat the butter and sauté the celery, carrot, and onion until the vegetables are tender, about 5 minutes. Whisk in the flour and cook for 2 minutes more, stirring constantly. Slowly add the broth, about 1 cup at a time, stirring until the soup thickens after each addition. When all of the broth has been added, add the half-and-half and sherry. Season with the salt and pepper. Add the cooked rice. Turn off the heat, let cool, and refrigerate until party time.

3. The day of the party, reheat the soup over very low heat just until hot. Just before your guests arrive, stir in the almonds and parsley.

Serves 6 to 8

Cream of Broccoli and Cauliflower Soup

Sometimes it's hard to find frozen cauliflower. If you can't, you can use fresh or even one of the frozen prepared dishes, like cauliflower with cheese sauce. Either one will work just fine.

Two 10-ounce packages frozen chopped broccoli

One 10-ounce package frozen cauliflower, or ½ head fresh cauliflower, separated into flowerets, or one 10-ounce package frozen cauliflower in cheese sauce

2 **cups chicken broth (canned is fine)**

1 **cup half-and-half**

1 **teaspoon salt**

½ **teaspoon pepper**

2 **cups grated Swiss cheese**

1. In a 4-quart stockpot, cook the broccoli and cauliflower in the broth until tender, about 15 minutes. Let cool. Puree in a blender or food processor, leaving the soup a little chunky. Return the soup to the stockpot. Add the half-and-half, salt, and pepper. Let cool and refrigerate until party time.

2. The next day, reheat the soup over very low heat for about 45 minutes. Just before your guests arrive, stir in the Swiss cheese.

Serves 4 to 6

Spicy Tomato Soup

This will be the hit of any meal. It's just sensational—so much better than what comes in the can!

½ cup (1 stick) plus
3 tablespoons butter

½ cup all-purpose flour

1 medium onion, diced

2 cloves garlic, diced

3 cups chicken broth
(canned is fine)

One 29-ounce can tomato
sauce

One 29-ounce can diced
tomatoes, with juice

2 dashes of your favorite hot
sauce, such as Tabasco

¼ cup honey

1 tablespoon dried dill weed

½ teaspoon pepper

1 teaspoon chili powder

1 teaspoon dried basil

Homemade croutons
(see Note)

1. In a 4-quart heavy-bottomed saucepan, melt half (5½ tablespoons) of the butter. When melted, whisk in the flour and stir until very smooth. Cook over low heat for about 5 minutes, until very thick and smooth.

2. In a small skillet, melt the remaining butter. Sauté the onion and garlic over low heat until the onion is translucent, 3 to 4 minutes. Add the onion and garlic to the flour mixture and combine. Slowly add the chicken broth, about 1 cup at a time, stirring well after each addition and allowing the soup to thicken slightly before adding more broth. When all the broth is added, begin adding the tomato sauce and the diced tomatoes, about 1 cup at a time, stirring well, then allowing the mixture to thicken before adding more. When all the tomato sauce and diced tomatoes have been added, season the soup with the hot sauce, honey, dill weed, pepper, chili powder, and basil. Turn off the heat, let cool, and refrigerate until party time.

3. The day of the party, reheat the soup over very low heat for about 45 minutes so that the flavors can blend. Stir frequently, as the soup will stick to the bottom of the pot. Garnish with homemade croutons.

Note: To make croutons, brush day-old French bread slices with olive oil. Sprinkle with garlic salt or a spice blend of your choice. Toast in a 300°F oven until very dry. Cut into small cubes. Store in an airtight container or bag until party time.

Serves 6 to 8

Cheese-Squash Casserole

No southern cook is worth her salt without a good squash casserole recipe. This one's a classic.

6 medium yellow summer squash (approximately)

1 small onion, chopped

1½ cups grated sharp Cheddar cheese

½ cup mayonnaise

10 soda crackers, crumbled

1 egg, lightly beaten

2 tablespoons butter, melted

Salt and pepper

1. Preheat the oven to 350°F. Spray an 8-inch square baking dish with vegetable oil cooking spray.

2. Peel the squash with a vegetable peeler and cut into ¼-inch slices. Place the squash and onion in about 2 inches of salted water in a medium saucepan. Bring to a rolling boil, then reduce the heat to medium-low and simmer until the squash is very tender, about 10 to 12 minutes. Drain the squash. In the same pot, mash the squash and onion with a fork; you should have about 2 cups of cooked squash. Add ½ cup of the cheese, the mayonnaise, and crumbled soda crackers. Stir in the egg and butter. Taste; add salt and pepper as needed. Pour into the prepared baking dish. Top with the remaining 1 cup cheese. Bake for 25 minutes, or until the cheese is melted and the casserole is bubbly.

Serves 8 to 10

Broccoli Casserole

This never-fail recipe is a great favorite with everybody.

Two 10-ounce packages frozen chopped broccoli, cooked and drained

1 **cup mayonnaise**

1 **cup grated sharp Cheddar cheese**

One 10¾-ounce can condensed cream of mushroom soup

2 **eggs, lightly beaten**

2 **cups crushed Ritz or cheese crackers**

2 **tablespoons butter, melted**

1. Preheat the oven to 350°F. Spray a 13-by-9-inch baking dish with vegetable oil cooking spray.

2. In a large mixing bowl, combine the broccoli, mayonnaise, cheese, soup, and eggs. Mix well with a metal spoon (the mixture is rather stiff and could break the handle of a wooden spoon). Place the mixture in the prepared baking dish. Top with the crushed crackers and pour the melted butter evenly over the crackers. Bake for 35 minutes, or until set and browned.

Serves 8 to 10

Suzie's Peach Pickles

Susan Greene makes her own peach pickles, but you can often find them in the grocery store. Southerners often have peach pickles on a relish tray for Thanksgiving.

For each quart canning jar:

- 1 cup white vinegar
- 2 cups sugar
- 14 very small peaches, peeled, each stuck with 2 to 4 cloves
- Cinnamon sticks (optional)
- 1 tablespoon allspice in a mesh boiling bag (optional)

Bring the vinegar and sugar to a boil. Add the peaches and cook until tender. Cinnamon sticks may be boiled with the peaches and added to the jars. Allspice in a mesh boiling bag may be boiled with the peaches, but do not put into the jar. Place the peaches into sterilized quart jars and cover with syrup. Seal according to the canning instructions that come with the jars. Serve cold.

Puttin' It All Together

New Year's Day Soup Lunch for the Neighbors

You know, there's no nicer way to start off the New Year than by enjoying a cup of homemade soup while catching up with the neighborhood news in a friend's kitchen. Well, that's just what this party is all about. It's a great way for neighbors to reconnect before the onslaught of a new year. The meal is inexpensive, simple, tasty, and appreciated by all those who made the resolution to start counting calories after the holidays. If any of your neighbors happen to be vegetarians, this menu will make them happy, too. Last but not least, this party provides a way to get rid of all those leftover Christmas sweets.

Here are some tips to make this informal get-together easy for you and special for your guests:

Make your soups several days beforehand, undercooking everything slightly so that they're still at the peak of perfection when reheated. Begin reheating the soups over very low heat about 45 minutes before the party.

Compose and print out invitations on the computer and distribute them several days before the party. Or, if you have all of the addresses, why not just use e-mail? No RSVP required, as leftovers can be frozen or taken to friends who are recovering from the holiday blahs.

This is a one-hour party. I always plan mine for 12:00 noon to 1:00, as the football kickoffs are usually at 1:30 on New Year's Day. You could go earlier, 11:30 to 12:30, if you don't have party animals for neighbors. My crowd are generally on the mature side, and noon to one has always suited them.

Leave up your holiday decorations. Throw all the clutter into a plastic trash bag and toss it into a closet until after the party. If you have something blooming in the yard, clip a few blooms and place them in glass vases to add a little freshness to your decorations, or make a quick trip to the grocery florist. Turn on all the Christmas lights, and light every candle you have in the house, even though the party is midday.

Serve the soups straight from the pots on the stove. Have heatproof throwaway cups and extra spoons handy. Plastic is okay for this party; in fact, plastic is advisable if your guests want to taste several soups. (Sometimes, they taste them all!) Pick up some cute napkins that say something fun about the New Year. You don't need paper plates unless you feel a real need.

Have condiments (grated cheese, crumbled bacon, homemade croutons) grouped in interesting bowls in the center of an island or on the kitchen table. Have the tiny corn muffins in a cute basket next to the condiments.

Assemble assorted chocolates, pralines, peppermints, cookies, slices of fruitcake, and any other goodies you've been given for Christmas in pretty dishes for dessert. You won't get rid of all of it, but with twenty people picking at it, you are bound to have fewer sweets around to tempt you than you did before the party. Coffee, hot or iced tea, lemonade, hot chocolate, and ice water are perfect beverages for this get-together.

The recipes that follow, in the quantities suggested, serve twenty moderate eaters.

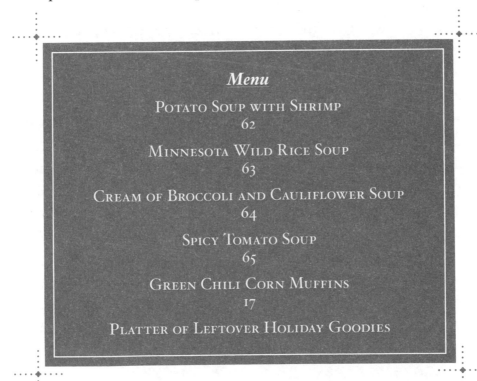

Menu

POTATO SOUP WITH SHRIMP
62

MINNESOTA WILD RICE SOUP
63

CREAM OF BROCCOLI AND CAULIFLOWER SOUP
64

SPICY TOMATO SOUP
65

GREEN CHILI CORN MUFFINS
17

PLATTER OF LEFTOVER HOLIDAY GOODIES

A Georgia Bulldawg Parking Lot Tailgate

Alison and Danny Mahfet are huge Dawg (as in Georgia Bulldawg) fans. Alison graduated from the University of Georgia in 1997, and her brother, Will Ronning, graduated in 1993. Years ago, Alison, Will, and some of their closest friends pooled their resources to buy a parking space (along with their season tickets) near the Georgia stadium, where, each home game, they set up an elaborate tailgate party. Now the group has grown to include new husbands, like Danny, who graduated from UGA in 1996, and assorted boyfriends, girlfriends, and soon, some new babies!

Here's the way Alison describes game day: "When we lived in Atlanta, all of our friends would meet at our house to load up all of our chairs and food coolers. (For really big games, we rent a huge van!) Once the cars are loaded and decorated with flags and magnets, we hit 316, the road to Athens. Wonderful Bloody Marys in red plastic cups are served to everyone except the driver. All the way down, the guys talk about how important this game is. The girls talk about what great red-and-black outfits we each have on. We always listen to a homemade Larry Munson (world-famous voice of the Georgia Bulldawgs) highlights CD. Route 316 is always packed with fellow Dawg fans—you are sure to see tons of friends along the way!

"Finally, we pull into one of the coveted Hull Street parking spots. We unload the supplies and the party really starts! The earlier you can get to Athens, the better. Now that we can no longer buy two-dollar student tickets, we are always sure to be in our seats in time for the kickoff. After the BIG WIN (always!), we return to tailgate some more until the traffic dies down and then we head back home to Atlanta."

It's not unusual to find this kind of devotion in Georgia folks. In fact, my sons, Jamie and Bobby, and my brother, Bubba, are three of the most avid Georgia Bulldawg fans you could ever meet. Even though none of them attended the university, that didn't keep them from going on the Internet to bid on lockers belonging to Tony Milton, Reggie Brown, and DJ Shockley. They each got a locker with a high bid of $1,200 (apiece, y'all). Now, is that nuts or what? So, happy as three little boys with new toys, they were off to Athens to haul back their treasures. Jamie's and Bobby's lockers are proudly displayed here at the restaurant in their office. Bubba's locker is currently in storage, awaiting the opening of Uncle Bubba's Oyster House, where he will put it in its place of honor.

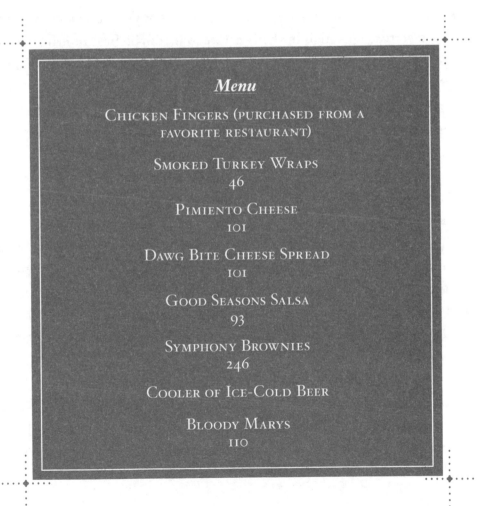

Menu

CHICKEN FINGERS (PURCHASED FROM A FAVORITE RESTAURANT)

SMOKED TURKEY WRAPS
46

PIMIENTO CHEESE
101

DAWG BITE CHEESE SPREAD
101

GOOD SEASONS SALSA
93

SYMPHONY BROWNIES
246

COOLER OF ICE-COLD BEER

BLOODY MARYS
110

Hunt Lunch in the Field

My girlfriend Susan Greene is just about the cutest little southern girl you ever saw. I still think of her as a girl; actually, she's a grandmother now. By the way, her grandchildren call her Bubbles, which suits her perfectly. Well, Bubbles is a fabulous cook and entertainer. When Bubbles started telling me about this latest party she threw, I just began to holler with laughter and said, "Damn, girl, only you would take that one on!"

I was born and raised in Albany (pronounced All-benny), Georgia, in the southwest corner of the state, slap kadab in the heart of some of the best hunting land in the South. I remember as a little girl seeing President Dwight Eisenhower coming there often to participate in the quail hunts.

Bubbles's husband, Phil, is a big hunter himself, and this is where it all started. Phil wanted to entertain around seventy-five of his friends for lunch before an early-afternoon dove shoot on the opening day of dove season, which is always at the beginning of October. The catch? He wanted to feed them in the field, and he wanted the field to look like a beautiful dining room under all the massive live oak trees!

Bubbles realized that she was going to need some buddy help, so she turned to Margaret Jo Hogg and decorator friend Linda Sailers. These three women brought in an oak hutch and dining room table and chairs and created an outdoor living room. They rented round tables and chairs and covered the tables with fall print tablecloths. Beautiful centerpieces of gold and red autumn foliage graced each of the tables, and the place settings were brown quail china and white linen napkins secured with miniature china doves.

The party was a smashing success! In fact, it was so successful that the meal has become a tradition, although it has been scaled down a little bit. And to think that these three women pulled off this fabulous party in the field . . . and the closest running water was two miles away! Aren't they something?

Menu

Bert's Southern Fried Chicken
136

Wild Rice Salad
54

Rene's Coleslaw
55

Suzie's Peach Pickles
68

Buttermilk Corn Bread
16

Maggie's Decadent Brownies
247

Lemon Blossoms
239

Keen-ager Casserole Luncheon

Martha Nesbit's mother, Alice Jo Giddens, and I have a lot in common: we were single mothers, and had to work hard to support our families. While I was busy in a restaurant kitchen, Mrs. Giddens was teaching at the Alice in Wonderland Kindergarten, a schoolroom attached to her house in Valdosta, Georgia. She taught every morning for thirty-five years, and tutored in the afternoons. Neither of us had much time for parties.

When Mrs. Giddens retired, she got involved with a church group of people aged fifty-five and older called the Keen-agers. For a number of years, Mrs. Giddens and a small committee of men and women have been preparing delicious home-cooked meals for as many as ninety Keen-agers from her church and other congregations four times a year.

Here are some of Mrs. Giddens's tips on preparing food for large groups:

"Have people sign up or RSVP in advance so you know exactly how many people are coming; otherwise, you might run out of food. Count on each of these casseroles serving about eight to ten. Multiply out the ingredients needed to feed the folks who've signed up, mix them in big bowls, and cook them in large casserole dishes at the church."

"Make more than you think you'll need. It's the horror of cooking for crowds not to have enough for everyone. You can always take the leftovers to shut-ins. Of course, I never have any leftovers."

"Don't do things that are complicated. In fact, two of my favorite recipes—a cranberry gelatin salad and a hot chicken salad—are two of the easiest. They have very few ingredients, but the blend of flavors is perfect."

"Think about traffic flow. We place two identical food tables in the middle of the room with the eating tables on either side. One side of the room goes to one table and the other side goes to the other. That way, you don't have a bottleneck or an overly long line."

As for making the place look pretty, Mrs. Giddens is a whiz at making a silk purse out of a sow's ear. She bought a dozen small glass vases at the dollar store a few years back, and usually fills them with something seasonal—hydrangeas, azaleas, or even wildflowers from the ditches in the Valdosta countryside. Baskets of popcorn are popular centerpieces on movie day; hollowed-out cantaloupes filled with fresh fruit chunks is another favorite edible centerpiece.

The Keen-agers aren't shy about voicing their opinions about the food. They love anything homemade! Mrs. Giddens, by the way, gets many of her ideas from the Food Network. She gives my show a thumbs-up! "You tell it like it is, and I like the way you're not afraid of using a convenience item if you want to."

This particular menu makes a beautiful plate, but what I really like is the way these flavors blend when you're eating this meal. Mrs. Giddens recommends two trifle-like desserts; the men particularly like the chocolate version.

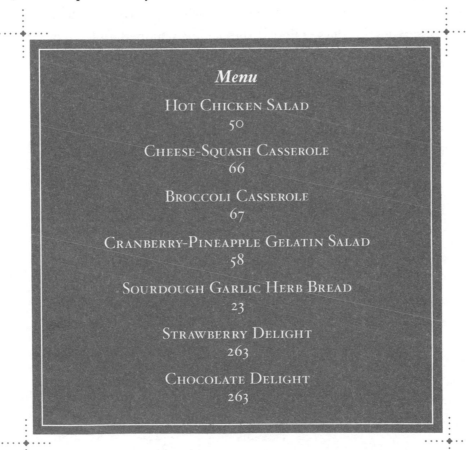

Menu

HOT CHICKEN SALAD
50

CHEESE-SQUASH CASSEROLE
66

BROCCOLI CASSEROLE
67

CRANBERRY-PINEAPPLE GELATIN SALAD
58

SOURDOUGH GARLIC HERB BREAD
23

STRAWBERRY DELIGHT
263

CHOCOLATE DELIGHT
263

A Working Lunch

This menu is very near and dear to my heart. You might ask, "Why is that, Paula?" Well, it was exactly sixteen years ago that I took responsibility for my own life. The first step in doing this was creating a business that would afford my sons and me financial independence. I felt like there might be folks out there chained to their desks during lunch hour with growling bellies, so I decided that I would prepare wonderful little bag lunches and send my sons out to sell 'em. I named my business The Bag Lady. Boy howdy, I had no idea how right I was! Before I knew it, I was feeding a couple hundred people a day. I lovingly prepared these meals fresh every morning; some of them cold, some of them hot, some of them fattening, some of them light. The recipes I've chosen to share with y'all in this menu remind me very much of those Bag Lady days. These dishes can be whipped up from last night's leftovers and are just perfect to pack up for today's lunch.

So, y'all remember these recipes the next time you're having a working lunch and you're asked to bring a covered dish. I promise they'll be a big hit!

Menu

SALMON SALAD
51

CURRY CHICKEN SALAD
47

CORN, AVOCADO, AND TOMATO SALAD
57

BAKERY CROISSANTS, SLICED

GOURMET POTATO CHIPS

DOUBLE RUM CAKE
221

BROWN SUGAR CHEWIES
243

Run for the Roses

Imagine having a party so memorable, people still talk about it twenty-five years later! That's precisely the situation Jane and Gilbert Wells, who have a successful bath and kitchen design business in Savannah, find themselves in. Jane and Gilbert, both native Kentuckians, had a Derby Day party in Savannah back in 1980, and people today are still asking Jane when she's having another. "It's the funniest thing," Jane remarks. "They think they've been dropped from the list. They are so relieved when they discover that we've been too busy to do another Derby party, and they always remind me not to forget them if I plan one."

Fans who watch the races from home plan an event centered around mint juleps (the classic Derby drink made with fresh mint, good Kentucky bourbon, and sugar syrup, and traditionally served ice cold in a silver julep cup), the television set, and good food, including what Jane considers Kentucky's finest delicacy: fresh-off-the-farm salt-cured country ham, complete with a moldy exterior. "I like to buy them directly from the farmers," Jane says. "If I were doing a Derby party, I'd call Gilbert's brother in Kentucky and have him send us one." (You can order a salt-cured ham from Smithfield Farms; see page 104 for ordering information.)

You don't have to be from Kentucky or serve a country ham to have a bona fide Derby party, however. Sue and Lou Off, of Tybee Island, Georgia, invited friends in for mint juleps (of course); cheese straws; pimiento cheese spread; marinated shrimp; beef tenderloin; a salad of green beans, walnuts, and feta cheese; and chocolate bread pudding with bourbon sauce. The supplies, including the mint julep cups, were ordered from www.atasteofkentucky.com. When guests arrived, they picked the name of a Kentucky Derby winner out of a hat, and found the matching place card. Everyone wore hats, and the guests played Derby trivia, with the male winner receiving a bottle of Kentucky bourbon and the female a flower centerpiece.

Jane agreed to go through her files to resurrect the recipes for her famous party, including the treasured recipe for how to cook a country ham that is in Gilbert's mother's handwriting, and other favorites culled from a collection of Kentucky cookbooks dating back to 1959. In addition to her made-from-scratch meal ("I just have to do everything from scratch; I drive my family crazy"), Jane served Kentucky Fried Chicken. "Colonel Sanders really did exist, and I met him," Jane explains.

Should Jane and Gilbert have another Derby party (they promise they will soon, folks!), they have 120 mint julep glasses from Churchill Downs, a box from each year of the race since 1963. Now, that's planning ahead! If Jane was serving twenty people, she'd definitely use her sterling silver julep cups.

Menu

GILBERT'S MINT JULEPS
109

BEER CHEESE
100

KENTUCKY COUNTRY HAM AND SOUTHERN BISCUITS
128 AND 21

STORE-BOUGHT FRIED CHICKEN

TOMATO ASPIC WITH COTTAGE CHEESE DIP
102

KENTUCKY SPOON BREAD
13

TASSIE CUPS WITH LEMON CURD FILLING
233

CHOCOLATE CHIP PIE
223

APPETIZERS & DRINKS

The Lady & Sons Crab-Stuffed Shrimp

I've been asked over and over to publish this recipe in one of my books. Well, ya'll, here it is!

1 tablespoon butter

3 green onions, finely chopped

½ cup finely chopped green bell pepper

¼ teaspoon garlic powder

¼ cup whipping cream

1 tablespoon Dijon mustard

Dash of cayenne pepper

½ cup saltine cracker crumbs

¼ cup mayonnaise

1 egg

2 tablespoons minced fresh parsley

Juice of ½ lemon

1 pound crabmeat, picked through twice for shells

1 pound extra-large or jumbo shrimp, peeled (tails on) and deveined

12 slices bacon, halved crosswise

Basil Cream Sauce

2 tablespoons (¼ stick) butter

1 tablespoon olive oil

1 teaspoon minced garlic

3 tablespoons minced yellow onion

¼ cup white wine

2 cups whipping cream

1 chicken bouillon cube, crushed, or 1 teaspoon granulated bouillon

3 tablespoons store-bought basil pesto

1. Preheat the oven to 350°F.

2. Melt the butter in a large skillet over medium heat and sauté the green onions, green pepper, and garlic powder until the pepper is limp. Place in a mixing bowl and add the cream, mustard, and cayenne pepper. Mix well.

3. Add the cracker crumbs, mayonnaise, egg, parsley, and lemon juice. Mix well. Gently fold in the crabmeat.

4. Split the shrimp down the bottom center to the tail, being careful not to cut through the back. Stuff each shrimp with a small mound of the crabmeat mixture. Wrap the shrimp in bacon and secure with a toothpick. Place the shrimp on a baking sheet and cook in the top third of the oven for 15 to 20 minutes, until the bacon is cooked through. Turn the oven to broil and broil for 4 minutes to crisp the bacon.

5. While the shrimp are cooking, make the Basil Cream Sauce: Heat the butter and olive oil in a skillet over medium heat. Add the garlic and onion and cook until light brown, about 3 minutes. Add the wine and reduce by half. Add the cream and bouillon cube or granulated bouillon and reduce by half again. Add the pesto, bring to a simmer, and heat until slightly thickened, about 2 to 3 minutes.

6. To serve, arrange 4 shrimp on each plate. Drizzle the shrimp with the Basil Cream Sauce.

Serves 5

Sensational Shrimp Mold

People on the coast make something called shrimp butter, which is nothing but ground-up shrimp held together with butter, with a little sherry for zap. This is one notch up from that, because in place of butter, it's got one of my other favorite ingredients—cream cheese!

1 pound small or medium shrimp

1 8-ounce package cream cheese, softened

½ cup mayonnaise

1 green onion, finely chopped, white and green parts

2 teaspoons Dijon mustard

Dash of hot sauce, favorite brand

1. Bring 2 cups water and 1 teaspoon salt to a boil in a medium saucepan and add the shrimp. When the water returns to a boil, turn off the heat, cover the pot, and allow the shrimp to sit for 5 minutes. Drain, peel, and devein.

2. Place the shrimp in a food processor and pulse about eight to ten times, until they are finely chopped but not mushy. Mix together the cream cheese, mayonnaise, green onion, mustard, and hot sauce in a small glass bowl, until well combined. Stir in the shrimp.

3. Line a 2-cup mold or glass bowl with plastic wrap, leaving lots of overhang. Place the shrimp mixture into the mold, packing tightly with a spatula. Cover with the plastic wrap overhang and chill in the refrigerator for at least 2 hours or overnight.

4. When ready to serve, unwrap the overhang and invert the mold onto a plate. Remove the plastic wrap. Allow to come to room temperature before serving with water crackers or other favorite snack cracker.

Serves 12 to 15 as part of a buffet

Smoked or Poached Salmon Mousse with Dill Sauce

Let's use our heads, girls. Buy the dad-gum poached salmon. It's the sauce that's so terrific!

1 envelope unflavored gelatin

½ cup mayonnaise

1 tablespoon fresh lemon juice

1 tablespoon fresh lime juice

1 tablespoon grated onion

2 drops hot sauce

½ teaspoon paprika

1 teaspoon salt

2 cups poached or smoked salmon, flaked into small pieces

2 tablespoons capers, drained

1 cup whipping cream, whipped

1 lemon, sliced paper thin, each slice cut into 2 half moons

1 bunch parsley or watercress, washed and dried

Dill Sauce

1 English cucumber, peeled, grated, and drained for at least 1 hour

1 cup sour cream

1 cup mayonnaise

2 tablespoons fresh lemon juice

1 small clove garlic, minced

1 teaspoon salt

⅔ cup fresh dill, finely chopped

1. Grease a 4-cup fish mold with butter or mayonnaise. Soften the gelatin in ¼ cup cold water. Add ½ cup boiling water and stir well, until the gelatin has completely dissolved. Add the mayonnaise, lemon juice, lime juice, onion, hot sauce, paprika, and salt and mix well. Stir in the salmon and capers and mix well. Fold in the whipped cream and continue folding until everything is well combined. Pour the mixture into the prepared mold. Cover with plastic wrap and chill in the refrigerator for at least 4 hours or overnight.

2. When ready to serve, unmold onto a large plate. Take lemon slices and create a "tail" on the back of the fish. Surround with parsley or watercress. Serve with the dill sauce.

3. To make the dill sauce: Combine all of the ingredients in a medium bowl. Cover with plastic wrap and chill for at least an hour to allow the flavors to blend. Serve next to the salmon mousse in a glass bowl with a serving spoon.

Serves 16 to 20 as part of a buffet

Note: You'll have a totally different taste depending on which type of salmon you choose; I like 'em both.

Crab Mousse

One 10¾-ounce can condensed cream of mushroom soup

One 8-ounce package cream cheese

1 envelope unflavored gelatin, softened in ¼ cup cold water

½ pound lump crabmeat, picked through for shells and cartilage

1 cup finely chopped celery

¼ cup chopped green onion, white and green parts

1 tablespoon fresh lemon juice

1 teaspoon Worcestershire sauce

¼ teaspoon seasoned salt

1. Grease a 3-cup seafood mold.

2. Combine the soup, cream cheese, and softened gelatin in a glass bowl. Heat for 2 minutes in the microwave, until very hot. Stir well to make sure that the gelatin is completely dissolved and there are no lumps. Add the crabmeat, celery, green onion, lemon juice, Worcestershire sauce, and seasoned salt. Stir gently but thoroughly.

3. Spoon the mixture into the mold and smooth the top. Cover with plastic wrap and chill until firm. When ready to serve, loosen the edges of the mousse, then invert onto a serving dish. The mousse will slip out in a few minutes. Serve with good crackers, such as Carr's Table Water Crackers.

Serves 8 to 10

Crabbies

These are soooooo good!

½ cup (1 stick) butter, softened

8 ounces (1 cup) sharp Cheddar cheese spread, any variety

2 teaspoons mayonnaise

¼ teaspoon garlic powder

½ teaspoon seasoned salt

½ pound fresh crabmeat, picked through twice for shells

6 regular-size English muffins, split

Paprika

1. In a medium bowl, combine the butter, cheese spread, mayonnaise, garlic powder, and seasoned salt. Mix well. Gently fold in the crabmeat.

2. Spread the mixture on the muffin halves and sprinkle with paprika. Cut into quarters. Place on a baking sheet and cover with plastic wrap. Freeze for 20 minutes.

3. While the crabbies are freezing, preheat the oven to 350°F.

4. Remove the plastic wrap and bake the frozen crabbies for 20 minutes, until the topping is browned and bubbly.

Makes 48 crabbies

Purist's Lump Crab Salad

Some of you won't be able to make this because you can't get lump crabmeat like we can. This is the ultimate luxury dish, even for those of us who live on the Georgia coast.
For the best flavor, make this at the last minute.

1 pound jumbo or regular lump crabmeat

Grated zest of 2 lemons

Seasoned salt

Juice of 2 lemons

About 1 tablespoon mayonnaise (just enough to hold it all together)

Just before serving, combine all of the ingredients, adding seasoned salt to taste; stir gently so as not to break up the crabmeat. Serve with water crackers or toast points.

Serves 10 to 12 as part of a buffet

Suzie's Peach Pickles (page 68); Buttermilk Corn Bread (page 16)

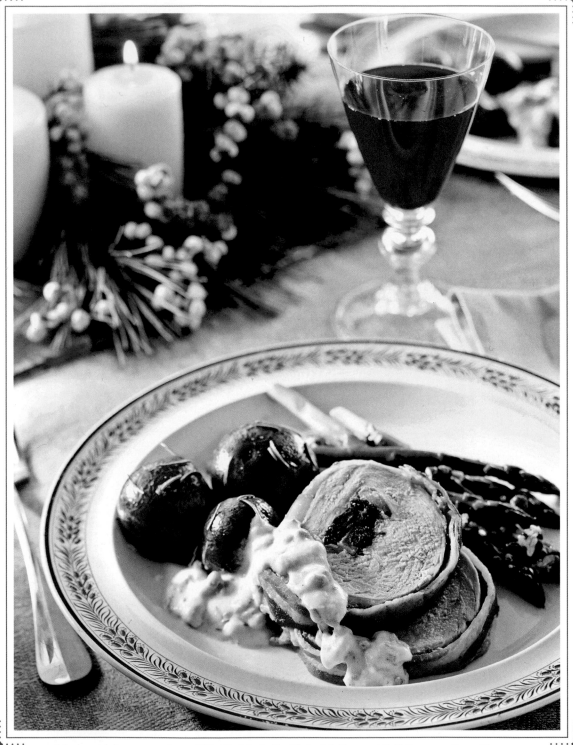

Marinated Asparagus (page 179); Veal Loin Stuffed with Roasted Bell Peppers, Goat Cheese, and Basil (page 124); Rosemary and Garlic Roasted New Potatoes (page 175)

Clockwise, from top: Apple Martini (page 111); Plantation Iced Tea (page 106);
Irish Jasper Green (page 107); Fuzzy Navel (page 108)

Artichoke Rice Salad with Shrimp (page 52); Marinated Tomatoes (page 191);
Grilled Pork Tenderloin (page 126)

Bloody Marys (page 110); Pimiento Cheese (page 101); Smoked Turkey Wraps (page 46)

Magnolia Lace Trumpets (page 238); Benne Seed Cookies (page 257); Paula's Ultimate Oatmeal
Cookies (page 250); Ginger Cookies (page 258); Mexican Wedding Cookies (page 260);
Savannah Bow Ties (page 248); Chocolate Sandwich Cookies (page 254)

Maple-Glazed Salmon with Pineapple Salsa (page 152)

Potato Soup with Shrimp (page 62); Green Chili Corn Muffins (page 17)

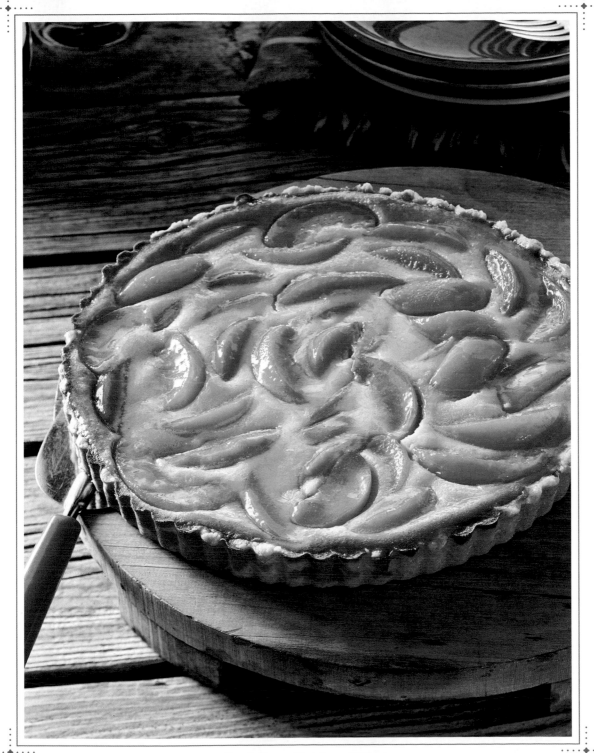

Peach Cream Tart (page 229)

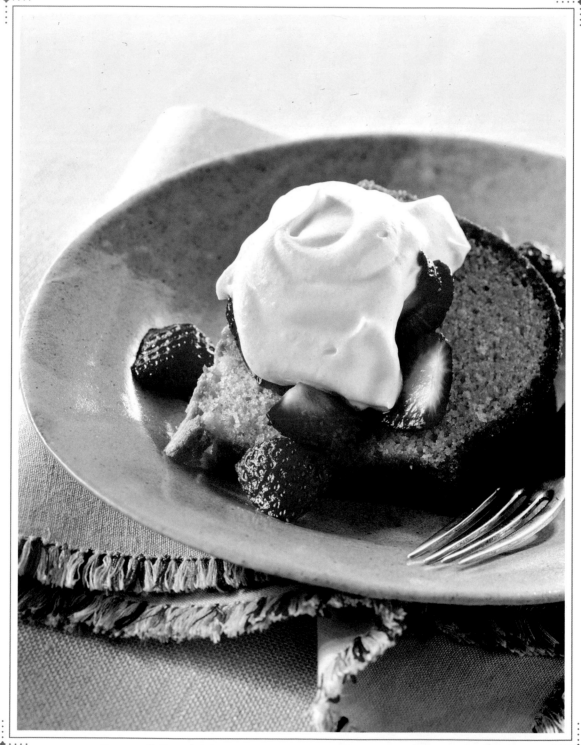

Buttermilk Pound Cake with Strawberries and Whipped Cream (page 210)

Beer-in-the-Rear Chicken (page 134)

Raspberry and Sherry Trifle (page 232)

Wild Rice Salad (page 54); Rene's Coleslaw (page 55); Bert's Southern Fried Chicken (page 136)

Shrimp and Grits (page 149)

Clockwise, from right: Fruit Kebabs (page 269); Almond Danish Swirls (page 26);
Sausage Swirls (page 8); Breakfast Casserole (page 4)

Bacon-Wrapped Grilled Corn on the Cob (page 184); Green Beans with New Potatoes (page 180)

Bacon Crisps

These delicious crisps can be frozen after they're cooked. Place the frozen crisps on a baking sheet and reheat them for 5 minutes in a 350°F oven.

½ **cup freshly grated Parmesan cheese**

1 **pound sliced bacon, cut in half**

1 **sleeve buttery rectangular crackers**

1. Preheat the oven to 250°F.

2. Place 1 teaspoon of the cheese on each cracker and wrap tightly with a strip of bacon (no toothpick required!). Place the wrapped crackers on a broiler rack on a baking sheet and put the baking sheet on the oven rack; bake for 2 hours, or until the bacon is done. Do not turn. Drain on paper towels. Serve hot or at room temperature.

Makes 3 dozen

Note: We were a little impatient during our testing and baked these at 350°F for about 40 minutes, with good results.

Teriyaki and Buffalo Chicken Wings

Serve the wings with celery sticks and blue cheese dressing.

36 fresh or frozen chicken wings, tips trimmed

Salt and pepper

Vegetable oil, for deep frying

Teriyaki Sauce

½ cup soy sauce

3 tablespoons light brown sugar

3 cloves garlic, minced

1 teaspoon grated fresh ginger

2 tablespoons dry sherry

Buffalo Sauce

4 tablespoons (½ stick) butter, melted

2 tablespoons hot sauce

1 teaspoon red wine vinegar

1. Thaw the frozen wings under running water until the glaze has melted. Dry the wings thoroughly. Salt and pepper to taste.

2. In a Dutch oven or an electric frying pan, pour in 3 inches of oil and heat to 360°F. Using tongs, lower each wing individually into the oil. Fry until the wings are crisp and brown, about 12 to 14 minutes. Drain on paper towels. You will have to cook the wings in several batches. This can be done several hours before the party. Leave at room temperature, covered loosely with foil, after they have cooled completely.

3. Preheat the oven to 350°F.

4. Combine the teriyaki sauce ingredients in a small measuring cup. Combine the Buffalo sauce ingredients in another small measuring cup. Place 18 wings in one baking dish and the remaining 18 wings in another baking dish. Pour the teriyaki sauce on the wings in one dish and toss to coat. Pour the Buffalo sauce on the other wings and toss to coat. Place in the oven for about 5 minutes, until the sauces have glazed the wings and the wings are heated through.

Serves 6

Chopped Liver

Jane Feiler used this recipe for The Hard Lox Café, an annual fund-raiser for Temple Mickve Israel.

3 tablespoons butter

1 pound chicken livers, cleaned

1 medium onion, chopped

½ teaspoon ground dried thyme

Salt and pepper

3 hard-boiled eggs, roughly chopped

1. Melt the butter in a skillet and cook the livers and onion until the onion becomes translucent, about 4 minutes. Add the thyme and generous amounts of salt and pepper while cooking. Drain the mixture but reserve any liquid.

2. Pulse the livers and onion four or five times in a food processor. Add the eggs and pulse again four or five times. Add some of the cooking liquid if needed; you want a smooth spreading consistency but not a paste. Serve with party rye or crackers.

Serves 10 to 12

Macho Nachos

This is a winner every time you serve it.

One 13.5-ounce bag white
corn tortilla chips

One 16-ounce can refried
beans, traditional, low-
fat, or vegetarian

1 medium yellow onion,
chopped

1 cup (¼ pound) shredded
pepper Jack cheese

1 fresh or pickled jalapeño
pepper, seeds and veins
removed, very finely
sliced crosswise, plus
extra for garnish

One 15-ounce can chili,
with or without beans

1 cup (¼ pound) grated
sharp Cheddar cheese

1 cup sour cream

½ cup chopped green onions

1 tomato, diced

1. Preheat the oven to 350°F.

2. On a large ovenproof platter, spread out a layer of tortilla chips. In a small saucepan over low heat, warm the refried beans until they are loose enough to spoon onto the chips. Put a teaspoon of beans on each chip. Working quickly, sprinkle the chips with onion, Jack cheese, and jalapeño slices. Spoon on the chili and top with the Cheddar.

3. Place the platter in the oven and bake until the cheeses have melted, 5 to 10 minutes.

4. Remove from the oven and place on a trivet or heatproof surface. Top the nachos with the sour cream, green onions, diced tomato, and extra jalapeño slices, for garnish. Serve hot.

Serves 10

Good Seasons Salsa

I really didn't think this would work, but it does. When you stir in the cheese, it soaks up the dressing and creates a delicious "sauce."

4 small tomatoes, chopped

One 3.8-ounce can sliced black olives, drained

One 4-ounce can green chilies, chopped

4 green onions, white and green parts, chopped

1 package Good Seasons salad dressing mix, prepared according to package directions

One 8-ounce package shredded Mexican cheese

Corn chip scoops (like Fritos Scoops)

In a medium glass bowl, combine the tomatoes, olives, chilies, green onions, and dressing. Cover with plastic wrap and refrigerate. Just before serving, stir in the cheese. Serve with corn chip scoops.

Note: Mexican cheese consists of Monterey Jack, Cheddar, and other mild cheeses combined; it's available in most supermarkets in the dairy/cheese section.

Tomato Tarts

These tarts smell so delicious when they are cooking, your guests will want to pluck them straight from the pan, but you need to let them cool or you'll burn your tongue! The recipe originally came from Savannah caterer Trish McLeod. You'll need a biscuit cutter for this recipe; take it with you when you shop for the tomatoes, so your tomatoes and pastry rounds are the same size.

1 sheet frozen puff pastry dough

Olive oil

½ cup grated white Cheddar cheese

4 or 5 Italian plum tomatoes, cut into ¼-inch slices

Salt and pepper

2 tablespoons fresh thyme leaves, chopped fine

Approximately ½ cup freshly grated Parmesan cheese

1. Preheat the oven to 375°F. Spray a baking sheet with vegetable oil cooking spray.

2. Remove the puff pastry sheet from the freezer and allow it to thaw for 20 minutes. Unfold the pastry on the counter, and using a 1½- or 2-inch biscuit cutter, cut out rounds of dough. Place the puff pastry rounds on the prepared baking sheet. Prick the surface of the pastry with a fork. Brush each round lightly with olive oil and top with a small amount of the Cheddar cheese, then with a tomato slice. Sprinkle salt and pepper to taste over the tomato, then sprinkle on a pinch of thyme and about 1 teaspoon of Parmesan cheese.

3. Bake for about 15 minutes. Let cool for 2 to 3 minutes before serving.

Makes about 10 tarts

Green Chili Squares

This is a quiche without the crust. The squares look pretty on the plate next to the enchiladas loaded down with toppings.

Three 4-ounce cans diced green chilies, with juice

2 **cups (½ pound) grated Monterey Jack cheese**

2 **cups (½ pound) grated sharp Cheddar cheese**

½ **teaspoon salt**

½ **teaspoon pepper**

Splash of hot sauce

6 **eggs, beaten**

1. Preheat the oven to 300°F. Spray a 12-by-8-inch baking dish with vegetable oil cooking spray.

2. Spread out the diced green chilies evenly over the bottom of the dish. Mix the cheeses together and sprinkle them evenly over the chilies.

3. Add the salt, pepper, and hot sauce to the beaten eggs. Pour the eggs over the chilies and cheese. Pat the mixture down with the back of a spoon.

4. Bake for 45 minutes, until the center is firm. Allow to sit for about 10 minutes, then cut into small squares with a bread knife. Serve warm.

Makes about 24 pieces

Slice-and-Bake Cheese Straws

Many a southern cook's reputation has been founded on cheese straws. These aren't made with a cookie press. Just roll the dough into a log using waxed paper, refrigerate, and slice as you would refrigerator cookies.

½ cup (1 stick) butter, softened

1 pound grated sharp Cheddar cheese

1½ cups all-purpose flour

½ teaspoon baking powder

½ teaspoon salt

¼ teaspoon cayenne pepper

1. Combine the butter and cheese in a food processor. Sift together the flour, baking powder, salt, and cayenne and add to the food processor bowl. Pulse until the dough forms a ball. Turn out onto waxed paper and roll into small logs. (I make several small ones for ease of handling.) Wrap each log in the waxed paper and twist the ends to keep airtight. Refrigerate until firm enough to slice.

2. Preheat the oven to 350°F. Line cookie sheets with parchment paper or nonstick baking mats, or use nonstick sheets.

3. Cut the dough into ¼-inch slices and place ½ inch apart on the prepared cookie sheets. Bake for 12 to 15 minutes, until lightly browned. Cool completely before placing into airtight tins. Dough may be placed into resealable plastic freezer bags and frozen. Baked cheese straws may be frozen in tins. To reheat, place frozen cheese straws in a 300°F oven for 5 minutes.

Makes 8 dozen

BLT Appetizer

This recipe came from Phyllis Curlee, of Savannah, who served it during visits with her brother and sister-in-law at Lake Oconee. It's messy but good!

Mix any leftovers together and serve as a salad with peeled, cooked shrimp and Cheddar cheese cubes, or fried chicken strips, chopped.

1 **cup mayonnaise**

1 **cup sour cream**

1 **pound lean bacon, cooked crisp and crumbled**

Iceberg lettuce, shredded

2 **large vine-ripe tomatoes, chopped**

Sea salt bagel chips

1. Combine the mayonnaise, sour cream, and half of the bacon in a small bowl with a snap-on lid. When well mixed, refrigerate until serving time.

2. When ready to serve, place the lettuce in a large serving bowl. Place the mayonnaise mixture on top of the lettuce. Top with the tomatoes and the remaining bacon. Serve with bagel chips.

Serves 8

Fresh Asparagus with Curry Dip

I don't steam asparagus; I boil them quickly. Just don't get distracted while the asparagus are cooking, or you'll wind up with limp spears. Allow one or two asparagus per person.

A little of this goes a long way; one recipe is usually enough, unless you've got a huge party. Then you can double the recipe.

1 **cup mayonnaise**

1 **teaspoon curry powder**

½ **tablespoon fresh lemon juice**

1 **tablespoon grated onion**

1 **red bell pepper**

1. Combine the mayonnaise, curry powder, lemon juice, and onion in a small bowl. Cover with plastic wrap and chill.

2. Cut the bell pepper in half lengthwise, remove the core and seeds, and serve the curry dip in pepper "bowls."

Serves 15 to 18

Cranberry Holiday Brie

This is one of those dishes that is just beautiful to see. When you bring it to the table, the puff pastry dough is browned and beautiful, and then, when you slice into the cheese, the Brie oozes out and the cranberries peek through. The white on red makes this a perfect dish for the holidays—any occasion between Thanksgiving and Valentine's!

1 sheet (½ package) frozen puff pastry dough

1 egg

¾ cup apricot preserves

2 tablespoons orange juice

⅓ cup dried cranberries

¼ cup toasted sliced almonds

1 Brie cheese, about 13 ounces

Water crackers

1. Allow the pastry sheet to thaw in the package about 30 minutes, until pliable. Preheat the oven to 400°F. In a small bowl, beat the egg with 1 teaspoon water to make an egg wash. Set aside.

2. Lightly flour a large wooden cutting board and roll out the pastry dough into a 14-inch square. Cut off the corners to make a circle. Save the extra dough to cut into decorative shapes for a garnish. Spread the apricot preserves on the pastry, leaving a 2-inch margin all around the edge.

3. Pour the orange juice into a small glass dish and add the cranberries, allowing them to absorb the flavor of the orange juice for about 5 minutes, until the cranberries are soft. Drain the cranberries. Arrange the cranberries evenly on top of the apricot preserves. Arrange the almonds evenly on the cranberries. Place the Brie on top of the almonds. Brush the edges of the puff pastry with the egg wash. Completely seal the Brie in the puff pastry. Seal the edges by brushing the egg wash on one edge, as if you are gluing the edges together.

4. Spray a baking sheet with vegetable oil cooking spray. Place the Brie seam-side down on the sheet. Decorate the top with pastry cutouts, rerolling scraps of dough, if desired. Brush the top with the remaining egg wash.

5. Bake for 20 minutes. Allow to sit for at least 30 minutes before serving; the cheese will be runny if you cut it too early! Serve with crackers.

Serves 12

Hot Spinach-Artichoke Dip

This is the only thing that needs to go in a chafing dish. Use it to anchor one end of the dining-room table, because it will draw a crowd. Make sure the heat under the chafing dish is set very low so the dip doesn't scorch. Nobody can ever quite figure out what's in this, but they like it, and that's all that matters.

One 10-ounce package frozen chopped spinach, cooked in the microwave for 5 minutes and squeezed until dry

Two 13¾-ounce cans artichoke hearts, drained and chopped in a food processor (about five or six pulses)

½ **cup mayonnaise**

½ **cup sour cream**

1½ **cups freshly grated Parmesan cheese**

1 **cup grated pepper Jack cheese**

Bagel chips

1. Preheat the oven to 350°F. Grease a 2-quart casserole dish.

2. Combine all of the ingredients in a large bowl. Stir well with a metal spoon. Place in the prepared casserole dish and bake for 30 minutes. Transfer to a chafing dish. Keep warm over a low flame. Serve with bagel chips.

Serves 16 to 20 as part of a buffet

Beer Cheese

Jane Wells says something cheesy is a requirement at a Derby party. Cheese straws, store-bought or homemade, are also an option.

1 pound grated sharp Cheddar cheese

1 teaspoon cayenne pepper

1 teaspoon salt

1 clove garlic, minced

¼ small onion, grated

2 tablespoons flat beer

Place the cheese, cayenne, salt, garlic, onion, and beer in a food processor and process until smooth. Pack the cheese into crocks or serving bowls. Cover with plastic wrap and refrigerate. Allow to come to room temperature before serving with water crackers or crisp celery stalks.

Makes about 2 cups, enough for a party of about 25

All-Purpose Cheese Spread

Good cook Patty Ronning made this recipe famous at her children's weekend riverhouse get-togethers. Serve it with crackers or celery sticks, crusty French bread, or smear it on baked potatoes on steak night. Yum!

One 6-ounce roll cheese food

One 8-ounce package cream cheese, softened

½ cup mayonnaise

½ cup (1 stick) butter, softened

Place all of the ingredients in a small mixing bowl. Mix well with a handheld electric mixer for about 3 minutes, scraping down the sides of the bowl, until completely combined. Store in a plastic container with a snap-on lid in the refrigerator. Serve at room temperature.

Makes 2 cups

Pimiento Cheese

Serve this cheese on Wheat Thins or as a sandwich filling. Some people also use it to stuff celery sticks.

One 8-ounce package shredded sharp Cheddar cheese

One 8-ounce package shredded extra-sharp Cheddar cheese

One 4-ounce jar pimientos, with juice

¼ cup mayonnaise

Salt and pepper

Mix the shredded cheeses together with the pimientos, with juice. Stir in the mayonnaise. With a metal spoon (pimientos will stain plastic or wood), stir until the mixture is well blended. Add salt and pepper to taste and stir again. Keep covered in the refrigerator until ready to use. It is easier to spread if left out on the counter for about 30 minutes before serving.

Makes 3½ cups

Dawg Bite Cheese Spread

This really has a kick. Serve at room temperature with crackers.

1 pound Velveeta cheese, cut into 1-inch cubes

1 cup mayonnaise

One 5-ounce bottle prepared horseradish

In a large glass mixing bowl, melt the Velveeta in the microwave on high power for about 90 seconds. Stir. If not soft and easy to stir, heat for 30 seconds more. Stir in the mayonnaise and half of the horseradish. Taste, and add more horseradish if you want more "bite." Stir again. Cover with plastic wrap and refrigerate.

Makes 2 cups

Tomato Aspic with Cottage Cheese Dip

At her next party, Jane intends to serve the tomato aspic in a horseshoe-shaped mold from The Wilton Store (www.wilton.com). She likes to fill the center of the aspic with a savory cottage cheese dip.

Aspic

- 1 envelope unflavored gelatin
- 1¾ cups V8 vegetable juice
- 2 tablespoons fresh lemon juice
- 2 teaspoons Worcestershire sauce
- 1 tablespoon prepared horseradish
- 2 teaspoons salt
- Dash of Tabasco
- ¼ teaspoon sugar

Cottage Cheese Dip

- 1 pound large-curd cottage cheese, 2% or 4% milkfat
- 1 cup grated sharp Cheddar cheese
- ½ cup chopped Spanish olives
- 1 tablespoon grated onion
- ½ teaspoon salt
- Dash of Worcestershire sauce
- Dash of Tabasco
- 2 tablespoons mayonnaise

1. To make the aspic: Soften the gelatin in ¼ cup cold water. Place the V8 juice in a 4-cup glass measuring cup and heat in the microwave for 2 minutes, until very hot. Add the softened gelatin to the hot juice and stir with a metal spoon until the gelatin is completely dissolved. Add the lemon juice, Worcestershire sauce, horseradish, salt, Tabasco, and sugar and stir well. Pour into a 2½-cup ring mold (sprayed with vegetable spray) and chill until set. Unmold by inverting onto a serving platter and allowing to sit for about 30 minutes; or dip the mold into warm but not hot water for 10 to 15 seconds, then insert carefully onto a serving platter. Serve a small sliver of aspic with a dollop of cottage cheese dip.

2. To make the dip: Combine the cottage cheese, Cheddar cheese, olives, onion, salt, Worcestershire sauce, Tabasco, and mayonnaise. Stir together gently but thoroughly. When ready to serve, mound into the center of the aspic. It also makes a good sandwich spread!

Serves 25

Black-Eyed Pea Dip

This tastes like southern salsa—it's particularly refreshing in summer, but is a hit any time it's served.

Two 15-ounce cans black-eyed peas, drained

One 15-ounce can whole kernel corn, drained

One 10-ounce can Ro-Tel tomatoes or any spicy canned tomatoes, chopped

1 cup chopped red bell pepper

1 cup chopped green bell pepper

¼ cup chopped fresh jalapeño pepper

½ cup chopped yellow onion

One 4-ounce jar chopped pimientos, drained

Dressing

½ cup red wine vinegar

1 tablespoon balsamic vinegar

1 teaspoon salt

½ teaspoon pepper

1 tablespoon Dijon mustard

¼ teaspoon sugar

Pinch of dried oregano

½ cup olive oil

½ cup vegetable oil

Corn chips, for serving

1. In a large bowl, combine the black-eyed peas; corn; tomatoes; red, green, and jalapeño peppers; onion; and pimientos.

2. In a glass jar with a tight-fitting lid, combine the wine and balsamic vinegars, salt, pepper, mustard, sugar, oregano, and olive and vegetable oils. Shake until the ingredients are blended.

3. Add the dressing to the pea mixture and stir gently but thoroughly. Cover and refrigerate until serving time. Allow to come to room temperature before serving. Stir well. Serve with corn chips.

Serves 10 to 12

Chutney Butter

Place this in a small crock near some store-bought shaved turkey or store-bought shaved country ham. Do not buy "hot" chutney.

1 cup (2 sticks) butter, softened

1 tablespoon cranberry chutney, any brand

Store-bought shaved turkey or store-bought shaved country ham

Combine the butter and chutney in a small bowl, stirring well with a spoon. Taste; add more chutney if desired. Store in the refrigerator until ready to serve. Serve in crocks; allow to stand about 30 minutes at room temperature to soften before serving.

TO ORDER A COUNTRY HAM

Country ham shaved thin and served on homemade biscuits is a big southern treat. Some people still opt to buy the whole bone-in ham, scrub off the mold that always comes with it, soak it, and bake it (see Jane and Gilbert Wells's "Run for the Roses" party, page 80, for details). Others are happy to have other people do the work. One very good source for purchasing country ham is www.smithfieldfarms.com; or call (800) 222-2110. Expect to pay about $70 for a 7- to 9-pound ham. Have it shaved by a friendly butcher.

Sweet Tea

The hotter the weather gets, the sweeter we want our tea! I like mine with fresh mint.

7 tea bags
1 cup sugar
  Mint sprigs
  Lemon wedges

Bring 4 cups water to a boil in a kettle. Add the tea bags and turn off the heat immediately. Place the lid on the kettle and allow the tea to steep for 1 hour. Remove the tea bags and pour the tea into a pitcher. Add the sugar and stir to dissolve. Add 4 cups cold water. Serve over ice with a sprig of mint and a lemon wedge.

Makes 2 quarts, about 10 servings

Lemonade

Our lemonade at the restaurant is so popular, we have to make it in tremendous batches, which is hard to break down for home use. We don't make ours from a mix—it's made from scratch.

3 cups sugar
2 cups fresh lemon juice
1 lemon, sliced
  Mint sprigs, for garnish

Put the sugar and 1 cup hot water in a 1-gallon container and stir until the sugar is dissolved. Add the lemon juice. Fill the container with cold water. Stir until well mixed. Serve over ice, with a squeezed lemon slice on top and garnished with mint.

Makes 1 gallon, about 20 servings

Plantation Iced Tea

Patty Ronning serves this at luncheons where no alcohol is permitted.

7 tea bags

12 mint leaves

½ cup sugar

   One 6-ounce can frozen
   lemonade concentrate

   One 12-ounce can
   pineapple juice

Pour 4 cups boiling water over the tea bags, mint, and sugar in a pitcher. Steep for 30 minutes. Remove the tea bags, squeezing out excess liquid. Remove the mint. Prepare the lemonade according to the instructions and add to the tea. Add the pineapple juice and stir. Serve over ice.

Makes 2 quarts, about 10 servings

Fruit Punch

Keep this in milk jugs for easier pouring.

   Two 6-ounce cans frozen
   orange juice concentrate

   Two 6-ounce cans frozen
   lemonade concentrate

   One 48-ounce can
   pineapple juice

3 cups sugar

2 pints strawberries, hulled

   One 2-liter bottle of
   Sprite

1. Combine the orange juice, lemonade, and pineapple juice and stir well.

2. Bring 3 cups water and the sugar to a boil in a heavy saucepan and boil until the sugar is dissolved, about 5 minutes. Let cool. Add the syrup to the fruit juices.

3. Place the whole strawberries into a ring mold that will float in your punch bowl. Pour in enough fruit juice to fill the mold. Freeze. Refrigerate the remaining juice.

4. When ready to serve, pour the fruit juice into a punch bowl and add the Sprite. Float the strawberry ice ring in the punch.

Makes 1 gallon, about 20 servings

Strawberry Slush

This was served by Molly Gignilliat, of Savannah, at a wedding shower.

One 3-ounce package strawberry gelatin dessert mix

1 cup pineapple juice

1 cup lemonade, made from frozen concentrate

2 cups crushed fresh strawberries

¼ cup sugar

Dissolve the gelatin in 1 cup boiling water. When completely dissolved, place in a blender with the remaining ingredients and 1 cup cold water. Blend. Add about 1 cup crushed ice or several ice cubes and blend again. Mixture will be thick.

Serves 4 to 6

Irish Jasper Green

Serve this on St. Patrick's Day. Sgt. William Jasper fought and was mortally wounded in the Siege of Savannah. He became famous because he picked up a fallen flag and rallied the troops. The Irish Jasper Green Company of the National Guard is still in existence in Savannah today.

2 scoops lime sherbet

1 cup lemonade, made from frozen concentrate

1 tablespoon honey

Splash of cream

Mint sprigs, for garnish

Place the sherbet, lemonade, honey, cream, and ½ cup crushed ice in a blender. Blend until smooth. Serve garnished with fresh mint.

Makes 2 drinks

Margaritas

When I'm having a social drink, this is the one for me.

One 6-ounce can frozen limeade concentrate

¾ cup gold tequila

¼ cup triple sec (orange liqueur)

Fresh lime slices

Salt

1. Place the limeade in a blender. Add the tequila (fill the empty limeade can) to the blender. Add the triple sec to the blender. Fill with ice and blend.

2. Take a lime slice and rub it around the rim of a glass. Dip the glass in salt. Fill with frozen margarita.

Makes 6 drinks

Fuzzy Navel

This is delicious!

3 medium peaches, peeled and cut from pit

One 6-ounce can frozen orange juice concentrate

¼ cup rum, light or dark

¼ cup sugar

Mint sprigs for garnish

Place the peaches, orange juice, rum, sugar, and 1 cup crushed ice in a blender. Blend until smooth. Serve garnished with fresh mint.

Makes 4 drinks

Gilbert's Mint Juleps

Gilbert Wells learned to make these in his hometown of Glasgow, Kentucky. He served these in California when he and his wife, Jane, lived there, and continues the tradition in Savannah. Get a good start, as the syrup needs to be made a week in advance and will keep up to thirty days. Be careful! Juleps are delicious and smooth; the alcohol sneaks up on you!

3 cups sugar

Leaves from 15 to 20 mint sprigs

Kentucky bourbon

Fresh mint sprigs, for garnish

1. Place 4 cups water and the sugar in a heavy saucepan and stir. Add the mint leaves and bring the mixture to a boil. Reduce the heat to medium and simmer for 10 minutes. Let cool. Put the sugar syrup into a jug and refrigerate for at least a week and up to 30 days to let the flavor fully develop.

2. When ready to serve, pour 1½ ounces of the cold syrup and 3 ounces of bourbon over crushed ice in a julep cup. Stir. Add a sprig of fresh mint and serve with short straws.

Makes enough syrup for 25 drinks

Bloody Marys

This recipe is adapted from a recipe made famous by Herb Wardell, of Savannah. Herb and his wife, Eloise, are family friends of the Ronnings.

One 46-ounce can V8 vegetable juice

1 teaspoon pepper

1 teaspoon salt

1 tablespoon Worcestershire sauce

Juice of 1 lemon

1 cup vodka

1 tablespoon celery seed

4 shakes of Tabasco or other hot sauce

Celery sticks, for garnish

Pour the juice into a large pitcher. Add the pepper, salt, Worcestershire sauce, lemon juice, vodka, celery seed, and hot sauce. Stir well. Pour into jars with lids for traveling. Serve over ice with celery sticks as stirrers.

Makes enough for about 10 drinks

Apple Martini

Don't ask me why, but martinis are all the rage in our bar at The Lady & Sons restaurant in Savannah. Our bartender, Shaky (her real name is Laura Schexnayder-Thomas), said this is how she makes them.

1½ ounces Absolut vodka

1¼ ounces Sour Apple Pucker schnapps liqueur

    Dash of Cointreau

Combine the vodka, liqueur, and Cointreau. Shake like crazy with ½ cup crushed ice until only slivers of ice are left. Strain into a martini glass.

Makes 1 drink

Irish Coffee

For coffee lovers, this is the best way to jump-start a new year.

For each drink

    Lime slice

    Sugar

¾ cup hot, strong black coffee

1 ounce Irish whiskey

2 tablespoons lightly whipped cream

Rub the lime slice around the rim of a glass coffee mug. Dip the rim in sugar to coat. Pour in the coffee. Add 1 to 2 teaspoons sugar and the whiskey and stir. Slide the whipped cream off a spoon so that it floats on top of the coffee.

Hot Cranberry Cider

This smells so good when it's percolating. Once you've used your coffeepot to make it, however, it always has the smell of cloves and cinnamon sticks in it! We recommend you dedicate a cheap percolator to this recipe.

¼ cup packed brown sugar

3 cinnamon sticks, plus additional sticks to use as stirrers

1 tablespoon whole cloves

6 cups cranberry juice

8 cups apple juice

Put the sugar, cinnamon sticks, and cloves in the basket of a coffee percolator. Put the juices in the bottom of the percolator. Let the mixture perk as if making coffee. Serve with cinnamon stick stirrers if desired.

Makes 3½ quarts, about 18 servings

Puttin' It All Together

A BIG Cocktail Buffet
114

A BIG Cocktail Buffet

After the September 11, 2001, tragedy in New York City, Simon Macfadyen, a young Englishman and a vice president of Marsh Limited in London (an insurer of airlines, including United), was sent to New York on business. He needed a getaway, and went to Washington, D.C., to see Mallory Crosland, a friend he'd met when she interned at Lloyd's of London. Through Mallory, he met Elizabeth Lientz (Barbie's daughter, of bridge club supper fame). Well, it was love at first sight, which is something my Michael and I know all about if you've been watching my show!

Anyway, Simon and Elizabeth were married in Savannah on March 27, 2004, and 130 Brits came for the wedding, including Pat Rowan, Simon's ninety-two-year-old grandmother! There was so much good food, including an oyster roast, which the Brits loved.

When Elizabeth's Savannah high school friends—Julia Holliday, Katherine Donovan, Benjamin Levy, and Meg Butler—heard that she was engaged, their parents wanted to throw a party when all the twentysomethings would be home for the holidays. The party was at the Donovans' house in Ardsley Park, and each of the host families contributed part of the food—a great idea for giving a large party. Elizabeth requested a menu the families had traditionally served during the holidays through the years.

Here's a little secret: When you're doing the cooking for a big party, do buy some quality prepared foods to help yourself out. At Elizabeth's Christmas cocktail buffet, the hosts and hostesses bought a boneless country ham and a boneless turkey breast, and had both shaved for make-your-own sandwich platters. No need to cook the meat when someone else can do it for you! They also bought just-baked yeast rolls and lemon bars from a local bakery. If you'd like to make your own lemon bars, we've provided a terrific recipe.

The centerpieces for the cocktail party were striking amaryllis in full bloom that Katherine's mother, Carolyn, had purchased from an annual garden club sale. The bulbs were tied together and accented with giant gold bows, and fresh greenery from the yard filled the base of the flowerpots.

Ms. Donovan had this tip for anyone planning a large cocktail buffet, and it's one I agree with totally: Do splurge on having someone in the kitchen to keep trays replenished and to clean up as the evening goes on. The hosts also hired a bartender, but you could also appoint your best young drink-mixer to this task. That way, girls, you can enjoy your own party and not have to face a mess when it's over!

We've selected some of the best recipes to create this rather elaborate menu. If you don't want to tackle the whole thing, you may pick and choose from the menu to prepare your own cocktail party for out-of-town family and friends.

Menu

STORE-BOUGHT SHAVED
COUNTRY HAM

STORE-BOUGHT SHAVED
SMOKED TURKEY BREAST WITH
CHUTNEY BUTTER AND STORE-
BOUGHT HONEY MUSTARD
104

TOMATO SANDWICHES
41

SMOKED OR POACHED SALMON
MOUSSE WITH DILL SAUCE
86

FRESH ASPARAGUS WITH
CURRY DIP
97

SENSATIONAL SHRIMP MOLD
85

HOT SPINACH-ARTICHOKE DIP
99

PURIST'S LUMP CRAB SALAD
88

SLICE-AND-BAKE
CHEESE STRAWS
96

BACON CRISPS
89

LEMON BARS
240

MINI CHOCOLATE ÉCLAIRS
234

CHOCOLATE-DIPPED
STRAWBERRIES
269

MAIN DISHES

Texas Brisket

When I fixed this brisket on my show, I cooked it for five hours, and lots of viewers wrote in to say they made it, and how moist and delicious it was. Later on, when I visited the Memphis barbecue festival, I learned that the real brisket cookers smoke their meat for ten to twelve hours! We tested this on a conventional charcoal grill and a gas grill. The flavor using charcoal was better, but you can't beat the ease of a gas grill; it's so easy to control the temperature. The most important thing is to allow enough time to cook the meat until it's falling-apart tender.

One 5- to 6-pound brisket, trimmed, but left with a layer of fat about ¼ inch thick

6 tablespoons House Seasoning (page 119)

3 tablespoons chili powder

1½ teaspoons dark brown sugar

1½ teaspoons onion powder

1 teaspoon dried oregano

1 teaspoon cayenne pepper

6 cups hickory wood chips, soaked in water for 30 minutes

1. Rinse the brisket thoroughly under cold water and pat dry with paper towels. In a small bowl, mix together the House Seasoning, chili powder, sugar, onion powder, oregano, and cayenne. Rub the brisket with the spice rub on all sides. Place the brisket fat-side up in a large disposable aluminum pan and let it sit while your grill/smoker heats.

2. Follow the directions on your grill/smoker for indirect grilling. Place the soaked chips into the chip box, or make a pouch with tinfoil for the chips and place the pouch directly on the coals. Place the pan with the brisket in the center of the grate and cover the grill.

3. Slow-grill the brisket until it is tender and an instant-read thermometer inserted in the center of the meat reads about 190°F, 10 to 12 hours. Add coals and wood chips as necessary to maintain a low temperature, 250° to 300°F.

4. Transfer the brisket to a cutting board to rest for about 30 minutes. (The meat will shred if you try to slice it right off the grill.) Slice the brisket across the grain to serve.

Serves 10 to 12

House Seasoning

You will notice I call for this in many recipes. I can't cook without it!

1 **cup table salt**

¼ **cup pepper**

¼ **cup garlic powder**

Mix the ingredients together and store in an airtight container for up to 6 months. Use as a seasoning on meat and when cooking vegetables.

Makes 1½ cups

Mama's Brisket

This recipe, developed by Inez Pachter, also works as the main course for a casual party, minus the white potatoes and baby carrots. Serve the chopped brisket in buns.

1 **beef brisket (4 to 5 pounds)**

2 **large onions, sliced**

Sauce

1 **cup ketchup**

1 **teaspoon salt**

½ **cup Worcestershire sauce**

3 **dashes of Tabasco**

1 **teaspoon chili powder**

1 **tablespoon brown sugar**

Four 14½-ounce cans whole white potatoes, drained

One 1-pound bag baby carrots

1. Preheat the oven to 400°F.

2. Place the brisket, fat side up, in a roasting pan. Brown in the oven, uncovered, for 30 minutes. Remove from the oven and lay the onions over the meat.

3. Bring all of the ingredients for the sauce to a boil in a small saucepan. Pour the hot sauce over the meat.

4. Reduce the oven temperature to 325°F and cook the brisket for 1½ hours, basting often. Remove from the oven and let cool. Cover with aluminum foil and refrigerate overnight.

5. When ready to serve, preheat the oven to 300°F. Remove any fat that has congealed. Slice the meat and return to the pan. Add the carrots and potatoes. Bake, covered, until the meat is very tender, about 1½ hours.

Serves 10 to 12

Marinated Filet Mignon

Okay, these are the best and, dad gum it, the most expensive! That's why this recipe is so perfect for that special daddy on Father's Day.

1 **small filet mignon per person, about 1¾ to 2 inches thick**

Marinade
(enough for 6 filets)

½ **cup olive oil**

1 **clove garlic, crushed**

2 **teaspoons finely chopped fresh rosemary**

2 **teaspoons finely chopped fresh thyme**

Flavored butter
(enough for 6 filets)

2 **tablespoons butter, at room temperature**

1 **teaspoon Worcestershire sauce**

1 **teaspoon Dijon mustard**

1. Place the filets in a resealable plastic bag. Combine the marinade ingredients in a glass bowl or measuring cup. Pour the marinade over the filets, seal the bag, and refrigerate for at least 1 hour or overnight.

2. When ready to cook, place the filets over hot coals and grill for about 10 minutes per side, or until the internal temperature is between 140° and 150°F (medium rare).

3. Thoroughly combine the butter, Worcestershire sauce, and mustard. Set aside until the steaks are cooked.

4. Remove the filets to a warm platter. Place about a teaspoon of flavored butter on top of each filet.

Stuffed Beef Tenderloin

When I really want to please Michael, I prepare a good piece of beef.

One 1½-pound beef tenderloin

1 tablespoon butter

¼ cup chopped shallots or yellow onion

1 cup chopped fresh mushrooms

Salt and pepper

Soy sauce

1. Preheat the oven to 400°F.

2. Butterfly the beef tenderloin by cutting the beef lengthwise down the center to within ½ inch of the other side. Set the beef aside.

3. In a medium skillet, melt the butter and cook the shallots or onion over low heat until tender, about 5 minutes. Add the mushrooms and cook over low heat about 5 minutes, or until the liquid is reduced by half.

4. To stuff the tenderloin, open the beef and sprinkle the inside with salt and pepper and rub with the soy sauce. Spoon the mushroom mixture down the center of the tenderloin. Bring the two sides of the tenderloin up around the filling to meet. Using butcher string, tie the tenderloin together at 2-inch intervals. Place the tenderloin in a roasting pan. Roast for 45 minutes for medium rare (150°F on a meat thermometer). Let stand for 10 minutes before slicing. Slice about 1½ inches thick.

Serves 2, with leftovers

Standing Rib Roast

This recipe is one of my family's favorites. You can start it early in the day, and finish it when it's time for dinner.

One 5-pound standing rib roast, bone in

1 **tablespoon House Seasoning (page 119)**

1. Allow the roast to stand at room temperature for at least 1 hour. Preheat the oven to 375°F.

2. Rub the roast with House Seasoning. Place the roast on a rack in a roasting pan with the rib-side down and the fatty-side up. Roast for 1 hour. Turn off the oven and leave the roast in the oven; do not open the door. About 1 hour and 10 minutes before serving time, turn the oven on to 375°F and reheat the roast for 30 to 40 minutes. Do not remove the roast or reopen the oven door from the time the roast is put in until the final roasting. Remove the roast from the oven and tent with foil. Allow the meat to rest for 25 to 30 minutes before carving.

Serves 8 to 10

Hamburger Pie

You can't season this enough. The meat flavors everything else. This is the same old recipe we did in Girl Scouts. You can't improve it.

1 pound ground beef, ground round, or ground chuck

Salt and pepper

1 large onion, thinly sliced

1 large baking potato, thinly sliced, peeled or unpeeled

4 carrots, thinly sliced, each carrot kept separate

Margarine or butter

1. Form the meat into four ½-inch-thick patties. Sprinkle generously with salt and pepper. Lay each patty on a large square of heavy-duty aluminum foil. Top each with a few slices of onion and potato, and 1 sliced carrot. Top with a generous tablespoon of margarine and add more salt and pepper. Wrap tightly in the foil, rolling ends to completely seal the package. Freeze or refrigerate. Pack in coolers.

2. When ready to eat, place packages directly in coals and cook for about 15 to 20 minutes. Check to see if the meat is cooked through; rewrap and cook a little longer if necessary.

Serves 4

Note: To prepare on the stovetop, form the meat into four ½-inch-thick patties. Generously sprinkle with salt and pepper and set aside. In a large skillet, melt the 2 tablespoons margarine, and cook the onions, potatoes, and carrots on medium high for 10 minutes or until tender and golden brown. Place vegetables in a casserole dish; set aside. Melt 2 tablespoons margarine over medium heat. Cook hamburgers until medium doneness for 8 to 10 minutes, turning once. Top vegetables with burgers and serve.

Each of these "pies" goes well with Rice-A-Roni, which can be cooked on a gas stovetop, or with a baked grilled potato. You might notice that we don't recommend turning wrapped foil packets. That's because the butter melts in the packets and will drip out and cause a flare-up if turned.

Veal Loin Stuffed with Roasted Bell Peppers, Goat Cheese, and Basil

Prepare this the day before the party so you won't be stressed. Yes, it's worth the money and the work! Have the butcher bone and trim all of the fat and membrane from a 4¾-pound center-cut veal rib roast, resulting in a 3-pound oblong boneless veal loin. If you are nervous about butterflying the loin at home, have the butcher do this as well.

2 large yellow bell peppers

One 3-ounce package cream cheese with chives, at room temperature

One 5.3-ounce package basil and roasted garlic goat cheese, or 6 ounces soft fresh goat cheese such as Montrachet, at room temperature

1 bunch arugula, well washed and dried, stems trimmed

16 large fresh basil leaves

1 boneless veal loin (3 pounds), butterflied

14 oil-packed sun-dried tomatoes, drained

2 tablespoons butter

Salt and pepper

8 slices bacon

1. Char the peppers over a gas flame or in the broiler, turning until they are blackened on all sides. Place in a paper bag for 10 minutes to loosen the skins. Peel, seed, and stem the peppers, then cut lengthwise into strips. Set aside.

2. Stir the cream cheese and goat cheese in a small bowl until blended. Set aside.

3. Plunge the arugula leaves into hot tap water with tongs; remove immediately. Drain and pat dry. Set aside. Repeat with the basil leaves.

4. Open the veal like a book and cover with plastic wrap. With a meat pounder or rolling pin, gently pound the veal to an approximately 10-by-12-inch rectangle of even thickness.

5. Overlap the arugula leaves down the center of the veal, forming a 2-inch-wide strip. Cover with half of the peppers, skinned side down. Top with the tomatoes, arranged in 2 rows.

6. Set aside ¼ cup of the cheese mixture for the sauce. Spoon the remaining cheese in an even log atop the tomatoes. Arrange the remaining peppers, skinned side up, over the cheese. Arrange the basil leaves over the peppers.

7. Fold the long side of the veal over the filling. Then begin rolling up the veal jelly-roll-style. Cover the ends of the veal with aluminum foil to enclose the filling completely.

8. Tie kitchen string around the veal roll to maintain a neat log shape. Wrap the string lengthwise around the veal to secure the ends. Cover the veal and reserved cheese separately and chill for at least 6 hours. (This can be prepared 1 day ahead.)

9. Preheat the oven to 375°F. Melt the butter in a large, heavy, shallow roasting pan over medium-high heat. Season the veal with salt and pepper. Brown the veal on all sides, turning frequently, about 10 minutes. Remove the pan from the heat. Drape the bacon over the veal, tucking in the ends.

10. Roast until a thermometer inserted into the center of the meat (not the filling) registers 140°F, about 45 minutes. Transfer to a work surface and let stand for 15 minutes. To serve, remove the aluminum foil, bacon, and string.

———◆———

Sauce

2¾ cups chicken broth (canned is fine)

3 medium shallots, finely chopped

¼ cup fresh lemon juice

2 tablespoons capers, drained

½ cup (1 stick) butter, cut into pieces, at room temperature

¼ cup reserved cheese mixture

2 tablespoons chopped fresh parsley

Salt and pepper

1. Combine the broth and shallots in a heavy medium saucepan. Bring to a boil over high heat and cook until the mixture is reduced to ½ cup, about 20 minutes.

2. Whisk in the lemon juice and capers. Reduce the heat to low; gradually whisk in the butter, reserved cheese mixture, and parsley. Add salt and pepper to taste.

3. To serve, cut the veal crosswise into even slices. Spoon a few tablespoons of sauce onto each plate. Top with 2 veal slices.

Serves 8

Grilled Pork Tenderloin

This pork tenderloin tastes better the longer it marinates. You can grill it the day before and serve it at room temperature.

1 pork tenderloin (2 to 2½ pounds)

Marinade

¼ cup soy sauce

2 tablespoons dry red wine

1 tablespoon honey

1 tablespoon brown sugar, dark or light brown

2 cloves garlic, minced

1 teaspoon minced fresh ginger

½ teaspoon ground cinnamon

2 green onions, chopped, white and green parts

1. Place the pork tenderloin in a resealable plastic bag. Place all of the marinade ingredients in a measuring cup and whisk to combine. Pour the marinade over the tenderloin and seal the bag. Marinate overnight in the refrigerator.

2. Preheat an outdoor grill, or preheat the oven to 350°F. Remove the tenderloin from the marinade and pat dry. Reserve the marinade. Grill the meat for about 35 to 40 minutes over medium heat, or roast in the oven for 45 minutes. Allow the meat to sit for about 10 minutes before cutting into 2-inch pieces for serving.

3. While the meat is grilling, gently simmer the reserved marinade in a small saucepan until it is reduced to about 2 tablespoons, stirring occasionally. Drizzle a small amount of marinade over each serving of meat.

Serves 6 to 8

Pork Chop and Pineapple Pie

Pork and pineapple are so good together. Leave out the green pepper if your kids don't care for it.

- 1 boneless pork chop per person
- 1 slice red onion per person
- 1 slice green bell pepper per person
- 2 canned pineapple slices per person
- 1 tablespoon teriyaki sauce per person
- 1 tablespoon margarine or butter per person

  Salt and pepper

1. For each serving, lay a pork chop on a large square of heavy-duty aluminum foil. Top each chop with the onion, green pepper, and pineapple slices. Drizzle with the teriyaki sauce. Top with the margarine and sprinkle generously with salt and pepper. Wrap tightly in the foil, rolling ends to completely seal the package. Freeze or refrigerate. Pack in coolers.

2. When ready to eat, place packages directly in coals for 15 to 20 minutes. Check to see if the pork chop is cooked through; rewrap and cook a little longer if necessary.

Note: To prepare this dish in the oven, preheat the oven to 400°F. Place each chop in a large square of heavy-duty aluminum foil or parchment. Top each chop with the onion, green pepper, and pineapple slices. Drizzle with the teriyaki sauce. Top with the margarine and sprinkle generously with salt and pepper. Wrap tightly, rolling the ends to completely seal the package. Place on a baking sheet and bake for 35 to 40 minutes. Check to see if the pork chop is cooked through; rewrap and cook a little longer if necessary.

Kentucky Country Ham

Jane and Gilbert Wells would never think of ordering a country ham over the Internet! They prefer to go to Kentucky themselves and buy a ham straight out of a farmer's barn. And they want the real thing—a ham that's been hanging from the barn roof for two years! The second-best scenario would be to call Gilbert's brother and have him buy the country ham from a farmer and send it. Preparing a country ham starts with taking it outside to wash the mold off with water and a stiff brush—no kidding! If that doesn't appeal to you, check out page 104 for a number where you can order a smaller, boneless country ham.

1 country ham (25 to 30 pounds)

4 cups cider vinegar

4 cups packed brown sugar

1. Take the ham outside and clean the skin under cold running water with a stiff brush. Soak the ham overnight in a large roasting pan in water to cover plus the vinegar.

2. Preheat the oven to 300°F. Remove the ham from the liquid and drain, reserving 4 cups of the soaking liquid. Return the ham to the pan fat side down. Mix 2 cups of the sugar with the reserved soaking liquid and pour over the ham. Bake, covered, for 15 minutes per pound, about 6 hours. Let cool in its liquid.

3. When cool, drain the cooking liquid. Skin the ham and score the top with a sharp knife. Pack the remaining 2 cups sugar over the top of the ham. Bake, uncovered, for 1 hour. Let cool.

4. When cool, slice wafer thin. Or take to a butcher and pay to have it shaved!

Makes enough for 80 sandwiches

Peanut Butter–Glazed Ham

Cooking a ham is easy if you start with premium meat. Ham goes well with any number of glazes, but this one is really yummy with the saltiness of the ham. You can use it over grilled ham slices, too.

One 10- to 12-pound whole smoked picnic ham, rinsed and patted dry, untrimmed

1 **cup chicken broth**

½ **cup creamy peanut butter**

¼ **cup honey**

1 **clove garlic, chopped**

2 **teaspoons soy sauce**

1. Position an oven rack in the lower third of your oven. Preheat the oven to 325°F.

2. Place the ham on a rack in a roasting pan. Place the pan in the oven and roast the ham for 20 minutes per pound. If the ham begins to burn, cover loosely with foil.

3. At the end of the cooking time, in a blender or food processor, combine the broth, peanut butter, honey, garlic, and soy sauce. Slather the glaze all over the surface of the ham and cook an additional 20 minutes.

4. Remove the ham from the oven and allow it to sit for about 15 minutes before carving.

Serve 12 to 14

Lamb Stew

I have never eaten or cooked much lamb, but lamb stew is just the perfect St. Patrick's Day dish for a party, so I altered one of my favorite beef stew recipes. I think you'll like the result as much as I do.

Salt and pepper

3 pounds leg of lamb meat, cut into 1½-inch cubes

¼ cup vegetable oil

¼ cup olive oil

6 celery stalks, chopped

2 large yellow onions, chopped

2 large leeks, chopped

2 cups finely chopped cabbage

½ teaspoon ground coriander

½ teaspoon ground thyme

2 cups canned beef consommé or beef broth

One 14.5-ounce can diced tomatoes, with juice

12 small new potatoes, scrubbed

1. Preheat the oven to 300°F.

2. Salt and pepper the lamb chunks. In a large oven-proof Dutch oven, sauté the meat in the oils until it is browned on all sides. Remove the meat from the Dutch oven and set aside.

3. In the same Dutch oven, sauté the celery, onions, leeks, and cabbage until limp, about 3 minutes. Season with the coriander and thyme. Add the consommé and tomatoes.

4. Return the meat to the Dutch oven, cover, and bake for 1 hour.

5. Using a vegetable peeler, remove a ring of peel around the middle of the potatoes. Add the potatoes to the stew after an hour. Cook the stew for another hour, or until the meat is fork-tender.

6. Serve the stew with a side dish of green peas.

Serves 8 to 10

Minted Lamb

You won't find a better marinade for lamb than this. The flavor of the mint really penetrates the meat. You definitely won't have folks hollering "Pass the mint jelly!"

1 small boneless lamb shoulder (about 3 pounds)

Marinade
½ cup olive oil

2 tablespoons chopped fresh thyme

2 cloves garlic, crushed

¼ cup honey

¼ cup wine vinegar

2 tablespoons chopped fresh mint

1. Place the lamb in a resealable plastic bag. Combine the marinade ingredients in a glass bowl or measuring cup. Pour the marinade over the lamb, seal the bag, and refrigerate for at least 1 hour or overnight.

2. Grill the lamb over indirect heat for about 45 minutes, until a meat thermometer registers 180°F.

Serves 4

Glazed Rock Cornish Game Hens Stuffed with Wild Rice

These are absolutely gorgeous when they come from the oven. And your whole house will smell delicious!

Glaze

⅔ cup light corn syrup or honey

2 tablespoons apple juice

2 tablespoons fresh lemon juice

2 tablespoons grated lemon zest

Wild Rice Stuffing

¼ cup (½ stick) plus 2 tablespoons butter

1 small onion, minced

1 carrot, diced

1 small celery stalk, diced

4 cups chicken broth (canned is fine)

1 bay leaf

Leaves from 1 sprig rosemary, chopped (discard stems)

Kosher or sea salt

¾ cup wild rice

1 cup white rice

Pepper

1. To prepare the glaze: Combine all of the ingredients in a small bowl. Set aside.

2. To prepare the stuffing: Melt ¼ cup of the butter in a large saucepan and sauté the onion, carrot, and celery until soft but not brown. Meanwhile, bring the chicken broth to a boil. When the vegetables are cooked, add the bay leaf, rosemary, 1¼ teaspoons salt, the wild rice, and 2 cups of the boiling broth. Cook, covered, over medium-low heat for 30 to 40 minutes, or until done. Stir several times to make sure the rice is not sticking. Remove from the heat and allow the rice to sit for 30 minutes to absorb the liquid. In the meantime, in a medium saucepan, combine the white rice, the remaining 2 cups boiling broth, the remaining 2 tablespoons butter, and 1 teaspoon salt. Cook the white rice over low heat for about 20 minutes, until the liquid is absorbed.

3. When the rices are cooked, drain off any extra broth, fluff with a fork, and remove the bay leaf from the wild rice. Combine the rices, and add salt and pepper to taste.

4. To prepare the hens: Preheat the oven to 350°F. Grease a baking dish large enough to hold the hens. If using whole hens, remove the giblets and necks. Rinse the hens, inside and out, with cold water and pat dry. Lightly season, inside and out, with garlic salt, seasoned salt, and pepper. Place a lemon slice inside each hen and stuff lightly with the rice mixture. (Place the remaining rice mixture in a microwavable dish, to be warmed later.) Tuck the wing tips

Cooking spray, oil, or butter for greasing baking dish

4 Rock Cornish game hens (¾ pound each is preferable, but may be up to 1 pound)

Garlic salt

Seasoned salt

4 lemon slices

of the hens back under the breast and tie the legs together with kitchen string. Place the hens in the prepared baking dish, and roast for approximately 1¼ hours, or until a leg can be moved easily up and down. Brush with the glaze about 15 minutes before the cooking time is complete and again after removing the hens from the oven. Let the hens stand for 5 minutes before serving.

5. To serve, warm the rice in the microwave. Spoon enough rice onto each of four dinner plates to make a bed for the hens. Place a hen on top of the rice.

Serves 4

Rosemary Chicken Quarters

I really like dark chicken meat—it's more flavorful and more tender than breast meat. Chicken quarters (thigh and drumstick) often go on sale, making this an inexpensive main course.

2 tablespoons butter per chicken quarter, softened

1 tablespoon finely chopped fresh rosemary per chicken quarter

1 chicken quarter per person

Salt and pepper

1. Mix the butter and rosemary until well combined. Lift up the skin covering the leg and thigh and massage 2 tablespoons of rosemary butter evenly underneath the skin of each chicken quarter. Sprinkle the chicken with salt and pepper to taste. Store in the refrigerator in a glass dish covered with plastic wrap.

2. When ready to cook, position the chicken over indirect heat and grill at medium heat until cooked through, about 45 minutes. Do not turn, as the butter will spill out of the pocket. The chicken will brown nicely on all sides.

Beer-in-the-Rear Chicken

1 chicken (3 pounds)

Lawry's Seasoned Salt

House Seasoning
(page 119)

One 12-ounce can beer

1 sprig rosemary

Assorted barbecue and hot
sauces, your choice

1. Wash and drain the chicken and pat dry. Coat the chicken inside and out with seasoned salt and House Seasoning. Refrigerate until ready to cook.

2. Prepare the charcoal grill. When the coals are hot and glowing, carefully push them over to the sides of the grill, leaving an open space in the middle of the grill. Open the can of beer and pour off approximately ¼ cup. Insert the sprig of rosemary into the can, then place the beer can, keeping it upright, into the rear cavity of the chicken. Carefully place the chicken, standing up on the beer can, in the center of the grill, facing one of the banks of coals, making sure not to spill the beer. Cover the grill and cook the chicken for approximately 1 hour, or until done, rotating the chicken as necessary. The chicken is done when the juice runs clear when pierced with a fork.

3. Carefully remove the beer can from the chicken using mitts and discard the can. Cut the chicken into halves or quarters. I personally don't want any sauce on this chicken, but I always offer barbecue sauces and hot sauces to my guests.

One chicken serves 2 to 4, depending on appetites. (My crowd can all eat half a chicken each, easy.)

Country-Fried Steak with Gravy

Chicken-fried steak is cubed steak floured, fried, and served with white gravy. Country-fried steak is cubed steak floured, fried, and served with a brown gravy, often with onions. Both are delicious, stick-to-your-ribs dishes.

8 to 10 pieces cubed steak (about 2½ pounds)

Salt and pepper

1 cup all-purpose flour

¼ cup vegetable oil

1 large yellow onion, sliced into thin rings

3 beef bouillon cubes or two 10.75-ounce cans condensed beef broth or 3 teaspoons granulated beef bouillon

1. Generously season the meat on both sides with salt and pepper. Place the flour in a resealable plastic bag and add the steak to the bag, several pieces at a time, shaking to coat all sides. Place the floured meat on a piece of waxed paper next to the cooktop.

2. Pour the oil into a heavy flat-bottomed 12-inch skillet with a tight-fitting lid. Heat the oil over medium-high heat for about a minute, then add the steak pieces. Brown the meat on each side until crispy and dark brown, about 3 minutes per side. It may all fit into the skillet, or you may have to brown the meat in two batches. After browning, place all the meat in the skillet and reduce the heat to low. Distribute the onion rings over the top of the meat.

3. Dissolve the bouillon cubes or granulated bouillon in 2½ cups water, or use the canned broth. Pour the beef bouillon over the meat and onions. Place the lid on the skillet, and cook over very low heat for about 45 minutes, until the meat is tender and the gravy has thickened.

4. Serve over white rice.

Serves 6 to 8

Bert's Southern Fried Chicken

You'll love the crust on this chicken. Be sure to season the chicken early in the day; otherwise, the seasoning just won't penetrate. Susan Greene likes to wrap her chicken in tinfoil to keep it warm, but I have to differ with her on that. I'd rather my chicken be room temperature and crispy than warm and not crispy. I put it in tinfoil pans and place parchment paper between the layers. Either way, it's hard to beat!

You'll need a well-seasoned cast-iron skillet to make this.

1 **chicken (3 pounds), washed and cut into 8 serving pieces**

Salt and pepper

2 **cups all-purpose or self-rising flour**

3 **eggs**

⅓ **cup milk**

Peanut oil for frying

1. Liberally sprinkle each piece of chicken with salt and pepper several hours before cooking. Place it in a dish, covered with plastic wrap, in the refrigerator.

2. Place the flour in a plastic kitchen storage bag. When ready to cook, beat the eggs with the milk. Dip the chicken pieces into the egg mixture, then place each piece in the bag. Shake until chicken is coated. Set the floured chicken on a plate while you heat the oil.

3. Pour enough oil into a cast-iron skillet to come only about halfway up the sides of the pan. This is important, as the oil rises when each piece of chicken is added. (You must be careful not to let the oil spill out while the chicken is frying; it can cause serious burns or cause a grease fire if the grease lands on a gas flame or electric cooktop.)

4. Turn the heat to medium high; test by adding a drop of water to the oil. If it sizzles, the oil is ready; this takes about 4 to 5 minutes. Place about 4 pieces of chicken into the hot oil. Allow to cook on the first side about 8 minutes, and on the second about 6 minutes, until brown and crispy. Pieces with large bones—the legs and thighs—may need an additional minute per side to get completely done. Remove the chicken from the oil and drain well on brown paper bags. Cook the second batch of chicken.

5. Wrap tightly in aluminum foil to keep warm (like Bubbles does) or place in aluminum pans with parchment paper between layers of chicken (like I do).

Serves 4 to 6

To season a cast-iron skillet, wash a new skillet with hot, soapy water and a stiff brush. Rinse and dry completely. With a paper towel, rub a layer of vegetable shortening on the entire surface, both inside and out, including the lid. Line the lower oven rack with aluminum foil to catch any drips, and place the skillet upside down in a prcheated 350°F oven for 1 hour. Turn the oven off and allow the skillet to cool before removing from the oven. After each use, clean with hot water and a stiff brush; never use soap or dishwashing liquid, and never place the seasoned pan in the dishwasher. Dry completely and place in a warm oven to completely dry out before storing.

We can get whole chicken cut into 8 pieces for frying. Buy the chicken parts you like best—breasts, thighs, wings, or drumsticks.

Chicken Divan or Chicken Florentine

Of the many chicken casserole–type dishes I've eaten, this one is just about the best. Adding broccoli makes it divan; adding spinach makes it Florentine. Everyone asks for the recipe.

Two 10-ounce packages frozen chopped broccoli (if making divan)

Two 10-ounce packages frozen chopped spinach (if making Florentine)

6 chicken breast halves (about 4 pounds), cooked, boned, and shredded

Two 10¾-ounce cans condensed cream of mushroom soup

1 cup mayonnaise

1 cup sour cream

1 cup grated sharp Cheddar cheese

1 tablespoon fresh lemon juice

1 teaspoon curry powder

Salt and pepper

½ cup dry white wine

½ cup freshly grated Parmesan cheese

½ cup soft bread crumbs

2 tablespoons butter

1. Remove the outer wrappers from the boxes of broccoli or spinach. Open one end of each box. Microwave on full power for 2 minutes, until thawed. Drain the broccoli or spinach and put into a large bowl. Add the shredded chicken.

2. In a medium bowl, combine the soup, mayonnaise, sour cream, Cheddar cheese, lemon juice, curry powder, salt and pepper to taste, and wine. Whisk together to make a sauce. Pour the sauce over the broccoli or spinach and chicken. Mix well with a spatula.

3. Place the mixture into an 11-by-7-inch casserole dish or two 9-inch square disposable aluminum foil pans that have been sprayed with vegetable oil cooking spray. Pat down evenly and smooth with a spatula. Combine the Parmesan cheese and bread crumbs and sprinkle over the top. Dot with the butter.

4. Wrap the uncooked casserole(s) securely with plastic wrap, then with aluminum foil. Place each pan into a plastic freezer bag and seal. Freeze. Prepare a label with these instructions: Allow casserole to thaw 24 hours in the refrigerator. When ready to bake, remove the plastic wrap and foil. Bake, uncovered, at 350°F for about 40 minutes, until bubbly.

5. If serving immediately, bake, uncovered, in a 350°F oven for about 30 minutes, until bubbly.

Serves 6 to 8

Enchiladas de Pollo
(Cream Cheese and Chicken Enchiladas)

Don't make these up too far ahead of the party, as they can get soggy. Go ahead and make the filling, and then assemble the enchiladas an hour or so before you want to cook them. Allow one enchilada per person; for a large crowd, you can even cut the enchiladas in half.

4 large chicken breasts, roasted or boiled, skin and bones removed, meat shredded

One 8-ounce package cream cheese, at room temperature

One 10.75-ounce can condensed cream of chicken soup

Two 4-ounce cans diced green chilies, with juice

6 green onions, chopped, including green tops

20 to 24 flour tortillas (7-inch diameter)

Two 10-ounce cans enchilada sauce

2 cups (½ pound) grated Monterey Jack cheese

4 cups (1 pound) grated sharp Cheddar cheese

Sour cream, for garnish

Shredded lettuce, for garnish

Diced tomatoes, for garnish

Salsa, store-bought or homemade, for garnish

1. Preheat the oven to 250°F. Spray two 13-by-9-inch casserole dishes with vegetable oil cooking spray.

2. Combine the chicken, cream cheese, soup, chilies, and green onions. Spoon 2 tablespoons of this mixture onto each tortilla and roll up.

3. Pour a very small amount of the enchilada sauce on the bottom of each casserole dish and tilt the dish so that the sauce covers the bottom. Place the enchiladas side by side on top of the sauce. When all of the enchiladas have been rolled and placed in the dishes, take the remaining enchilada sauce and pour it over the top of the enchiladas. Combine the Monterey Jack and Cheddar cheeses and sprinkle evenly over the casseroles.

4. Cover the dishes with foil and bake for 30 minutes. Uncover and bake for 10 more minutes. To serve, cut between the enchiladas and serve from the dish. Have bowls of sour cream, shredded lettuce, diced tomatoes, and salsa for garnish.

Makes 20 to 24 enchiladas

Chicken Breast Pie

You can include or omit ingredients to suit the tastes of your campers.

1 boneless chicken breast per person

Salt and pepper

1 tablespoon sun-dried tomato pesto per person

1 tablespoon feta cheese per person

1 slice country ham per person (available in the meat section of your supermarket or from the deli; other ham varieties won't be the same, but it's your recipe!)

1 tablespoon margarine or butter per person

½ teaspoon dried oregano per person

1. For each serving, lay a chicken breast on a large square of heavy-duty aluminum foil. Sprinkle with salt and pepper. Spread the tomato pesto over the chicken, top with the cheese, and wrap a slice of ham completely around the chicken and cheese. Top with the margarine and sprinkle with the oregano. Wrap tightly in the foil, rolling ends to completely seal the package. Freeze or refrigerate. Pack in coolers.

2. When ready to eat, place packages directly in coals for 15 to 18 minutes. Check to see if the chicken is cooked through; rewrap and cook a little longer if necessary.

Note: To prepare in the oven, preheat the oven to 375°F. For each serving, lay a chicken breast on a large square of heavy-duty aluminum foil. Sprinkle with salt and pepper. Spread the tomato pesto over the chicken, top with the cheese, and wrap a slice of ham completely around the chicken and cheese. Top with the margarine and sprinkle with the oregano. Wrap tightly in the foil, rolling the ends to completely seal the package. Bake for 25 to 30 minutes, or until chicken is done.

Turducken

You can order a turducken from the meat department in a large supermarket, or you may order a Cajun-style stuffed turducken from www.turducken.com. You should place your order several weeks in advance. Cooking instructions are included; be prepared to cook the turducken on a baking rack with a pan underneath for about 5 hours. When done, remove the turducken from the oven and place it on a carving board. Pour 3 cups water into the pan drippings in the bottom of the pan and use a wooden spoon to scrape up all of the drippings. This will be used for the brown gravy, below. After removing it from the oven, allow to cool about 15 minutes before carving. Slice thinly—there will be beautiful "ribbons" of the various meats.

One 15-pound turducken will serve about 20

———◆———

Brown Gravy

This is a beautiful caramel color and is yummy poured over dressing.

4 tablespoons (½ stick) butter

¼ cup all-purpose flour

3 cups pan drippings from the turducken or turkey

Salt and pepper

In a 1-quart saucepan over low heat, melt the butter. Whisk in the flour until the mixture is completely smooth. Strain 3 cups of pan drippings (to eliminate lumps) into a measuring cup. Slowly pour the drippings into the flour mixture, stirring constantly to keep the gravy smooth as it thickens over low heat. When it is the desired thickness, taste to see if it needs a little salt or pepper. Turn off the heat and cover the gravy until it is time to use. Reheat and pour into a gravy boat when ready to serve.

Makes 3 cups gravy, enough to serve about 20

Shrimp and Crab au Gratin

This dish is a treasure; it's the ultimate "I care" casserole. Why? Because it costs an arm and a leg and because you have to be willing to take the time to make an old-fashioned cream sauce.

½ cup (1 stick) butter

½ cup all-purpose flour

½ cup whole milk

½ cup dry white wine

Juice of 1 lemon

½ teaspoon black pepper

⅛ teaspoon cayenne pepper

1 pound small or medium shrimp, peeled and deveined

1 pound claw crabmeat, picked through for shells

1½ cups grated sharp Cheddar cheese

1. Melt the butter in a heavy-bottomed saucepan over very low heat. When the butter is completely melted, stir in the flour with a wooden spoon. Cook for about 1 minute over low heat, stirring constantly. Slowly add the milk. Using a whisk, stir briskly until you have a smooth sauce, about 2 minutes. Add the wine, lemon juice, black pepper, and cayenne and whisk again. Switch to the wooden spoon and keep stirring the white sauce until it is completely smooth and thickened, about the consistency of mayonnaise. Remove from the heat.

2. Bring 2 cups water and ½ teaspoon salt to a boil in a medium saucepan and add the shrimp. When the water returns to a boil, cook the shrimp for 1 minute. Drain immediately. Roughly chop the shrimp and put in a large mixing bowl. Add the crabmeat and, with your hands, toss gently to mix.

3. Pour the sauce over the seafood. With a large spoon, gently combine, taking care not to break apart the crabmeat.

4. Spray an 8-inch square disposable aluminum foil pan with vegetable oil cooking spray or use an 11-by-7-inch casserole dish. Pour the mixture into the pan. Place the grated cheese on top, completely covering the seafood mixture. Wrap the uncooked casserole securely with plastic wrap, then with aluminum foil. Place the pan into a plastic freezer bag and seal. Freeze. Prepare a label with these instructions: Completely thaw in the refrigerator. When ready to bake, remove the foil and plastic wrap. Bake at 350°F for about 25 to 30 minutes, until bubbly.

5. If serving immediately, bake in a 350°F oven, uncovered, for about 25 minutes, until bubbly.

Serves 4 to 6

Shrimp and Wild Rice Casserole

Just because this recipe is easy to put together doesn't mean it's not delicious!

1 package Uncle Ben's Original Wild Rice

1 pound medium shrimp, peeled and deveined

2 tablespoons butter

½ green bell pepper, chopped

½ onion, chopped

One 10¾-ounce can condensed cream of mushroom soup

2 cups grated sharp Cheddar cheese

Salt and pepper

1. Cook the rice according to package directions, minus ¼ cup water. Let cool.

2. Bring 2 cups water and ½ teaspoon salt to a boil in a medium saucepan and add the shrimp. When the water returns to a boil, cook the shrimp for 1 minute. Drain immediately and set aside.

3. Heat the butter in a saucepan and sauté the green pepper and onion until soft, about 5 minutes.

4. In a large bowl, combine the rice, soup, 1½ cups of the cheese, the shrimp, and vegetables. Add salt and pepper to taste. Mix well.

5. Spray a 9-inch square aluminum cake pan or an 11-by-7-inch glass casserole dish with vegetable oil cooking spray. Place the mixture in the pan and top with the remaining ½ cup cheese. Wrap securely with plastic wrap, then with aluminum foil. Place the pan into a plastic freezer bag and seal. Freeze. Prepare a label with these instructions: Completely thaw in the refrigerator. When ready to bake, remove the foil and plastic wrap. Bake, uncovered, at 325°F for 30 minutes, until bubbly.

6. If serving immediately, bake, uncovered, in a 325°F oven for about 20 minutes, until bubbly.

Serves 6 to 8

Shrimp and Scallop Lasagna

Martha Nesbit created this recipe for a column she writes for *Savannah* magazine. It's just delicious with pole beans, fresh sliced tomatoes, and blueberry muffins. For dessert, serve Mom's Banana Dessert (page 262), or my Buttermilk Pound Cake with Strawberries and Whipped Cream (page 210).

12 lasagna noodles

3 tablespoons butter

1 small onion, finely chopped

2 cloves garlic, minced

3 tablespoons all-purpose flour

2½ cups half-and-half

1 cup grated Romano cheese, preferably freshly grated

½ teaspoon salt

¼ teaspoon pepper

¾ pound medium shrimp, peeled and deveined

¾ pound sea scallops, cut in half or quartered if very large

½ cup grated Parmesan cheese (freshly grated adds the most flavor)

1. Preheat the oven to 375°F if cooking immediately. (Do not preheat the oven if you are preparing the casserole to take on a family vacation.) Spray a 13-by-10-inch aluminum foil pan with vegetable oil cooking spray.

2. In a large pot of boiling salted water, cook the lasagna noodles until they are just done, about 8 minutes. Drain and set aside.

3. Melt the butter in a large, heavy skillet and cook the onion over low heat until very soft, about 5 minutes. Add the garlic and cook about 1 minute more. Over medium-low heat, stir in the flour with a whisk, then gradually add the half-and-half, allowing the sauce to thicken slightly before adding more. When the sauce has thickened to about the consistency of whipping cream, add the Romano cheese and stir well. Add the salt and pepper and stir again. Add the shrimp and scallops and cook for about 5 minutes, just until the shrimp turn pink. Turn off the heat.

4. Spoon about 2 tablespoons of sauce from the skillet into the prepared pan. Cover the bottom of the pan with 4 noodles, placing them side by side. Spoon one-third of the sauce over the noodles, distributing half of the seafood evenly. Layer 4 more noodles, one-third of the sauce with half the seafood, the remaining 4 noodles, and the remaining sauce. For the top layer, do not spoon any seafood on top of the noodles; just use the sauce. Tuck in any edges of the noodles so they're all coated with sauce. Top with the Parmesan cheese.

5. The pan can be carefully wrapped for freezing and frozen at this point. Allow to thaw completely in the refrigerator before baking. When ready to bake, preheat the oven to 375°F. Bake for 20 to 25 minutes, uncovered, until bubbly. Allow to sit for 10 minutes before slicing.

Serves 8

Low-Country Boil

Low-Country boil is more of a technique than a recipe, and I'm about to tell ya just how to do it so that you have the best dish you could ever hope for. You have to start with quality ingredients, and you have to follow the directions exactly to have all of the ingredients come out perfectly cooked.

Sometimes, my husband, Michael, will pull out the sausage, potatoes, and corn and put them into a cooler to stay warm. Then he will cook the shrimp separately in the seasoned water. This way, there is no chance the shrimp will get overcooked.

¼ pound fully cooked smoked sausage per person, cut into 1-inch pieces

¼ cup Old Bay seasoning, or more to taste

2 small new potatoes per person

1 ear fresh corn per person, shucked, silked, and broken in half

½ pound large fresh shrimp per person (16 to 20 count size), shell on

Tartar Sauce (page 147)

Cocktail Sauce (page 147)

Potato Sauce (page 147)

Fill a large pot with enough water to cover all of the ingredients. Add the sausage and Old Bay seasoning and allow to boil for about 20 minutes so that the sausage can flavor the water. Taste, and add more Old Bay if you think you need more. Add the potatoes and boil for about 15 minutes. Add the corn and boil about 10 minutes more. Finally, add the shrimp and allow to cook for 3 minutes. Taste a shrimp, and if it is cooked through, drain immediately and serve on an oversize platter or, as we do, on a table covered with newspaper! Serve with the three sauces.

Tartar Sauce

Leftovers will keep, covered and refrigerated, about two weeks. Great with any seafood.

½ cup chopped green onion
½ cup chopped dill pickle
1½ cups mayonnaise
½ teaspoon House Seasoning (page 119)
1 teaspoon dried dill weed

In a glass dish, stir together all of the ingredients. Cover and refrigerate until serving time.

Makes about 2 cups

Cocktail Sauce

Leftovers will keep, covered and refrigerated, about two weeks. Delicious with fried shrimp or scallops.

2 cups ketchup
1 tablespoon prepared horseradish
1 tablespoon fresh lemon juice
1 teaspoon Worcestershire sauce

In a glass dish, stir together all of the ingredients. Cover and refrigerate until serving time.

Makes about 2¼ cups

Potato Sauce

If I serve potatoes and no potato sauce, I am in trouble, big-time!

¾ cup mayonnaise
¼ cup sour cream
2 cups finely chopped yellow onion
Salt and pepper

In a glass dish, stir together the mayonnaise, sour cream, and onion. Add salt and pepper to taste. Cover and refrigerate until serving time. Serve with buttered new potatoes.

Makes about 3 cups

Teriyaki Shrimp

Don't be tempted to cook these shrimp with their shells on. They'll stick to the grill and the shells will be almost impossible to remove.

1 **pound large shrimp, peeled and deveined**

Marinade

1 **tablespoon fresh lime juice**
¼ **cup dry sherry**
¼ **cup olive oil**
¼ **cup teriyaki sauce**

1. Place the shrimp in a resealable plastic bag. Combine the marinade ingredients in a glass bowl or measuring cup. Pour the marinade over the shrimp, seal the bag, and refrigerate for at least 2 hours or overnight.

2. One hour prior to grilling, start soaking wooden skewers.

3. When ready to cook, thread the shrimp on the skewers, leaving a little space between each shrimp. Place the skewers in a grill basket sprayed with vegetable oil cooking spray. Grill over high heat for about 5 minutes on each side, or just until cooked through. Serve hot or cold.

Serves 2 or 3

Shrimp and Grits

Here it is, y'all! Martha's beloved shrimp and grits recipe! If you have everything chopped and measured before you start cooking, it takes only about fifteen minutes to prepare. It's perfect as a one-dish meal for family.

1 **cup stone-ground grits**
Salt and pepper

¼ **cup (½ stick) butter**

2 **cups shredded sharp Cheddar cheese**

1 **pound shrimp, peeled and deveined, left whole if small and roughly chopped if medium or large**

6 **slices bacon, chopped into tiny pieces**

4 **teaspoons fresh lemon juice**

2 **tablespoons chopped fresh parsley**

1 **cup thinly sliced green onions, white and green parts**

1 **large clove garlic, minced**

1. In a medium saucepan, bring 4 cups water to a boil. Add the grits and salt and pepper to taste. Stir well with a whisk. Reduce the heat to the lowest possible setting and cook the grits until all the water is absorbed, about 10 to 15 minutes. Remove from the heat and stir in the butter and cheese. Keep covered until ready to serve.

2. Rinse the shrimp and pat dry. Fry the bacon in a large skillet until browned and crisp, then drain on a paper towel. Add the shrimp to the bacon grease in the skillet and sauté over medium heat just until they turn pink, about 3 minutes. Do not overcook! Immediately add the lemon juice, parsley, green onions, and garlic. Remove the skillet from the heat.

3. Pour the grits into a serving bowl. Pour the shrimp mixture over the grits. Garnish with the bacon bits.

4. If you are serving this as an appetizer, spoon ¼ cup of the grits onto a bread or salad plate. Top with ¼ cup of the shrimp mixture. Garnish with a sprinkling of crisp bacon bits and serve immediately.

Serves 8 as an appetizer or 4 as a main course

Shrimp Étouffée

The word *étouffée* means "smothered." You start with a roux—which is just butter and flour cooked until it turns a caramel color and is used to thicken the sauce. Don't let your roux burn, or you'll have to throw it out and start from scratch. The salmon color of this dish is just beautiful served over white rice!

6 tablespoons (¾ stick) butter

¼ cup all-purpose flour

1 cup chopped yellow onion

½ cup chopped green bell pepper

1 cup chopped celery

3 cloves garlic, finely minced

2 pounds small shrimp, peeled and deveined

½ teaspoon black pepper

½ teaspoon cayenne pepper, or to taste

1 teaspoon Cajun seasoning

⅓ cup minced green onions

⅓ cup minced fresh parsley

2 to 3 dashes of Tabasco sauce

One 14.5-ounce can diced tomatoes, with juice

1 to 2 teaspoons salt

Diced green onions, for garnish

1. Melt the butter in the bottom of a large, heavy saucepan over low heat. Gradually whisk in the flour to form a paste. Continue cooking over low heat, stirring with a wooden spoon occasionally, until the mixture turns a caramel color, 15 to 20 minutes.

2. Add the onion, green pepper, celery, and garlic and cook over low heat about 5 minutes, until the vegetables are limp.

3. Add the shrimp and stir to coat in the roux. Add the black pepper, cayenne pepper, Cajun seasoning, green onions, parsley, and Tabasco to taste.

4. Add 1 cup water and stir until blended. Add the tomatoes and their juice and stir to blend. Taste for seasoning. Add the salt, starting with 1 teaspoon, then add more if needed. Bring the mixture to a boil, then reduce the heat to low and simmer for 10 to 15 minutes, until the shrimp are firm and pink and the flavors have blended.

5. Transfer the étouffée to a tureen or serving bowl. Garnish with the green onions.

Serves 6 to 8 as a main course, or 10 to 12 as part of a buffet

Patty's Shrimp Creole

This is another one of Patty Ronning's good ol' standbys. A friend told me recently that the kids in her family don't like shrimp creole, so on shrimp creole night, the kids always get sloppy joes. Well, the kids had been bragging about their aunt's famous sloppy joes for years, and asked their mom to get the recipe. Our friend asked her sister for the recipe, and it turns out it was Manwich out of the can! See? Everything tastes better when you're on vacation!

3 tablespoons vegetable oil

½ cup chopped onion

½ cup chopped celery

1 clove garlic, minced

One 14½-ounce can stewed tomatoes

One 8-ounce can tomato sauce

¾ teaspoon salt

1 teaspoon sugar

½ to 1 teaspoon chili powder

1 tablespoon Worcestershire sauce

Dash of hot sauce

2 teaspoons cornstarch

¾ pound small shrimp, peeled and deveined

½ cup chopped green bell pepper

Cooked rice

1. Heat the oil in a large, heavy skillet and cook the onion, celery, and garlic over low heat until tender, about 5 minutes. Add the tomatoes, tomato sauce, salt, sugar, chili powder, Worcestershire sauce, and hot sauce. Simmer, uncovered, for 45 minutes, stirring occasionally to keep the mixture from sticking.

2. Mix the cornstarch with 1 tablespoon cold water. Stir the cornstarch into the tomato mixture and cook for about 2 minutes. If you are going to serve this immediately, add the shrimp and green pepper and cook for about 8 to 10 minutes, until the shrimp are done. The shrimp should turn pink. Taste one to see if it is done to your liking. If you are preparing this to take on vacation, allow the tomato mixture to cool, then pack into a freezer bag and freeze until ready to use. When ready to prepare, thaw, place the mixture into a heavy saucepan or skillet, and bring to a simmer. Add the shrimp and green pepper and cook for 8 to 10 minutes. Serve over rice.

Serves 6

Maple-Glazed Salmon with Pineapple Salsa

There just ain't no better fish for grilling than salmon. Salmon's rich flavor and the smoke from the grill make for a delicious combination. This is almost better the next day, served cold in a salad. Yum!

1 **salmon fillet (6 ounces) per person**

Marinade
(enough for 4 fillets)

  1 **tablespoon maple syrup**

  1 **tablespoon teriyaki sauce**

  1 **tablespoon pineapple juice**

  1 **teaspoon minced fresh ginger**

  1 **clove garlic, crushed**

  1 **tablespoon Southern Comfort or other bourbon**

1. Place the salmon fillets in a resealable plastic bag. Combine the marinade ingredients in a glass bowl or measuring cup. Pour the marinade over the fillets, seal the bag, and refrigerate for at least 1 hour or overnight.

2. In a grill basket sprayed with vegetable oil cooking spray, grill the salmon skin-side down over hot coals. Do not turn! Watch for the fish to cook from the bottom up; it takes about 15 to 20 minutes. Serve with Pineapple Salsa: Two variations are given on page 153.

Pineapple Salsa I

We've included two recipes for pineapple salsa because we love them both and can't decide which one we like more! The first is cooked; the second isn't and doesn't have the tomato.

1 medium ripe tomato, chopped into small cubes

¼ cup chopped bell pepper

2 pickled jalapeño pepper slices, finely chopped

½ cup pineapple chunks, fresh or canned in juice or syrup

1 teaspoon salt

1 tablespoon sugar

1 tablespoon white vinegar

Place all of the ingredients in a small saucepan. Simmer over low heat for about 5 minutes. Let cool. Cover with plastic wrap and refrigerate until ready to serve with salmon.

Pineapple Salsa II

This recipe was contributed by Sue Off, of Tybee Island, near Savannah. She also serves it with grilled mahi mahi.

1 cup fresh pineapple, finely diced

¼ cup chopped red bell pepper

¼ cup chopped green bell pepper

½ fresh jalapeño pepper, seeded and finely minced

1 tablespoon finely minced red onion

2 tablespoons minced cilantro leaves

1 tablespoon fresh lime juice

1 teaspoon sugar

Place all of the ingredients in a small glass bowl and toss to combine. Cover with plastic wrap and refrigerate until ready to serve with salmon.

Pecan-Coated Fish with Remoulade Sauce

A chef taught Martha how to cook fish like the restaurants do. Although this recipe calls for grouper or snapper, you could use any 1-inch-thick fish fillet. There are two steps: searing the fish on the stovetop, then completing the cooking in a preheated oven.

You can usually fit only four 6-ounce fillets in a pan, so if you're cooking for more, you'll have to use a second skillet.

4 grouper or snapper fillets, cut about 1 inch thick, 4 to 6 ounces each

½ cup (1 stick) butter, melted

1 cup pecans, ground into crumbs in a food processor

1 tablespoon butter

1 tablespoon vegetable oil

1. Preheat the oven to 350°F.

2. Rinse the fish and pat dry. Dredge the fish in the melted butter. Spread the ground pecans on a plate and press the fish into the crumbs to coat. Turn the fillets and coat the other side.

3. In a cast-iron or other heavy, ovenproof skillet, heat the tablespoon of butter with the oil. When it begins to sizzle, sear the fish about 3 minutes per side. Place the skillet in the oven for 6 to 10 minutes, depending on the thickness of the fillets and your preference for degree of doneness. Serve immediately with Remoulade Sauce (page 155) on the side.

Serves 4

Remoulade Sauce

This is just a snazzed-up mayonnaise. It's delicious with any kind of seafood, but it's also yummy on the asparagus, or on your finger!

⅓ cup chopped fresh parsley

⅓ cup chopped green onions, white and green parts

2 tablespoons capers, with juice

1 clove garlic, minced

1 cup mayonnaise

3 tablespoons olive oil

2 tablespoons fresh lemon juice

½ teaspoon Dijon mustard

Place the parsley, green onions, capers, and garlic in a blender or food processor and combine. Add the mayonnaise, olive oil, lemon juice, and mustard. Blend well. Chill until ready to serve with seafood. This keeps in a covered container in the refrigerator for several weeks.

Makes 1½ cups

Blackened Fish

What could be tastier after a long day of hiking than fish that you've cooked outdoors? You'll probably need a portable gas stove to keep the skillet hot enough for this dish.

1 tablespoon paprika

2 teaspoons salt

1 teaspoon onion powder

1 teaspoon garlic powder

¼ teaspoon cayenne pepper

¼ teaspoon black pepper

½ cup (1 stick) butter

1 fish fillet per person (redfish, pompano, red snapper, or any fillet no more than ½ inch thick)

1. Combine the seasonings and place in a shaker bottle to take with you on the trip.

2. When ready to cook, melt the butter in an aluminum foil cake pan over the grill. Place a large cast-iron skillet over high heat and heat it until you see white ash in the bottom, about 5 to 6 minutes.

3. Dip each fillet in the melted butter, then sprinkle generously on both sides with the seasonings. Place the fillets in the hot skillet and pour 1 teaspoon of melted butter over each fillet. Cook, uncovered, over high heat until the underside looks done, about 3 minutes. Turn the fillets, top each with 1 teaspoon butter, and cook until the second side is done, about 3 minutes. Serve hot.

Note: To prepare on the stovetop, prepare as above, cooking in the skillet over medium-high heat.

Puttin' It All Together

A Cooking Shower

I was working myself silly at The Lady restaurant in the Best Western motel in Savannah in the mid-1990s when I received a call from Martha Nesbit, who was the food editor of the *Savannah Morning News*. She wanted the recipe for my son Jamie's chicken salad, one of our popular menu items, and I was thrilled to pieces to share it with her!

Martha and I have been food friends ever since. And let me tell you, that girl can cook! Bobby Flay's team came to Savannah to tape a segment for the Food Network's *FoodNation with Bobby Flay,* and Bobby spent a morning in Martha's kitchen because she had agreed to prepare shrimp and grits for a segment on the show. Several years later, Bobby and I were out in L.A. taping a *$25,000 Pyramid* show together. Bobby made a point to tell me hands down that Martha's shrimp and grits were the best he'd ever tasted. He said (with a big laugh) that normally he shares the food with his staff, but this particular dish, he ate the whole thing—by himself!

When we started this book, I told Martha I had one request: Please, please, give me the recipe for the shrimp and grits so I can share it with my reader friends.

Martha and her husband, Gary, served this menu one night to a very special engaged couple, Alison Ronning, who had been Martha's babysitter for many years, and Danny Mahfet. Martha asked Alison and Danny to invite several couples who enjoyed cooking, and they spent a casual evening in Martha's kitchen while she showed them how to prepare these recipes. Kinda like your own personal cooking show! They ate the tomato tarts straight off the cookie sheet, and shrimp and grits ladled right out of the pot onto Martha's grandmother's gold-rimmed bread plates. Then the group retired to the dining room for the rest of the meal and the presents, which were, of course, all culinary tools.

Alison reports that she and Danny still consider this their favorite meal, and it's one they prepared for all of their friends in Atlanta, where they lived and worked before returning to Savannah. Their "Georgia Bulldawg Parking Lot Tailgate" is featured on page 72. Alison's appreciation of good food and entertaining runs in the family: her mother, Patty, is one of Savannah's best cooks. Those Ronning women are women with good taste!

Menu

TOMATO TARTS
94

SHRIMP AND GRITS
149

PECAN-COATED FISH WITH REMOULADE SAUCE
154

ROSEMARY AND GARLIC ROASTED NEW POTATOES
175

FRESH ASPARAGUS WITH LEMON BUTTER
178

FRESH FRUIT TART
228

A Bridge Club Supper

Before I can tell you about Barbie's Bridge Club Supper, I have to tell you about Barbie. Barbie lives in Savannah with her attorney husband, John Lientz. She's just about the most caring, unselfish person you ever could meet—to know her is to love her. For example, when she heard that John's cousin needed a kidney transplant, she offered right then and there to donate her own kidney. But when Barbie started the donation process, she found out that she had a possibly fatal kidney disease that needed treatment. The bottom line is this: Barbie's unselfishness wound up saving her own life. By the way, Barbie is fine, and John's cousin got his kidney.

Barbie, who has a long history of serving her community in organizations like the Junior League, Second Harvest Food Bank, and her church's mission outreach committee, also likes to have fun! She tells me: "When my daughter was in preschool, Janet Barrow and I decided to organize a little bridge group. We played during the morning from nine to twelve, making a mad dash to pick up the children by noon. Most of the original members of the Isle of Hope Bridge Club have come and gone, but the group still continues. We celebrated our twenty-fifth anniversary in 2004!"

Barbie served this menu buffet style in her dining room, using real china and silver. She says there never seem to be enough occasions to use china and silver, and so she decided, What the heck! We'll use the good stuff, even if my guests are in shorts and sandals!

Menu

Grilled Pork Tenderloin
126

Artichoke Rice Salad with Shrimp
52

Marinated Tomatoes
191

Garlic Cheese Biscuits
20

Angel Chocolate Mousse Pie
226

Comfort Food

When one of your friends is hurting—she's just gotten divorced, her child has been in a car accident or gotten into trouble, her mother has had surgery, or when a member of the family has died—that's when you spend the afternoon making your best casserole, soup, cake, or pie to deliver for dinner as a show of support. These dishes are comfort food, pure and simple.

When we were looking for someone who always provides for those in need, we turned to Patty Ronning, of Savannah. She'll wash dishes, rearrange your refrigerator, and clean out your closets, if necessary. This lady epitomizes Southern hospitality, thoughtfulness, and fortitude. She's a real steel magnolia.

Patty has this observation for cooks who want to contribute to a meal following a tragedy: "I have found when working 'funeral kitchens' that desserts come up short, or the desserts are all supermarket cakes. I sometimes think I'm the only person still baking. A homemade cake or pie is always appreciated by the family."

For this particular menu, we've collected a variety of recipes that have been particularly popular with the people who have received them. We've included some soups and casseroles that hold up well in transport and freeze well in the event the bereaved family has too much food on hand. We've also supplied several special desserts that are sure to help your hurting friends feel better.

Menu

Quick Crab Stew
60

Gumbo
61

Chicken Divan or Chicken Florentine
138

Shrimp and Crab au Gratin
142

Shrimp and Wild Rice Casserole
143

Cream Cheese Pound Cake
220

Raspberry and Sherry Trifle
232

Black Bottom Pie
225

The Saturday Night Grill Party

In the South, we can dine outdoors for much of the year (okay, so we fight the gnats and the mosquitoes, but we enjoy the outdoors anyway). What's so nice about an outdoor party is that the guests can stand around, chat, watch, and smell the main course cooking. There's nothing to pique the appetite like the smell of something on the grill!

You may decide to eat outdoors, if you have the right setting and nice weather, or you may choose the comfort of air-conditioning. Whichever way you go, choose plates in summer colors—Fiestaware comes to mind—and lots of candles to set the mood. A simple bowl of fresh summer fruit can serve as a centerpiece.

When planning a Saturday Night Grill Party, by all means keep it simple. I happen to like cold accompaniments with my grilled meat—a classic potato salad and sliced vine-ripe tomatoes suit me to a T. For those who want something a little more sophisticated, I've included a tomato salad with crumbled blue cheese. The Vidalia onion corn bread is the perfect taste to round out the meal. You can have everything done before the party so you can stand around and sniff with your guests.

Polish off the evening with a peach cream tart, which you can make with fresh peaches, if you're lucky like we are in June, or canned peaches if you live where the fresh peaches taste like cardboard.

I always opt not to serve an appetizer. Why spoil your appetite for the main course? Here are some grilling tips:

- Allow the meat to marinate up to 24 hours if possible.
- Buy grill baskets with nonstick coating for easier cleanup, and spray them with vegetable oil cooking spray to keep foods from sticking.
- Have your grill very hot before you add the food.
- Don't leave grilling food even for a minute. If you have a flare-up, your entire meal is ruined.

Choose whatever turns you on from the dishes that follow, or do what I sometimes do and cook a little bit of everything and let your guests have a mixed grill!

Menu

ROSEMARY CHICKEN QUARTERS
133

MARINATED FILET MIGNON
120

MAPLE-GLAZED SALMON WITH PINEAPPLE SALSA
152

MINTED LAMB
131

TERIYAKI SHRIMP
148

POTATO AND EGG SALAD
173

TOMATOES WITH BLUE CHEESE
190

VIDALIA ONION CORN BREAD
14

PEACH CREAM TART
229

A Weekend Campout

Who would have thought that a show about cooking around a campfire would have been a hit? But the episode called "Campfire Cooking" was one of the most popular I have ever done. No matter how sophisticated we get, some people still like to spend the night out under the stars, thank goodness!

Lucky us to find Scoutmaster Robert English, of Savannah, who has been taking boys on camping trips for more than forty-six years! Mr. English has been known to dump out a boy's backpack before a camping trip, leaving behind all the candy bars and commercial snacks. Instead, he prefers to teach the boys how to dine around a campfire on chicken breasts or pork chops topped with fresh vegetables. Meals are often polished off with his famous Dutch-Oven Peach Cobbler (page 230). This is gourmet camping, y'all!

New coolers have really made the job of keeping food cold easier, Mr. English says. He also freezes water in milk jugs. The ice stays frozen longer, and there's very little mess. Keeping food cold on a camping trip is critical for food safety. Food defrosts quicker than you'd think in the South, so you will notice that we have suggested freezing all of our entrées and then packing them into the cooler just prior to the trip. Items will thaw out at different times, and you just pick the packages that are the most thawed and cook those first. If you are camping in climates where it's cool, you can skip the freezing step and safely refrigerate the items, and then pack in coolers and eat within three days. I freeze everything, because you might be gone several days and the item you want to cook on night three or four will have that long to defrost. You want to err on the side of safety. If food has reached room temperature, that is, 70 degrees, not cool to the touch, absolutely do not cook and eat it. Bacteria grows rapidly at room temperature, and food is to be considered questionable after two hours.

Safety also requires us to cook all meats until there is no pink showing. Cut through a sample piece of meat, and using a flashlight, visually inspect hamburgers, chicken, and pork to make sure that they are cooked through. This is particularly important when feeding children, who are even more susceptible than adults to food poisoning.

We recommend burning the used foil in the fire after you eat, which will greatly assist in your cleanup. Mr. English has done this successfully his entire camping career with no ill effects. The tinfoil burns away, leaving only a sliver of silver to pick up and dispose of when you leave your campsite.

Menu

HAMBURGER PIE
123

CHICKEN BREAST PIE
140

PORK CHOP AND PINEAPPLE PIE
127

BLACKENED FISH
156

BAKED GRILLED POTATOES
175

ZUCCHINI OR GREEN BEAN BUNDLES
187

BOB'S DUTCH-OVEN BREAD
19

S'MORES
235

DUTCH-OVEN PEACH COBBLER
230

TORTILLA DESSERT WRAPS
235

BEASON BREAKFAST BURRITOS
7

SIDE DISHES

Southern Corn Bread Dressing

This is a classic southern soft dressing.

Corn Bread

- 2 tablespoons bacon grease or vegetable oil
- 1 cup self-rising cornmeal
- ½ cup self-rising flour
- ¾ cup buttermilk
- 2 eggs

Dressing

- 1 recipe Corn Bread, crumbled
- 4 slices white bread, dried in the oven and crumbled
- 40 (1 sleeve) saltine crackers, crumbled
- ½ cup (1 stick) butter
- 2 cups chopped celery
- 1 large yellow onion, chopped
- 1 teaspoon salt
- ½ teaspoon pepper
- 2 teaspoons poultry seasoning
- 7 cups chicken stock
- 5 large eggs, beaten

1. Preheat the oven to 400°F. Grease an 8-inch square or round metal pan with the bacon grease or vegetable oil.

2. Combine the cornmeal, flour, buttermilk, and eggs in a 1-quart bowl and mix well with a metal spoon. Pour into the prepared pan and bake for about 20 minutes, until very lightly browned on the top. Remove from the oven and allow to cool in the pan until cool enough to handle. Crumble when cool.

3. In a large bowl, combine the crumbled corn bread, white bread, and saltine crackers. In a 12-inch skillet, melt the butter over low heat. Add the celery and onion and sauté until soft, about 10 minutes. Pour the sautéed vegetables over the corn bread mixture. Add the salt, pepper, and poultry seasoning.

4. About 1½ hours before you want to serve your meal, preheat the oven to 350°F. Spray a 13-by-9-inch baking dish with vegetable oil cooking spray.

5. Add the stock to the corn bread mixture. Stir in the eggs. The mixture will be very soupy. Pour the mixture into the prepared dish. Bake the dressing for 50 minutes, until puffed and lightly browned. Serve with turducken and brown gravy.

Serves about 20

Creamy Macaroni and Cheese

I didn't think my macaroni and cheese could be improved upon, but adding the Cheddar cheese soup gives it a wonderful, creamy texture and helps to "stretch" the dish.

2 cups uncooked elbow macaroni (an 8-ounce box isn't quite 2 cups)

2½ cups (about 10 ounces) grated sharp Cheddar cheese

3 eggs, beaten

½ cup sour cream

One 10.75-ounce can condensed Cheddar cheese soup

4 tablespoons (½ stick) butter, cut into pieces

½ teaspoon salt

1 cup whole milk

½ teaspoon dry mustard

½ teaspoon pepper

1. Preheat the oven to 350°F. Spray a 13-by-9-inch baking dish with vegetable oil cooking spray.

2. Boil the macaroni in a 2-quart saucepan in plenty of water until tender, about 7 minutes. Drain. Return the drained macaroni to the saucepan and add 2 cups of the cheese. Stir until the cheese melts while the macaroni is still hot. Add the eggs, sour cream, soup, butter, salt, milk, mustard, and pepper and stir well.

3. Pour the macaroni into the prepared dish. Smooth the top and sprinkle the remaining ½ cup of cheese on top. Bake for 40 minutes, until browned and bubbly.

Serves 12

Note: The macaroni and cheese can be prepared earlier in the day or the day before and refrigerated unbaked, covered, until needed. Allow to come to room temperature before baking.

Arroz con Tomate (Red Rice)

In Savannah, red rice is often served in place of potatoes. Here's the Low-Country version of the Mexican staple.

8 slices bacon

1 medium yellow onion, chopped

2 celery stalks, chopped

1 small green bell pepper, chopped

2 cups white rice

One 14.5-ounce can stewed tomatoes

1 cup regular or spicy tomato juice

1 teaspoon sugar

1 teaspoon salt

¼ teaspoon black pepper

¼ teaspoon cayenne pepper

2 drops hot sauce

1. Preheat the oven to 325°F. Spray a 3-quart baking dish with vegetable oil cooking spray.

2. Fry the bacon until it is crisp in a heavy Dutch oven. Remove the bacon and drain it on paper towels. Sauté the onion, celery, and green pepper over low heat in the bacon grease until the vegetables are soft, about 5 minutes. Crumble the bacon and return it to the pot. Add the rice and stir well to coat it with the drippings.

3. Whirl the tomatoes in the blender briefly until they are chopped; do not puree. In a quart measuring cup, place the tomatoes and the tomato juice. Add enough water to make 4 cups liquid. Add this to the rice mixture and stir well. Add the sugar, salt, black pepper, cayenne pepper, and hot sauce.

4. Transfer the rice to the prepared baking dish. Bake for 45 minutes, covered, until the rice is tender. The rice will not be sticky; it will still have a little crunch to it.

Serves 10 to 12

Potato and Egg Salad

This is just delicious. You can make it early in the day and refrigerate if you like it cold, or if you're like me and want it warm, you can make it at the last minute.

5 to 6 medium white potatoes, peeled and cubed

6 hard-boiled eggs, peeled and chopped

½ cup finely chopped celery

1½ cups mayonnaise

Salt and pepper

Boil the potatoes until tender, about 15 minutes. Drain and let cool. Place in a large bowl and add the eggs and celery. Gently stir in the mayonnaise, being careful not to mash the potatoes. Add salt and pepper to taste. Cover with plastic wrap and refrigerate until ready to serve.

Serves 4 to 6

Baked Sweet Potatoes with Butter and Brown Sugar

This is an alternative to the many sweet potato casseroles that are out there.

3 large sweet potatoes

6 tablespoons (¾ stick) butter

3 tablespoons light brown sugar

1. Preheat the oven to 350°F. Scrub the outside of the potatoes. Pierce the potatoes in several places with a sharp knife.

2. Place the potatoes in a baking pan and bake until soft, about 1½ hours.

3. When done, make a large slit in each potato and plump up the "meat" inside. Place 2 tablespoons butter and 1 tablespoon brown sugar down into each slit. Quarter the potatoes crosswise and place on a serving dish.

Serves 12

Twice-Baked Potato Casserole

There just isn't any better combination than meat and potatoes. This is such a great dish because you can make it the day ahead and you've still got that delicious flavor of baked potatoes.

8 medium baking potatoes, about 4 pounds

One 8-ounce package cream cheese, at room temperature

½ cup (1 stick) butter, softened

2 cups (½ pound) shredded sharp Cheddar cheese

1 pint sour cream

2 cloves garlic, minced

1½ teaspoons salt

½ teaspoon pepper

¼ cup chopped chives, for garnish

6 slices bacon, cooked crisp, drained, and crumbled, for garnish

1. Preheat the oven to 350°F. Pierce the potatoes and place on a baking pan. Bake the potatoes for 1 hour and 15 minutes, until very soft.

2. Peel and mash the potatoes in a large bowl with a potato masher or the back of a fork. Add the cream cheese, butter, 1 cup of the Cheddar cheese, and the sour cream. Stir well. Add the garlic, salt, and pepper and stir again.

3. Spray a 13-by-9-inch baking dish with vegetable oil cooking spray. Place the potatoes into the dish. The casserole may now be covered with plastic wrap and refrigerated until ready to bake.

4. When ready to bake, preheat the oven to 350°F. Remove the plastic wrap and bake the potatoes for 30 to 35 minutes, until hot. Sprinkle the remaining 1 cup Cheddar cheese over the top of the casserole and return to the oven for about 5 minutes, until the cheese melts. Garnish with the chopped chives and crumbled bacon before serving.

Serves 10 to 12

Rosemary and Garlic Roasted New Potatoes

You'll want to start these potatoes about an hour before you want to serve dinner. (When finished, let them rest on the countertop while you cook the fish.) The smell of the garlic and rosemary is terrific. Leave the skins on the potatoes for color.

2 tablespoons olive oil

2 cloves garlic, finely minced

2 tablespoons fresh rosemary, minced

Salt and pepper

16 large new potatoes, scrubbed and cut into relatively uniform chunks

1. Preheat the oven to 350°F. Spray a glass baking dish with vegetable oil cooking spray.

2. Place the olive oil, garlic, rosemary, and salt and pepper to taste in a large resealable plastic bag. Add the potatoes, seal, and toss to coat evenly. Pour into the prepared baking dish. Roast the potatoes for about 30 to 40 minutes, until crisp on the outside and tender inside.

Serves 6 to 8

Baked Grilled Potatoes

How long these take to bake depends on the size of the potatoes and how hot the coals are.

1 large baking potato per person

¼ cup (½ stick) butter per person, or to taste

Salt and pepper

Wash each potato and pierce all over with a fork. Wrap each potato in heavy-duty aluminum foil. Place the potatoes directly onto hot coals and cook for about 45 minutes, turning often, using long tongs. Split the potatoes and top with butter. Pass the salt and pepper.

Note: To prepare in the oven, prepare as above, and bake in 375°F oven for 1 hour.

Garlic Mashed Potatoes

Garlic mashed potatoes are all the rage in restaurants everywhere. And why not? They are terrific with beef dishes!

3 medium baking potatoes, peeled and coarsely chopped

1 teaspoon salt

4 tablespoons (½ stick) butter, at room temperature

¼ cup sour cream, at room temperature

1 teaspoon finely minced garlic

Whole milk, start with 1 tablespoon, at room temperature or warmed

Salt and pepper

1. In a medium saucepan, cook the potatoes in salted water until tender, about 15 minutes. Drain the potatoes and return them to the saucepan.

2. Add the butter, sour cream, and garlic. Mash the potatoes with a potato masher or the back of a fork until the ingredients are blended. Add the milk, 1 tablespoon at a time, until the potatoes are the desired consistency. Taste, and add salt and pepper if needed.

Serves 2, with leftovers

Phyllo-Wrapped Asparagus

These are beautiful to look at and very tasty, too!

8 or 9 asparagus spears

4 sheets frozen phyllo (filo) pastry from a 16-ounce package, thawed and covered with a clean, damp tea towel

4 tablespoons (½ stick) butter, melted

¼ cup freshly grated Parmesan cheese

1. Preheat the oven to 375°F. Snap off the tough ends of the asparagus.

2. Unwrap the phyllo pastry and cut the stack in half lengthwise. Remove 4 sheets of pastry. Reserve the rest for another use; store in an airtight freezer bag. Cover the phyllo lightly with a damp tea towel to keep it from drying out.

3. Take 1 piece of phyllo and brush lightly with melted butter. Sprinkle with cheese. Place 2 or 3 asparagus spears on the short end of the phyllo. Roll up, jelly-roll style. Fold over the ends to enclose the asparagus spears.

4. Place each roll, seam-side down, on a baking sheet. Brush with butter and sprinkle with cheese. Repeat until all of the asparagus spears are rolled. Bake for 15 to 18 minutes or until golden brown and crispy.

Serves 2

Fresh Asparagus with Lemon Butter

Trim the asparagus early in the day and roll in a damp towel to keep fresh.

5 or 6 asparagus spears per person, thin stalks preferred

¼ cup (½ stick) butter

Juice of 1 lemon

1. Rinse the asparagus. Line the spears up on a cutting board with the tops even. Even up the bottoms, and cut off any tough ends.

2. Bring a skillet or oval casserole filled half full of salted water to a boil.

3. In a small saucepan, melt the butter and whisk in the lemon juice. Set aside.

4. When the water comes to a boil, dump in the asparagus all at once. When the water returns to a boil, cook the asparagus for 2 to 5 minutes, depending on their size and your preference. Drain the asparagus but do not rinse. Return them to the hot pan and pour the sauce over. Serve immediately.

Marinated Asparagus

This is just beautiful—crunchy and delicious.

1½ **pounds fresh asparagus, ends trimmed**

¼ **cup sugar**

¼ **cup white vinegar**

¼ **cup soy sauce**

2 **tablespoons canola oil**

¼ **cup finely chopped pecans or walnuts, lightly toasted**

1. Fill a large frying pan with 2 inches of water and bring to a rolling boil. Plunge the asparagus into the water and remove after 1 minute. Drain immediately and pat dry. Place in a 13-by-9-inch casserole dish.

2. Combine the sugar, vinegar, soy sauce, and oil. Whisk vigorously. Pour over the asparagus. Cover and chill for at least 8 hours.

3. To serve, drain the marinade. Place the asparagus in a serving dish and sprinkle with the nuts.

Serves 8

Asparagus with Shallot Vinaigrette

Gail Levites contributed this one. The dressing is enough for about three dozen asparagus spears.

2 **tablespoons red wine vinegar**

1 **tablespoon Dijon mustard**

½ **cup extra-virgin olive oil**

2 **tablespoons finely chopped shallots**

Salt and pepper

4 **to 6 asparagus spears per person, steamed until tender**

Whisk the vinegar and mustard together in a small glass bowl. Slowly drizzle in the oil, whisking constantly. Add the shallots, and salt and pepper to taste, and mix well. Allow to sit at room temperature for 30 minutes. Drizzle over the hot asparagus. Serve at room temperature.

Green Beans with New Potatoes

My children's favorite green beans were cooked by their Great-Grandmother Paul. She used very little water and always wilted them. It dawned on me a couple of months back that while I had been cookin' these like Grandmama Paul did for years, I didn't have an exact formula. So the other day, I went into the kitchen at the restaurant and wrote down exactly everything I did. Well, I brought home that pot of beans and potatoes for Michael's supper. I served them alongside of Lace Hoecake Corn Bread (page 15) and sliced tomatoes with onions. We fixed our plates and started eating, when all of a sudden Michael put down his fork, looked at me, and said, "Paula, those are the best green beans I have ever eaten." Needless to say, that little statement made me very happy, and once again proved that Grandmama Paul was a fabulous teacher.

3 pounds fresh green beans

¼ pound salt pork, sliced

¼ cup bacon grease (pour this into a jar and keep on hand in the refrigerator to use as needed)

2 cups chicken broth, plus more if needed (canned is fine)

2 to 3 teaspoons House Seasoning (page 119)

12 small red potatoes, or more

1 onion, cut into slivers

1. Remove the ends from the beans. Snap the beans in two, place into a colander, wash, and set aside to drain.

2. Meanwhile, in a large, cast-iron Dutch oven, lightly brown the salt pork in the bacon grease over medium heat, turning often, for approximately 10 minutes.

3. Toss the green beans into the pot, stirring them with a wooden spoon to coat well with the pork fat. Add the stock and House Seasoning. Cook over medium-low heat, covered tightly, for approximately 30 minutes, or until the beans are half done.

4. While the beans are cooking, peel a center strip from each new potato with a potato peeler. At the end of 30 minutes, add the potatoes and onion to the beans; add ¼ cup more broth if needed. Cook, covered tightly, until the potatoes are tender, approximately 25 to 30 minutes, periodically checking the pot to make sure a small amount of liquid remains. When the potatoes are tender, tilt the lid slightly, off to the side of the pot, and continue to cook until the green beans are wilted, approximately 15 minutes.

Serves 8 to 10

Note: My tips for cooking phenomenal green beans: Stir often. Add additional chicken broth in small amounts as needed, but don't drown your beans.

Slow Cooker Pinto Beans

1 pound dried pinto beans

1 teaspoon chili powder

½ teaspoon dried oregano

½ pound ham hocks, or ¼ pound streak o' lean

1 yellow onion, chopped

2 tablespoons (¼ stick) butter (optional)

1 tablespoon House Seasoning (page 119)

1. Wash the beans and soak overnight in cold water. Or use the quick method and boil the beans in plenty of water for 2 minutes, then allow to sit for 1 hour.

2. Drain the beans and dump them into the slow cooker. Stir in the chili powder and oregano.

3. If using ham hocks, soak in a separate pot in 4 cups water for 2 hours. Add the ham hocks and soaking liquid to the slow cooker. If using streak o' lean, cut the meat into chunks and brown in a skillet. Remove the meat and put it in the slow cooker with the beans.

4. Sauté the onion in the fat in the skillet or sauté the onion in 2 tablespoons butter. Add the onion to the beans. Add the House Seasoning. Stir well.

5. Cover and cook on high until the beans are tender and have absorbed most of the liquid, about 5 hours.

Serves 10 to 12

Southern Pole Beans

Pole beans are large, flat green beans adored by southerners. You may substitute green beans if pole beans are unavailable.

3 pounds pole beans, ends and strings removed, snapped into 3-inch pieces

¼ pound salt pork, sliced thin, like bacon

¼ cup bacon grease

2 cups chicken broth

2 teaspoons House Seasoning (page 119)

1. Place the beans in a colander, wash, and set aside to drain.

2. In a large, cast-iron Dutch oven, lightly brown the salt pork in the bacon grease over medium heat, turning often, for about 10 minutes.

3. Add the pole beans to the pot and toss to coat with the bacon grease. Add the broth and House Seasoning. Cook over medium-low heat, covered tightly, for about 30 minutes (or longer), until the beans are tender and flavorful.

Serves 12

Brussels Sprouts with Onion and Bacon

My family really loves my green beans, but sometimes I serve brussels sprouts, which taste and look like sweet little cabbages.

½ pound lean bacon, finely diced

1 cup diced yellow onion

2 cloves garlic, minced

2 pounds brussels sprouts, trimmed

2 cups chicken broth

4 tablespoons (½ stick) butter

1. In a heavy-bottomed pot over medium heat, fry the bacon until crisp. Remove the bacon and drain on paper towels.

2. Sauté the onion and garlic in the bacon grease over low heat until soft, about 3 minutes. Add the brussels sprouts and stir them around so that they are coated with the bacon grease.

3. Add the broth and cook, covered, over low heat until the sprouts are easily pierced with a fork, about 12 to 15 minutes. Stir in the butter just before serving. Garnish each serving with bacon bits.

Serves 8

Bacon-Wrapped Grilled
Corn on the Cob

8 ears fresh corn, husks
   attached
8 slices bacon
   Butter

1. Gently pull back the husks, completely exposing the kernels, but do not remove the husks. Remove the corn silk and use a brush to make sure all the silk is removed. In a large pot filled with water, soak the corn for 30 minutes.

2. Preheat the grill to medium.

3. Remove the corn from the water and pat dry. Take a slice of bacon and wrap it spiral-fashion around an ear of corn. Fold the husk back over the corn and bacon. Tie the husk with butcher string. Repeat the process for each ear of corn. Place the corn on the hot grill and cook, turning occasionally, until the bacon is cooked and the corn is tender, approximately 15 to 20 minutes. The bacon will not be brown, which doesn't bother me one bit, but if it bothers you, gently pull the husks back and run the corn under the broiler for a few minutes until the bacon is brown. Serve with butter!

Serves 8

Fried Peanut Butter and Banana Sandwich (page 44)

Crab and Spinach Casserole (page 6); Baked Tomatoes (page 9); Blueberry Gems (page 24)

Mardi Gras King Cake (page 216)

Pecan Squares (page 242)

White Cake with Strawberry Icing (page 212); Strawberries Dipped in White Chocolate (page 268)

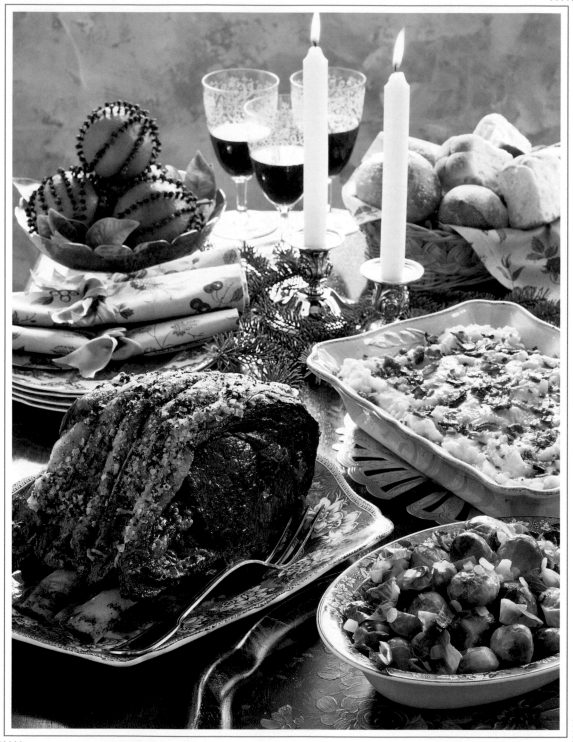

Standing Rib Roast (page 122); Twice-Baked Potato Casserole (page 174);
Brussels Sprouts with Onion and Bacon (page 183)

The Lady & Sons Crab-Stuffed Shrimp (page 84)

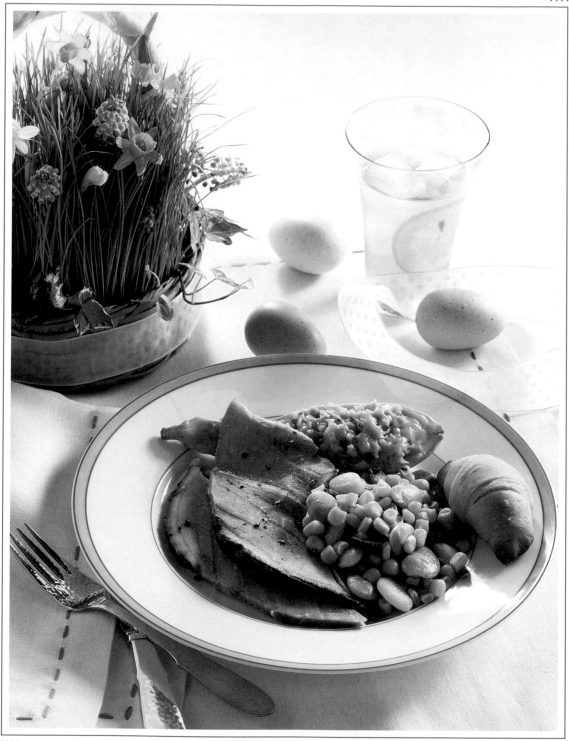

Peanut Butter–Glazed Ham (page 129); Squash Boats (page 188);
Butterhorns (page 22); Succotash (page 189)

Crème de Menthe Brownies (page 245)

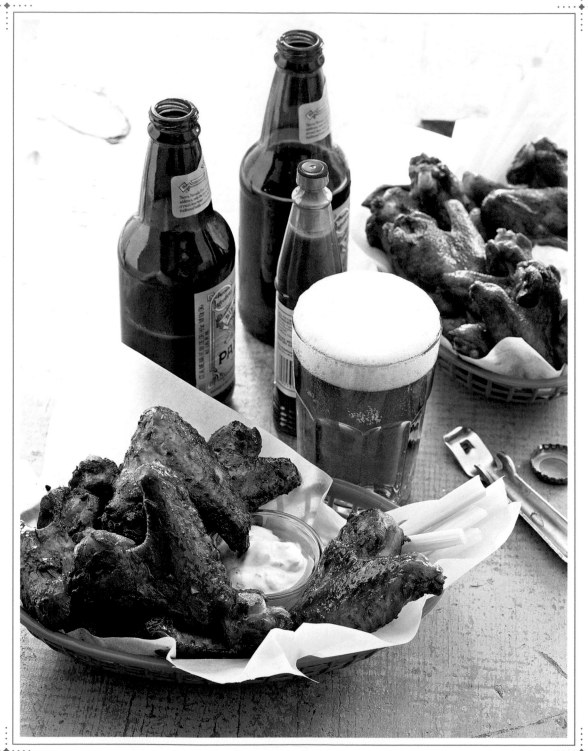

Left: Buffalo Chicken Wings (page 90); right: Teriyaki Chicken Wings (page 90)

On the serving stand, top to bottom: Lemon Cups (page 241), Pecan Squares (page 242),
Petticoat Tails (page 259); on the plate, clockwise from top: Ginger-Nut Sandwiches (page 43),
Cucumber Sandwiches (page 42), Cheese Sandwiches (page 42)

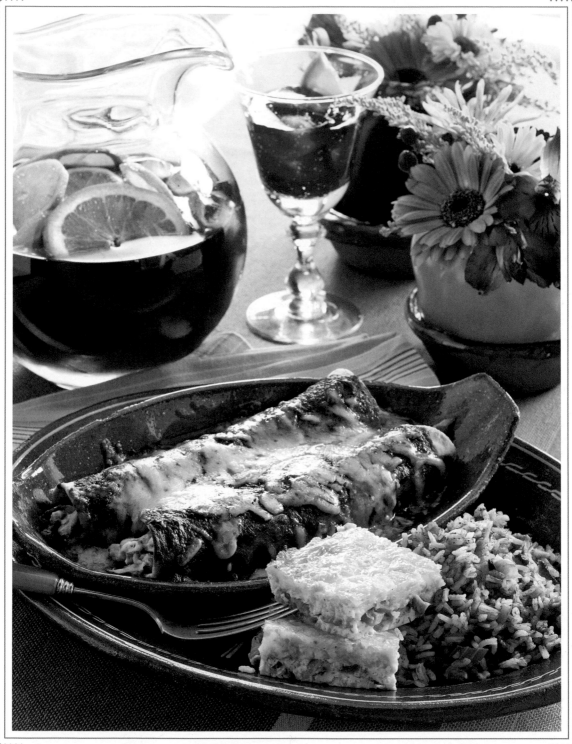

Sangria (recipe not included); Enchiladas de Pollo (Cream Cheese and Chicken Enchiladas) (page 139); Green Chili Squares (page 95); Arroz con Tomate (Red Rice) (page 172)

Small plate: Turtle Pizza (page 237); large plate: Pesto and Feta Pizza (page 37)

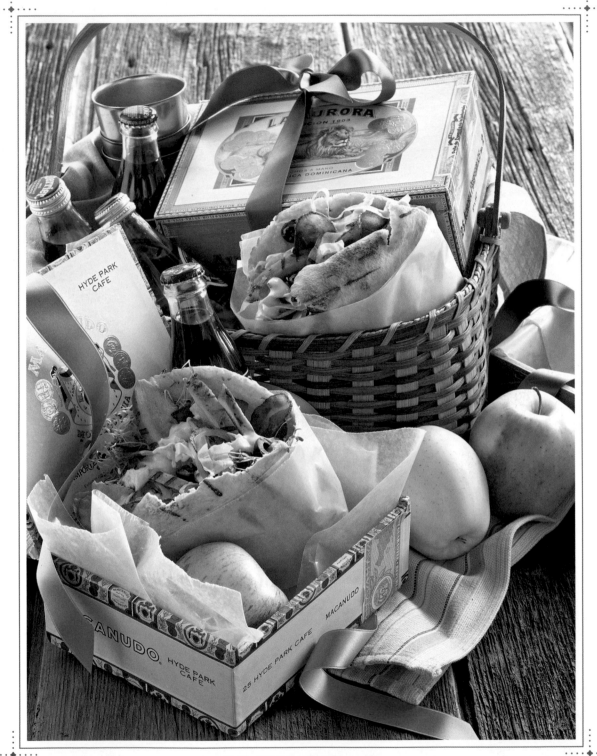

Grilled Chicken Pita (page 48)

Low-Country Boil (page 146) with (clockwise from top) Cocktail Sauce (page 147),
Potato Sauce (page 147), and Tartar Sauce (page 147)

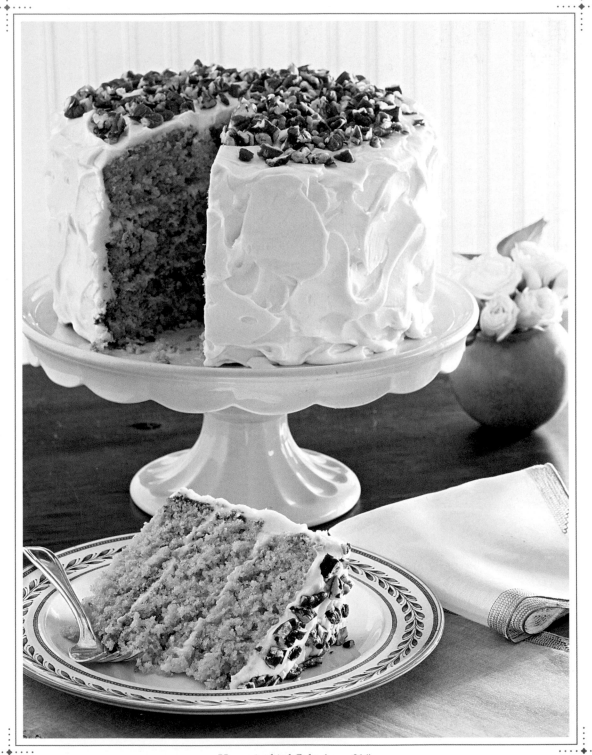

Hummingbird Cake (page 214)

Roasted Carrots

This is my son Jamie's favorite way to eat carrots. I buy the baby carrots already peeled and cleaned; they are uniform in size and cook evenly; but you can peel and quarter large carrots if you prefer. This dish is so simple, yet so delicious.

One 1-pound bag baby carrots

2 tablespoons olive oil

1 teaspoon House Seasoning (page 119)

2 tablespoons butter

2 tablespoons chopped fresh parsley

1. Preheat the oven to 350°F.

2. In a large bowl, coat the carrots with the olive oil. Toss with the House Seasoning and place in a 13-by-9-inch roasting pan. Roast until tender, approximately 30 minutes. Remove from the oven and toss the carrots with the butter and chopped parsley.

Serves 6 to 8

All-Day Mushrooms

Katherine assured me that this unusual recipe was worth the time, but I had my doubts. Katherine was right; these mushrooms were so delicious!

3 pounds whole button mushrooms

½ cup (1 stick) butter

2 cups Burgundy wine

1 tablespoon Worcestershire sauce

1 teaspoon minced garlic

1 teaspoon dried dill weed

½ teaspoon pepper

2 chicken bouillon cubes

2 beef bouillon cubes

With a wet paper towel, wipe any dirt from the mushroom caps and stems. Place the mushrooms in a large stockpot. Add the remaining ingredients to the pot. The liquid will not cover the mushrooms at first. Cook, covered, over very low heat for 4 hours, stirring occasionally so that the mushrooms are completely coated with cooking liquid. Remove the cover and cook for an additional 4 hours. The mushrooms will shrink by half and become saturated with cooking liquid. Remove with a slotted spoon and serve in a bowl.

Serves 8

Spinach-Swiss Casserole

Is this a spinach soufflé or a casserole? Who cares, when it tastes so good? You can serve it hot or at room temperature, and I think it makes a nice brunch or lunch dish, too. Baking the soufflé in a hot-water bath will give the dish a silky texture.

One 10-ounce package frozen chopped spinach

¼ cup finely minced yellow onion

4 tablespoons (½ stick) butter

3 tablespoons all-purpose flour

½ teaspoon salt

Pinch of cayenne pepper

¼ teaspoon black pepper

1 cup whole milk

1 cup (¼ pound) grated Swiss cheese

½ cup freshly grated Parmesan cheese

3 eggs, beaten well

1. Preheat the oven to 325°F. Spray a 1½-quart casserole with vegetable oil cooking spray.

2. Remove the spinach from the packaging and transfer to a microwave-safe bowl. Microwave on high for 2 minutes. Remove the spinach and squeeze dry with your hands. Place the spinach into a medium mixing bowl.

3. In a skillet, over medium-low heat, sauté the onion in 1 tablespoon of the butter until soft, about 3 to 4 minutes. Add the onion to the spinach.

4. In the same skillet, melt the remaining 3 tablespoons butter over medium-low heat. Whisk in the flour, salt, cayenne pepper, and black pepper. Stir until smooth. Slowly add the milk and continue stirring until the mixture thickens, 3 to 5 minutes. Turn off the heat. Stir in the Swiss and Parmesan cheeses and continue stirring until the mixture is smooth. Pour the sauce over the spinach in the mixing bowl. Add the eggs and stir well.

5. Pour the spinach mixture into the casserole. Place the casserole into a larger casserole filled with 1 inch of water (a hot-water bath) and bake for 45 minutes.

Serves 8 to 10

Squash Casserole

Robbie Hollander says a squash casserole is a requirement at a Shabbat dinner. This dish is great for any meal and is her children's favorite.

1½ pounds yellow squash, about 6 medium, ends trimmed, lightly peeled and sliced

¼ cup chopped onion

1 egg, beaten

¼ cup (½ stick) butter

1½ teaspoons sugar

½ teaspoon salt

½ teaspoon pepper

¼ cup soft bread crumbs

1. Preheat the oven to 375°F. Grease a 2-quart casserole dish.

2. Boil the squash until tender, then drain and mash. Add the onion, egg, 2 tablespoons of the butter, sugar, salt, and pepper. Place the squash mixture into the prepared casserole dish and smooth the top. Melt the remaining 2 tablespoons butter and pour over the top. Sprinkle with the bread crumbs. Bake for 30 minutes, or until brown.

Serves 6 to 8

Zucchini or Green Bean Bundles

These should be prepared at the campsite; you don't even need to put the vegetables in a cooler unless it's really hot. If it is, however, you'll need to keep them on ice or they will deteriorate rapidly.

1 zucchini per person, lightly peeled and thinly sliced, or 1 cup green beans per person, ends removed

1 tablespoon butter per person

Salt and pepper

For each serving, place the zucchini or green beans on a square of heavy-duty aluminum foil and top with the butter. Sprinkle generously with salt and pepper. Wrap tightly in the foil, rolling ends to completely seal the package. Place packages directly in coals for about 10 minutes for zucchini, about 15 minutes for beans.

Note: To prepare in the oven, prepare as above and place on baking sheet. Bake in preheated 375°F oven for 15 minutes.

Squash Boats

I'm not sure that there's any way to improve upon a good squash casserole, but these squash boats are fun and different.

4 medium yellow squash or zucchini

2 tablespoons (¼ stick) butter

1 small yellow onion, finely chopped

½ teaspoon salt

¼ teaspoon pepper

2 saltine crackers, crushed into crumbs

1 cup (¼ pound) shredded sharp Cheddar cheese

1. Preheat the oven to 350°F. Lightly butter a baking dish large enough to hold the squash on a small rimmed baking sheet.

2. Boil the whole squash in a medium saucepan in about 2 cups water over medium heat until the squash are tender, about 15 minutes.

3. Remove the squash from the water, drain, and allow to cool. Cut the squash in half lengthwise. Using a small spoon, gently scoop out the pulp, leaving the shape of the squash intact. Place the squash shells in the prepared dish.

4. In a small skillet, melt the butter and sauté the onion until tender, about 3 to 5 minutes. Add the salt and pepper. Add the squash pulp and cracker crumbs. Stuff the filling into the squash shells. Top each squash boat with enough cheese to cover the filling.

5. Bake for 20 minutes. Serve hot or at room temperature.

Serves 8

Succotash

Succotash is just fresh corn off-the-cob and baby butter beans or lima beans. What could be better? If you are lucky enough to get farm-fresh produce, then you will have the best ingredients. However, this dish is almost as good when you use frozen baby butter or lima beans and corn, or supermarket corn that you cut off the cob. The name succotash comes from an Indian word meaning "boiled corn."

½ teaspoon House Seasoning (page 119)

½ teaspoon seasoned salt

1 chicken bouillon cube or 1 teaspoon granulated bouillon

One 10-ounce package frozen baby butter beans or lima beans

6 slices bacon, cut into tiny pieces

3 ears fresh corn, kernels cut from cob, or one 10-ounce package frozen corn kernels

2 tablespoons (¼ stick) butter

¼ teaspoon pepper

1. In a medium saucepan, add the House Seasoning, seasoned salt, and bouillon cube to 2 cups water. Add the butter beans or lima beans and bring to a boil. Reduce the heat, cover, and cook over low heat for about 20 minutes, until the butter beans are tender and some of the water has been absorbed.

2. In a medium skillet, sauté the bacon until it is very crisp.

3. Drain off all except 1 tablespoon grease. Add the corn to the skillet with the bacon pieces and cook over medium-low heat for about 10 minutes. Using a slotted spoon, add the butter beans to the skillet. Add a little of the butter bean liquid to create a sauce. Add the butter and pepper. Stir well and serve.

Serves 8 to 10

Tomatoes with Blue Cheese

This is one of those dishes you'll definitely eat with your eyes first! Use whatever type of lettuce looks freshest at the market, and the ripest tomatoes.

1 head romaine or 2 heads Boston lettuce, washed, dried, and chopped

2 ripe tomatoes, sliced

1 cup crumbled blue cheese

1 cup fresh basil leaves, cut into ribbons

Dressing

3 tablespoons fresh lemon juice

½ cup vegetable oil

2 tablespoons sugar

1 small clove garlic, crushed

½ teaspoon salt

½ teaspoon dry mustard

1. Arrange the lettuce on a large platter. Distribute the tomato slices, blue cheese, and basil attractively over the lettuce.

2. Make the dressing: In a glass jar with a tight-fitting lid, combine the dressing ingredients and shake well. Drizzle the dressing over the salad just before serving.

Serves 6 to 8

Marinated Tomatoes

The best thing about this recipe is that it makes even those awful winter tomatoes taste delicious. The leftover marinade can be used to dress a simple lettuce salad.

Dressing

- 3 tablespoons chopped fresh parsley
- 1 tablespoon sugar
- 1½ teaspoons garlic salt
- 1½ teaspoons seasoned salt
- ½ teaspoon pepper
- ¾ teaspoon dried oregano
- ¾ cup vegetable oil
- ½ cup red wine vinegar

- 4 to 6 large tomatoes, cored, each cut into six wedges

Place all of the ingredients for the dressing in a measuring cup and whisk thoroughly to combine. Place the tomatoes in a resealable plastic bag and pour in the dressing. Marinate for 4 to 5 hours or overnight in the refrigerator. Bring to room temperature before serving. Serve with a slotted spoon.

Serves 6 to 8

Alice Jo's Spaghetti Sauce

Alice Jo Giddens has served this sauce to hundreds of people who attend the Park Avenue United Methodist Church, in Valdosta. It's also eagerly anticipated at family get-togethers. Make it in advance and freeze it in pint- or quart-size containers.

1½ pounds ground beef

1 large onion, chopped

1 green bell pepper, chopped

1 clove garlic, chopped

Two 6-ounce cans tomato paste

One 8-ounce can tomato sauce

One 14½-ounce can stewed tomatoes

1 tablespoon Italian seasoning

1 tablespoon Worcestershire sauce

2 tablespoons sugar

1 teaspoon salt

Brown the beef in a large, heavy-bottomed pot, then drain off the fat. Add the onion, green pepper, and garlic, and sauté until the onion is tender, about 5 minutes. Add the tomato paste, tomato sauce, stewed tomatoes, 1 cup water, and seasonings. Simmer for 30 minutes. Let cool. The sauce will keep for several days, covered, in the refrigerator.

Serves 6 to 8

Ambrosia

I love to serve this traditional southern dish for Thanksgiving. Add the bananas at the last minute.

12 medium juice oranges

One 8-ounce can crushed pineapple, with juice

One 8-ounce can pineapple chunks, with juice

½ cup sweetened flaked coconut

¼ cup sugar

One 4-ounce jar maraschino cherries, drained and rinsed

½ cup chopped toasted pecans

2 bananas, sliced

1 cup whipping cream, whipped with 1 tablespoon confectioners' sugar

Peel and section the oranges, removing all the membrane. Place the sections into a large glass bowl. Add the pineapple, coconut, and sugar and stir to combine. Refrigerate until about 30 minutes before serving time. At that time, add the cherries, pecans, and bananas. Stir before serving. Serve with a slotted spoon in dessert dishes with a dollop of sweetened whipped cream, or over pound cake.

Serves 18 to 20

Sautéed Red-Skinned Apples

This is so easy and pretty on the plate next to those golden hens! Prepare the apples in advance and then just before serving, warm them in the microwave at medium setting to prevent over-cooking. Double or triple the recipe so that you can serve this the next night over ice cream. It's delicious!

4 medium, tart, red-skinned apples (such as Fuji or Gala)

6 tablespoons butter

½ cup sugar

1½ to 2 teaspoons ground cinnamon

1. Wash the apples in cold water and pat dry. Cut them into quarters, and cut out the core. Slice each quarter lengthwise into 4 slices.

2. Melt the butter in a medium frying pan over medium heat. Add the apples and sugar and mix well. Sprinkle the apple slices with the desired amount of cinnamon. Reduce the heat to medium low and continue cooking for 12 to 15 minutes, stirring frequently, until the apples have reached the desired degree of doneness. The cooking time will vary depending on the variety of apples being used. When the apples are done, the butter and sugar mixture will have become a delicious syrup. Serve warm.

Serves 4

Puttin' It All Together

The Boss Comes to Dinner

So the boss is coming for dinner. This is the night when you want to show off: your home, your children, your pets, your style, your culinary creativity. In searching for the perfect menu, we turned to Katherine Slagel, of Richmond Hill, near Savannah, who is both a boss (she's an established interior designer) and the wife of David, who has frequently entertained his boss (David's an engineer at International Paper).

Katherine developed a fall menu that will cost you at least $100, will take you several days to prepare, and will literally put you on the map as a couple to be reckoned with. This is not a menu for the faint of heart, but if you want to prepare a meal that the boss will still be talking about a year from now, this is the one to master.

"Timing is everything when issuing an invitation," Katherine says. "The holidays are filled with attempts to get together with family and friends, and you are neither to your boss. My mother has always said that it lacks creativity to center entertaining around a holiday; better to accomplish eight for dinner on a quiet October evening than to be a stop on the cocktail circuit in December.

"This is the night for all to glitter and can be a great excuse to hire your first housekeeper, especially if you're working. Up to one week before, iron the cloth napkins, polish the silver, and set the table. I turn plates and goblets upside down to avoid dust. October is still too warm for a fire in the Deep South, but candles of varying heights on a mirror can carry the table and the season if you can't cope with the thought of arranging flowers. On the morning of the party, I usually use a hollowed pumpkin as a bowl to be filled with evergreens, ivy, mums, hawthorne berries, and pomegranates on skewers for a fail-safe, long-lasting arrangement. Don't forget place cards, and please print them from the computer if your handwriting suffers. There's no need to get fussy with the napkin fold.

"Chicken isn't special, beef seems pretentious, and lamb doesn't appeal to all. Therefore, my staple years ago became a luscious veal loin ($18 a pound, y'all!) stuffed with roasted yellow peppers, goat cheese, and basil. Much of the preparation can be done a day ahead, and the butcher tackles the most difficult parts. In the oven, roast new potatoes alongside the veal. A crab mousse appetizer begins the meal, and dessert is my very yummy Pumpkin Roll Cake. I've never had a sliver of food remaining after this meal.

"Be sure to keep the cocktail hour to thirty minutes. This meal is too special to have tummies full. You and your husband will have just enough time to present your precious children and give a brief tour of the public areas of your home. Then, voilà! Two simple platters, one of meat and potatoes, the other of asparagus, need to be set on the table while your husband clears the salad plates. (You carved, covered, and placed the meat in the cooling oven during his tour.)

"The dessert should be displayed uncut on the sideboard; the coffee should be brewed during dinner. Don't forget sugar and spoon, cream, and sugar substitute. Serve a favorite pinot and remember to sip! This is your shining moment and you've done well!"

If you're not feeling quite so adventuresome and still need a stunning main course, try the recipes from my cousin-in-law Kelley Ort. Kelley is married to my cousin George, and they both grew up in Albany, Georgia, but they haven't lived there for a long time. They've lived the corporate life—seven homes, all over! They are now in Denver, where George is a partner with a large consulting firm. Kelley left her corporate career to be at home with their teenage sons. Kelley and George found that, moving around so much, entertaining was a great way to get to know people. They like to entertain formally because nobody does it much anymore! "We really enjoy surprising everyone with how we can pull off a fancy dinner. We have been fortunate enough to receive a lot of nice china from both of our mothers, who decided that their formal entertaining days had passed—and can you believe that they had chosen the very same china pattern when they each got married? So, needless to say, we can feed a lot of people on very nice, matching china!"

Kelley and George have served this meal to customers, bosses, friends, etc. Kelley says she always cooks extra because one time, when they had invited customers and expected only the principals, one customer brought his wife! They scrambled at the last minute and, as discreetly as possible, cut the hens in half and served them on this beautiful wild rice. Everyone had plenty. Now, that's a smart southern girl for ya!

Kelley's Menu

Glazed Rock Cornish Game Hens Stuffed with Wild Rice
132

Marinated Asparagus
179

All-Day Mushrooms
185

Good Bakery Rolls

Sautéed Red-Skinned Apples
194

Paula's Birthday Bash

Since my marriage, my family has doubled in size, which means so have the birthdays. And that's all right by me, because I just love throwing birthday parties for my family and close family friends. Because some months have multiple birthdays, I've found that it was easier if I picked one Sunday in each month and celebrated all the birthdays for that month on the same day. Take March, for example. This past March we had five birthdays, which meant five cakes, because one of the rules is "Everybody has his own cake." For this I have to confess I just go to the local grocery store, head straight for the bakery department, and order each guest of honor a personalized birthday cake. Then I bake a homemade pound cake and serve it along with fresh sweetened strawberries, ice cream, and fresh whipped cream. That gives everybody a traditional cake as well as that scrumptious homemade cake. Well, I'm really getting ahead of myself with this story, though, because before anyone can sing, blow out their candles, and eat birthday cake, there are a lot of things that have to happen first!

A few years back, I realized that our childhoods were getting further and further behind us, and that made me sad. So I set out to find a way to step back in time and recapture a small piece of that time when our lives were worry free. I decided one way to do this was through the wonderful, silly games we all played at our childhood birthday parties. Well, needless to say, when I announced that this birthday celebration was going to involve games, the moans and groans commenced. All the adult children said, "But we don't want to play games," and my response was, "If you're physically able, you must play the games, or no cake for you." Well, it took all of about three minutes for the hoots and hollers of laughter to begin. To this day, I cannot tell you who had the most fun—Jamie and Bobby playing pin the tail on the donkey, or Michelle and Anthony running the three-legged race. I also found that the guys love bashing a piñata.

So I'm happy to say, now on Birthday Sundays, when I clap my hands and yell, "Okay, let the games begin," everybody is eager to play. I also found that these games really work up a hearty appetite. So after the games and before the birthday cake we all share a scrumptious meal together. Michael and I always make sure to plan a meal that is easy to prepare for a large crowd. Michael does the outside cooking while I prepare the inside dishes. It's really a toss-up between the most requested meal, but it's almost always a Low-Country Boil (page 146) or a Beer-in-the-Rear Chicken (page 134).

Michael and I would like to share with y'all one of our Birthday Bash menus and hope that your family and friends enjoy it as much as ours do.

Menu

BEER-IN-THE-REAR CHICKEN
134

BACON-WRAPPED GRILLED CORN ON THE COB
184

GREEN BEANS WITH NEW POTATOES
180

LACE HOECAKE CORN BREAD
15

ROASTED CARROTS
185

SOUTHERN BISCUITS
21

BUTTERMILK POUND CAKE WITH STRAWBERRIES
AND WHIPPED CREAM
210

DESSERTS & SWEETS

Cheesecake Cupcakes

These taste just like miniature cheesecakes without the crust. Decorate with fresh seasonal fruit—a sliver of strawberry (if available) or kiwi for Christmas, a dollop of fruit topping or jam, or a fresh raspberry or blueberry in summer. You can eat about a dozen, so be careful!

Three 8-ounce packages cream cheese, softened

1 cup sugar

4 eggs

1½ teaspoons vanilla extract

Topping

1 cup sour cream

¼ cup sugar

1 teaspoon vanilla extract

Kiwi or strawberry slivers, fruit topping or jam, blueberries or raspberries, for garnish

1. Preheat the oven to 325°F. Line 24 regular muffin cups with paper cupcake liners.

2. In a large mixing bowl, beat the cream cheese until very smooth. Add the sugar and mix well. Add the eggs and vanilla and mix well.

3. Fill the cups about half full with the batter. Bake for about 25 minutes, until the cupcakes are set and golden brown.

4. Make the topping: Combine the sour cream, sugar, and vanilla and stir well with a metal spoon or spatula. Spoon about a teaspoon on top of each cupcake and return to the oven for 5 minutes to glaze.

5. Remove the cupcakes from the oven. When they can be handled safely, remove them from the muffin tins and let cool completely on wire racks. When completely cool, place them in plastic containers with lids and refrigerate until ready to serve. Just before serving, decorate with slivers of freshly cut seasonal fruit, or jam or fruit topping, or 1 or 2 whole blueberries or raspberries. Serve at room temperature.

Makes 2 dozen

Peanut Butter Brownie Cupcakes

Make these any time you're asked to "bring brownies." They are so pretty, and people love it when they hit the peanut butter.

One 18½-ounce package Duncan Hines Chewy Fudge Brownie mix

One 12-ounce package peanut butter chips or 24 miniature peanut butter cups

1. Preheat the oven to 350°F. Line 24 regular muffin cups with paper cupcake liners.

2. Prepare the brownie mix according to package directions for cakelike brownies. Fill the cups half full with brownie batter. Place about 1 tablespoon peanut butter chips in the center of the batter, or press 1 peanut butter cup into the batter in each muffin cup until the batter meets the top edge of the peanut butter cup. Bake for 18 to 20 minutes, until the cupcakes are set. When they can be handled safely, remove them from the muffin tins and let cool completely on wire racks. Store in an airtight container.

Makes 2 dozen

Individual Birthday Cakes

This recipe calls for 6-inch cake pans; you can find them at a kitchen or baking supply store, or order them from www.wilton.com.

Frosting

One 3-ounce package cream cheese, softened

½ **cup (1 stick) butter, softened**

One 1-pound box confectioners' sugar (about 3¾ cups)

⅓ **cup milk**

Cake

2 **eggs**

1 **teaspoon vanilla extract**

1¼ **cups all-purpose flour**

½ **teaspoon baking powder**

¼ **teaspoon salt**

⅓ **cup milk**

Sprinkles or small candies, for garnish

1. Preheat the oven to 350°F. Grease and flour three 6-inch round cake pans.

2. To make the frosting: In a large mixing bowl, beat the cream cheese and butter with an electric mixer until smooth. Add the confectioners' sugar slowly, and beat at low speed until smooth. Add the milk and blend until smooth and creamy. Reserve 1½ cups of frosting and set aside.

3. To make the cake: With the mixer at low speed, add the eggs to the remaining frosting mixture in the bowl. Add the vanilla and beat until blended. Sift together the flour, baking powder, and salt. Add the flour mixture to the cake batter alternately with the milk, beating after each addition until well blended. Pour the batter into the prepared pans. Bake for 25 minutes, or until a toothpick inserted into the center comes out clean. Let cool for 5 minutes, then remove from the pans and allow to cool completely on wire racks.

4. While 3 cakes are baking, make a second batch of frosting and batter. Make 3 more cakes.

5. The next morning, place each cake on a piece of waxed paper. Give each guest about 2 tablespoons of frosting and a popsicle stick. Allow each girl to ice her own cake and decorate it with sprinkles or candies.

One recipe makes 3 cakes

Coconut Pound Cake with 7-Minute Frosting

I always make a coconut cake for Christmas, always frosted with this fluffy frosting or with whipped cream and coconut, and decorated with holly sprigs.

2 cups (4 sticks) butter, at room temperature

2 cups sugar

2 cups all-purpose flour

6 eggs

One 7-ounce package sweetened flaked coconut (2⅔ cups)

1 teaspoon vanilla extract

Glaze

1 cup sugar

1 teaspoon coconut extract

7-Minute Frosting (opposite)

1. Preheat the oven to 350°F. Generously grease and flour a 10-inch springform tube pan.

2. Cream the butter and sugar with an electric mixer. Add 1 cup of the flour and mix well. Add the eggs, one at a time, and mix. Add the coconut with the remaining 1 cup flour and mix well. Add the vanilla and blend.

3. Pour the batter into the prepared pan. Bang the pan on the counter a couple of times to get rid of any air bubbles. Bake the cake for 1 hour and 15 minutes.

4. Remove the cake from the oven and set aside to cool for about 10 minutes. Meanwhile, make the glaze: In a small saucepan, simmer the sugar with ½ cup water until the sugar has dissolved, about 10 minutes. Stir in the coconut extract.

5. Run a knife around the outside edge of the cake. Remove the outer rim from the tube pan. While the cake is still hot, prick the top with the tines of a fork, and spoon the glaze over the top. Cool the cake on a wire rack.

6. Run the knife around the inner tube of the pan and under the bottom of the cake to loosen it. Take a plate and invert the cake onto it. Remove the bottom of the pan, then turn the cake back over so that the glazed part is on top. When completely cool, you can ice with 7-Minute Frosting. Store in an airtight container and serve at room temperature. Refrigerate leftovers.

Makes 12 to 16 servings

7-Minute Frosting

2 egg whites

2 teaspoons light corn syrup

Dash of salt

1 teaspoon vanilla extract

⅓ cup toasted coconut, for garnish

Place the egg whites, corn syrup, salt, and ½ cup cold water into the top of a double boiler. With an electric mixer, whip the ingredients for 1 minute. Cook over gently boiling water, beating with the electric mixer, until the frosting forms stiff peaks, about 7 minutes. Remove the top of the double boiler and add the vanilla to the frosting. Continue beating the frosting for 2 minutes more, until the frosting reaches spreading consistency. Frost the top and sides of the cooled coconut cake, then sprinkle with the toasted coconut.

Buttermilk Pound Cake with Strawberries and Whipped Cream

Buttermilk gives this cake its delicious tang.

3 cups all-purpose flour

½ teaspoon baking soda

½ teaspoon baking powder

½ teaspoon salt

1 cup (2 sticks) butter, softened

½ cup vegetable shortening

3 cups sugar

5 eggs

1 cup buttermilk

1 tablespoon vanilla extract

1. Preheat the oven to 325°F. Grease and flour a 10-inch Bundt pan.

2. Sift together the flour, baking soda, baking powder, and salt and set aside.

3. Using an electric mixer, cream the butter, shortening, and sugar until fluffy. Add the eggs one at a time and mix well after each addition. Add the dry ingredients and the buttermilk alternately to the butter mixture, beginning and ending with the flour. Add the vanilla and mix well.

4. Pour the batter into the prepared pan. Bake for 1¾ hours, or until the cake is done. (The cake will pull away from the sides of the pan when ready, and a toothpick inserted into the center of the cake will come out clean.) Remove the cake from the oven and let cool in the pan for 10 minutes. Invert onto a cake plate and serve each big slice of cake topped with strawberries and whipped cream.

Serves 8

Fresh Strawberries

½ cup sugar

2 pints strawberries, hulled and sliced

Dissolve the sugar in ⅓ cup warm water, add to the strawberries, and toss. Let stand, tossing a few times before serving. They will make their own juice in about 30 minutes.

Makes 3½ cups

Fresh Whipped Cream

1 cup whipping cream

¼ cup sugar

Using an electric mixer, beat together the cream and sugar until stiff.

Makes approximately 2 cups, enough for a dollop on 8 slices of strawberry-topped cake

White Cake with Strawberry Icing

This simple cake has become a family favorite. It looks, tastes, and smells like spring!

One 18.25-ounce package white cake mix

½ cup (1 stick) butter, softened

3 large eggs

Icing

4 tablespoons (½ stick) unsalted butter, softened

4 cups sifted confectioners' sugar, about 1 pound

6 ripe strawberries, hulled and mashed

6 whole strawberries, for garnish

1. Preheat the oven to 375°F. Grease and flour a 13-by-9-inch baking pan.

2. Blend the cake mix, ⅔ cup water, the butter, and the eggs in a large bowl with an electric mixer until well blended, about 3 minutes.

3. Pour the batter into the pan and bake for 28 to 30 minutes, until the center of the cake springs back when pressed. Cool in the pan on a wire rack for about 15 minutes.

4. Make the icing: Place the butter and 2 cups of the sugar in the bowl of an electric mixer. Beat at low speed until blended. Add the mashed strawberries and mix at medium speed until well combined. Add the remaining 2 cups sugar and beat until creamy and smooth. The icing should be thick enough to stand up on a spoon. If too thin, add more confectioners' sugar. If too thick, add a teaspoon or two of milk.

5. Frost the cooled cake in the pan. For decorative effect, make swirls in the frosting with a clean spatula. Garnish with the whole strawberries. Cut into 12 to 16 pieces, and store, covered, in the refrigerator for up to 5 days.

Serves 12 to 16

Flag Cake

The icing will hide any flaws in your layering.

One 6-ounce package cherry-flavored gelatin

One 1-pound loaf pound cake, any brand

Two 8-ounce packages cream cheese, softened

½ cup confectioners' sugar

2 cups whipping cream, whipped

1 pint fresh strawberries

1 pint fresh blueberries

1. Boil 1½ cups water. In a glass dish, stir the water into the gelatin, stirring about 2 minutes, until all of the gelatin is thoroughly dissolved. Add 2 cups cold water and stir. Refrigerate this mixture for about 15 minutes, until it has begun to thicken but is still loose enough to spread.

2. Spray a 13-by-9-inch baking pan with vegetable oil cooking spray. Cut the pound cake into thin slices and lay them evenly over the bottom of the pan. Spread the partially gelled gelatin evenly over the cake. Refrigerate for several hours, until the gelatin has set and formed a firm layer over the cake.

3. Beat together the cream cheese and sugar until very fluffy. Fold in the whipped cream. Spread this evenly over the gelatin layer. Refrigerate until ready to serve.

4. Not more than 30 minutes before serving, slice the strawberries in half. Decorate the top of the cake in a flag pattern, using the strawberries for the "bars" and the blueberries for the "stars."

Serves 20

Hummingbird Cake

I like having a showstopping cake on the buffet table for special events. This old favorite is so easy—you just dump all of the ingredients into a bowl and stir!

3 cups self-rising flour

2 cups granulated sugar

¾ cup vegetable oil

½ cup finely chopped pecans

2 very ripe large bananas, mashed

One 8-ounce can crushed pineapple, with juice

1 teaspoon vanilla extract

1 teaspoon ground cinnamon

4 large eggs, beaten

Icing

One 1-pound box confectioners' sugar

One 8-ounce package cream cheese, at room temperature

6 tablespoons (¾ stick) butter, softened

1 teaspoon vanilla extract

1 tablespoon milk, or more, if needed

½ cup finely chopped pecans

1. Preheat the oven to 325°F.

2. Grease and flour three 8-inch round cake pans. In a large mixing bowl, combine the flour, sugar, oil, pecans, bananas, pineapple, vanilla, cinnamon, and eggs. Stir well with a spoon until the batter is smooth.

3. Pour the batter into the prepared pans. Bake for 26 to 28 minutes, until the tops spring back. Cool in the pans for about 10 minutes, then loosen from the pans and invert onto wire racks to cool completely.

4. To make the icing, mix the sugar, cream cheese, butter, vanilla, and 1 tablespoon milk in a large mixing bowl with an electric mixer until the icing is smooth. If needed, add more milk, 1 teaspoon at a time, to achieve the proper spreading consistency. Ice between the cake layers, and on the sides and top of the cake. Sprinkle the top with the pecans. Refrigerate until ready to serve.

Serves 12

Carrot Cake

What could be more appropriate at Easter than carrot cake for all those somebunnies you love! This dense, sweet cake is delicious, and the icing is downright addictive.

2 cups granulated sugar

1½ cups vegetable oil

4 eggs

2 cups all-purpose flour

2 teaspoons ground cinnamon

2 teaspoons baking powder

2 teaspoons baking soda

1 teaspoon salt

2 cups shredded carrots, about 4 medium carrots

¼ cup chopped walnuts

Icing

½ cup (1 stick) butter, softened

3 cups confectioners' sugar

One 8-ounce package cream cheese, softened

¼ cup chopped walnuts

1. Preheat the oven to 350°F. Spray a 13-by-9-inch baking pan with vegetable oil cooking spray and dust with flour.

2. In the bowl of an electric mixer, combine the sugar, oil, and eggs. Mix at medium speed until smooth.

3. Sift together the flour, cinnamon, baking powder, baking soda, and salt. Add the flour mixture to the egg mixture and combine at low speed until smooth. With a spoon, stir in the carrots and walnuts.

4. Place the batter in the prepared pan and place on the middle rack in the oven. Bake for 50 minutes, or until a toothpick inserted in the cake comes out clean and the top of the cake springs back when touched. When the cake is done, remove from the oven and allow to cool on the countertop for 15 minutes before icing.

5. To make the icing: Beat the butter, sugar, and cream cheese in a medium bowl until smooth. Stir in the walnuts. Ice the cake when it is warm, not hot; this improves the icing's spreadability. The icing will firm up in the refrigerator. Keep the cake cold until ready to serve.

Serves 12 to 16, depending on the size of the pieces (It's very rich!)

Mardi Gras King Cake

Is this a bread or a cake? You decide! This is the traditional cake eaten at Mardi Gras parties in New Orleans. Typically, a tiny plastic pink baby or an uncooked red bean is baked in the dough; whoever gets the piece with the baby or bean has to make the next cake. I do warn you, however, that the last time I made this, I cooked it with a red bean, which was swallowed by the little girl who happened to get that piece of cake! (She was fine.) The sprinkles are the traditional colors of Mardi Gras: purple, gold, and green, representing justice, power, and faith.

½ cup (1 stick) butter, softened

⅔ cup evaporated milk

¾ cup plus 1 teaspoon granulated sugar

1 teaspoon salt

2 envelopes active dry yeast, regular or rapid rise

3 eggs

Grated zest of 1 lemon

6 cups all-purpose flour

4 tablespoons (½ stick) butter, melted

1 egg white, for glazing

Cinnamon-Sugar Filling

½ cup granulated sugar

1 teaspoon ground cinnamon

White Icing

2 cups confectioners' sugar

2 tablespoons whole milk

Colored Sugar

¾ cup granulated sugar

Yellow, green, red, and blue food coloring

1. Melt the butter in the microwave in a medium mixing bowl. Add the evaporated milk, ¾ cup of the sugar, and the salt. Stir so that the sugar dissolves. Allow to cool.

2. Dissolve the yeast in ¼ cup lukewarm water and stir in the remaining teaspoon sugar. Allow to stand for 10 minutes, until foamy. If the yeast does not foam up, it is no good, so you'll have to start over with new yeast and sugar.

3. Add the yeast mixture to the butter and milk mixture. Add the eggs and lemon zest and whisk together vigorously, until well blended.

4. Whisk in the flour, 1 cup at a time, until you have a thick paste—about 3 cups flour. Then switch to a wooden spoon and continue adding flour and mixing well. Do not add more than 6 cups flour, or your cake will be too dense. When you have added all the flour, turn the dough out onto a lightly floured wooden board and knead it with your hands, which you have dusted with flour, until the dough is smooth and elastic, about a dozen turns.

5. Place the dough into a large clean bowl that you have sprayed with vegetable oil cooking spray. Turn the dough to coat all sides with spray. Cover the bowl with a tea towel and allow the dough to rise in a warm place until doubled, about 1 hour.

6. Make the cinnamon-sugar filling: Combine the sugar and cinnamon in a small dish and stir well.

7. Punch the dough down and divide the dough in two. Roll out each half into a 10-by-15-inch rectangle. Brush each rectangle with half of the melted butter and then sprinkle each rectangle with half of the cinnamon-sugar filling mixture. Roll up along the long end like a jelly roll. Press the roll together at the seam, sealing with water if necessary. Wind the two rolls together, forming one thick piece. On a baking sheet sprayed with vegetable oil cooking spray, form the dough into a circle and seal the ends together.

8. Cover with a tea towel and allow the cake to rise in a warm place for about 1 hour (when it rises, the center will close up and it will look like a bumpy "cake"), until it almost doubles in size.

9. Preheat the oven to 350°F. Whisk the egg white with 1 tablespoon water. Brush the top of the cake with the egg white. Bake the cake for 35 minutes, until it is browned and sounds hollow when tapped.

10. Make the white icing: Combine the sugar and milk in a small dish and whisk until smooth. If the mixture seems too thin, add a little more sugar. If it won't drizzle, add a little more milk, ½ teaspoon at a time.

11. Make the colored sugar: Place ¼ cup sugar in each of three custard cups. Put 1 drop of yellow food coloring into one, then, using your fingers, grind the color into the sugar until all of the granules are colored. Do the same using green food coloring, and in the third cup, blend 1 drop of red coloring and 1 drop of blue coloring to make purple.

12. Allow the cake to cool for a few minutes on a wire rack. Drizzle with icing and sprinkle the colored sugar in random patterns over the white icing. Slice across the width of the cake into thin slices to serve.

Makes about 24 thin slices

Pumpkin Cheesecake

This is very rich and dense—a little sliver is all you need.

1¾ cups graham cracker crumbs

2 tablespoons light brown sugar

1 teaspoon ground cinnamon

½ cup (1 stick) butter, melted

Three 8-ounce packages cream cheese, at room temperature

1½ cups granulated sugar

2 tablespoons all-purpose flour

1 teaspoon vanilla extract

⅛ teaspoon freshly grated nutmeg

⅛ teaspoon ground cloves

3 large eggs

1 large egg yolk

One 15-ounce can pumpkin

¼ cup sour cream

Whipped cream, for garnish

Toasted pecan halves, for garnish

1. Preheat the oven to 350°F. Spray a 9-inch springform pan with vegetable oil cooking spray.

2. Combine the graham cracker crumbs, brown sugar, and ½ teaspoon of the cinnamon in a medium bowl. Pour the melted butter over the mixture and stir until all of the crumbs are moistened. Press this mixture on the bottom and about 1½ inches up the sides of the pan.

3. Beat the cream cheese with an electric mixer until it is very smooth. Add the remaining ½ teaspoon cinnamon, the granulated sugar, flour, vanilla, nutmeg, cloves, eggs, egg yolk, pumpkin, and sour cream and beat at low speed until the mixture is very smooth.

4. Spread the batter in the pan and place the pan on a baking sheet for easier handling. Place the baking sheet in the center of the oven and bake the cheesecake until the center is set, about 1 hour. Cool on a wire rack for 15 minutes.

5. To loosen the cheesecake from the springform pan, run a butter knife along the inside of the pan. Remove the outer ring and allow the cake to cool completely on a wire rack. Cover tightly and refrigerate for at least 4 hours before serving.

6. Bring to room temperature before serving with whipped cream and toasted pecan halves.

Makes 12 to 14 servings

Fresh Apple Cake

This gets better the longer it sits, so I suggest making it at least a day in advance.

2 cups plus 3 tablespoons sugar

3 teaspoons ground cinnamon

1½ cups vegetable oil

3 large eggs

3 cups chopped Granny Smith apples, peeled (about 3 medium apples)

2 teaspoons vanilla extract

¼ teaspoon freshly grated nutmeg

3 cups all-purpose flour

1 teaspoon baking soda

½ teaspoon salt

1 cup chopped pecans

½ cup raisins or coconut, your choice (or both!)

1. Preheat the oven to 325°F. Generously grease a 10-inch tube pan. Combine 3 tablespoons of the sugar and 1 teaspoon of the cinnamon and coat the inside of the pan with the mixture by shaking the pan all around until the sides and bottom are coated.

2. Beat the oil and the remaining 2 cups sugar with an electric mixer until well blended. Add the eggs, one at a time, beating well after each addition. With a spatula, stir in the apples and vanilla. Sift together the remaining 2 teaspoons cinnamon, the nutmeg, flour, baking soda, and salt. Add the flour mixture to the apple mixture and mix well with a spatula. Add the pecans and raisins or coconut. The batter will be very thick.

3. Spoon the batter into the prepared pan and smooth the top. Lift the pan from the counter about 2 inches and drop it back down to get out all of the air bubbles.

4. Bake the cake for 1½ to 1¾ hours, until a tester inserted in the center comes out clean. Allow to rest on the countertop for at least 30 minutes before turning out onto a cake plate to cool completely.

Serves 12

Cream Cheese Pound Cake

This recipe makes a heavy, dense, beautiful pound cake. It freezes well, should there be any left for freezing!

1½ cups (3 sticks) butter, softened

One 8-ounce package cream cheese, softened

3 cups sugar

6 large eggs

3 cups cake flour, sifted twice

Pinch of salt

1 teaspoon vanilla extract

1 teaspoon almond extract

1. Preheat the oven to 325°F. Grease and flour a 10-inch Bundt pan.

2. Cream the butter and cream cheese with an electric mixer until well combined. Add the sugar. Mix for 7 minutes, until fluffy. Add the eggs, one at a time, beating after each until blended. Gradually add the flour, beating after each addition, until all is added and combined. Add the salt, vanilla, and almond extract. Mix again.

3. Pour into the prepared pan. Hit the pan gently on the counter about five times to help settle the batter and remove any air pockets. Bake for about 1½ hours. The cake is done when it pulls away from the sides of the pan and a toothpick inserted comes out clean.

4. Remove from the oven and let cool in the pan for about 15 minutes. Invert the cake onto a wire rack and let cool completely before putting it on a cake plate or wrapping in aluminum foil for delivery.

Serves 12

Double Rum Cake

Let's just say that no matter what meal you serve this after, it will end on a decidedly good note when you present this rum cake. The aroma of rum and the delectable color of the cake are a winning combination! The recipe comes from Jeanie Simmons, a Savannah preschool teacher who has contributed this cake to many a meeting.

One 18½-ounce package yellow cake mix

One 3½-ounce package instant vanilla pudding mix

½ cup rum, light or dark

½ cup vegetable oil

4 large eggs

½ cup chopped pecans

Rum Syrup

1 cup sugar

½ cup (1 stick) margarine

¼ cup rum, light or dark

1. Preheat the oven to 325°F. Liberally spray a nonstick 2-quart Bundt pan with vegetable oil cooking spray.

2. Using an electric mixer at low speed, blend the cake mix, pudding mix, rum, oil, and ½ cup water. Add the eggs, one at a time, beating well after each addition.

3. Evenly distribute the pecans in the bottom of the prepared Bundt pan. Pour the batter on top of the pecans. Bake for 50 to 55 minutes, until a knife inserted an inch from the center comes out clean; do not remove the cake from the pan.

4. Make the rum syrup: In a small saucepan, bring the sugar, margarine, rum, and ¼ cup water to a boil and cook for 3 minutes. With a fork, make holes in the top of the cake. Pour the syrup over the cake and let sit for 30 minutes while the syrup is absorbed.

5. Invert the pan onto a serving plate. Allow it to sit for several minutes; the cake will loosen from the pan.

Serves 12 to 16

Pumpkin Roll Cake

The English toffee pieces can be found in the supermarket next to the chocolate chips. They're a seasonal item in some markets.

Cake

- ¾ cup cake flour
- 1½ teaspoons ground cinnamon
- 1¼ teaspoons ground ginger
- ¾ teaspoon ground allspice
- 6 large eggs, separated
- ⅓ cup granulated sugar
- ⅓ cup packed light brown sugar
- ⅔ cup canned pumpkin
- ⅛ teaspoon salt

  Confectioners' sugar

Filling

- 1 teaspoon unflavored gelatin
- 2 tablespoons dark rum
- 1 cup whipping cream
- 3 tablespoons confectioners' sugar
- 10 tablespoons plus ½ cup English toffee pieces

  Confectioners' sugar
- 1½ cups purchased caramel sauce, warmed

1. To make the cake: Preheat the oven to 375°F. Line a 15-by-10-by-1-inch baking sheet with parchment paper, then spray with vegetable oil cooking spray.

2. Sift the flour, cinnamon, ginger, and allspice into a small bowl. Beat the egg yolks, granulated sugar, and brown sugar with an electric mixer until very thick. Add the pumpkin and combine at low speed until incorporated. Add the dry ingredients and beat at low speed until mixed. In a separate bowl, beat the egg whites and salt until stiff but not dry. Fold into the cake batter with a spatula until most of the white streaks are gone.

3. Spread the batter onto the prepared baking sheet and smooth out the top. Bake until a cake tester comes clean, about 15 to 18 minutes. While hot, dust the cake generously with confectioners' sugar. Loosen the edges and turn the cake out onto a kitchen towel. Fold the towel over the long edge of the cake and roll up lengthwise like a jelly roll. Let cool completely, seam down, for 1 hour in the refrigerator.

4. To make the filling: In a small saucepan, soften the gelatin in the rum. Stir over low heat until the gelatin dissolves. Let cool. Beat the cream and confectioners' sugar in a large bowl until peaks form. Fold in the gelatin and 6 tablespoons of the toffee pieces.

5. To assemble: Unroll the cake. Spread the filling over the cake, then sprinkle with 4 tablespoons of the toffee pieces. Starting at one long side and using the towel as an aid, roll up the cake. Place the cake, seam down, on a platter. The cake can be prepared 1 day in advance. Cover with aluminum foil and refrigerate.

6. To serve, trim the ends of the cake on a slight diagonal. Dust the cake with confectioners' sugar. Spoon some warm caramel sauce over the top, then sprinkle with ½ cup toffee pieces. Cut the cake crosswise into 1½-inch slices, using a serrated knife. Pass more warm sauce—and enjoy the compliments!

Serves 8 or 9

Chocolate Chip Pie

1 cup sugar

½ cup self-rising flour

½ cup (1 stick) butter, melted and cooled

2 eggs, lightly beaten

1 cup pecan pieces

1½ cups (9 ounces) semisweet chocolate chips

One 9-inch refrigerated piecrust, fitted into a 9-inch glass pie plate

1. Preheat the oven to 325°F.

2. Place the sugar, flour, butter, eggs, pecans, and chocolate chips in a medium bowl. Stir with a spatula until thoroughly combined. Pour into the piecrust. Bake for 50 to 60 minutes, until the filling is puffed and set. Let cool, then chill in the refrigerator. Allow to come to room temperature before serving. Cut into slivers to serve.

Serves 10

Green Grits Pie

There are a few recipes that have become a part of who I am and this is one of them. I can't tell you how many times I've served this pie. It's always a surprise to the people who are lucky enough to have a piece—they just can't believe the filling is made with our good ol' southern grits! The grits give this a taste very similar to chess pie, which is made with cornmeal.

⅛ teaspoon salt

¼ cup quick-cooking grits (not instant)

½ cup (1 stick) butter

Green food coloring

¾ cup sugar

2 tablespoons all-purpose flour

3 large eggs, lightly beaten

¼ cup buttermilk

1 teaspoon vanilla extract

One 9-inch frozen piecrust, thawed, or 1 refrigerated piecrust, unbaked, fitted into a 9-inch glass pie plate

1 cup whipping cream, whipped and sweetened with 1 tablespoon confectioners' sugar and colored with 1 drop of green food coloring

Strawberries, for garnish

1. Preheat the oven to 325°F.

2. In a small saucepan, bring ¾ cup water and the salt to a boil. Add the grits, reduce the heat, cover, and cook over low heat for 5 minutes, stirring several times, until the grits are very thick. Add the butter and 1 drop of food coloring and stir until the butter melts. Set the grits aside and allow them to cool slightly.

3. In a small bowl, stir together the sugar, flour, eggs, buttermilk, and vanilla. Stir well into the cooled grits. Pour the mixture into the piecrust. Bake for 35 to 40 minutes, until set.

4. Serve warm or cold with whipped cream, and garnish with strawberries.

Serves 8

Black Bottom Pie

This is an old southern favorite. It's a bit time-consuming, but after all, comfort food is a labor of love. It's from Patty Ronning's files.

Crust

5 tablespoons margarine or butter

30 gingersnaps, finely crushed

Filling

2 cups milk, scalded

4 eggs, separated, yolks beaten lightly

1 cup granulated sugar

1¼ tablespoons cornstarch

1½ ounces (1½ squares) unsweetened chocolate, coarsely chopped

1 teaspoon vanilla extract

1 envelope unflavored gelatin

¼ teaspoon cream of tartar

2 tablespoons rum, light or dark

1 cup whipping cream

2 tablespoons confectioners' sugar

½ ounce (½ square) unsweetened chocolate

1. To make the crust: Preheat the oven to 300°F. Combine the margarine or butter and cookie crumbs with a metal spoon. When well blended, pat evenly into a 9-inch pie plate. (Use a disposable aluminum foil pie pan or an inexpensive glass one that you can give as a gift.) Bake the crust for 15 minutes. Let cool completely.

2. To make the filling: Combine the milk, egg yolks, ½ cup of the sugar, and the cornstarch. Stirring constantly with a wooden spoon, cook in a double boiler for about 12 minutes, or until thickened to about the consistency of mayonnaise. Remove from the heat. Place 1 cup of the custard in a small bowl, add the chocolate, and stir until the chocolate melts and is combined. Add the vanilla. Pour into the pie crust and allow to cool completely before adding the next layer.

3. Soak the gelatin in ¼ cup cold water for 5 minutes. Add to the remaining hot custard and stir for about 2 minutes to make sure that the gelatin is completely dissolved and mixed into the custard. Beat the egg whites with the remaining ½ cup sugar and the cream of tartar until stiff. Gently fold into the custard. Add the rum.

4. As soon as the chocolate custard layer is cool, add the second custard layer. Chill the pie until both layers are set.

5. Whip the cream with the confectioners' sugar. Spread over the top of the chilled pie. Shave chocolate on top of the whipped cream. Refrigerate until ready to serve or take to a friend.

Serves 8

Angel Chocolate Mousse Pie

This is so rich, you can only manage a sliver! Make sure your bowl and beaters are absolutely clean and grease free, or your egg whites won't beat up nice and fluffy. The meringue does get soggy if it isn't eaten the first day after preparation, but the pie is still delicious.

½ cup chopped pecans

3 egg whites, at room temperature

1 teaspoon cream of tartar

½ cup sugar

Filling

One 12-ounce package semisweet chocolate chips

¼ teaspoon vanilla extract

2 cups whipping cream, whipped

Additional whipped cream for topping (optional)

1. Preheat the oven to 300°F. Grease, or spray with vegetable oil cooking spray, a 9-inch glass pie plate.

2. Place the pecans on an ungreased baking sheet and toast in the oven for 3 to 5 minutes. Check them after 3 minutes; you don't want them to burn! Remove the pecans to cool and reduce the oven temperature to 275°F. Grind 1 tablespoon of the nuts in a food processor and set aside.

3. Place the egg whites in a mixing bowl. Begin beating the egg whites with an electric mixer at low speed. When frothy, add the cream of tartar and gradually add the sugar, beating all the while, until the egg whites are stiff. When you lift the beaters, no egg white should fall from them. Gently stir in the chopped pecans.

4. Spread the meringue in the bottom of the prepared pie plate and bake for 1 hour. When you remove the meringue from the oven, it will be puffed up, but it will deflate as it cools, leaving a crater in the center for the pie filling.

5. To make the filling: Place the chocolate chips and 6 tablespoons water in a bowl and microwave for 2 minutes, until the chocolate is almost melted. Stir well, making sure that all the chips are completely melted (they will continue to melt as you stir). Let cool, then add the vanilla and fold in the whipped cream. Put the filling into the cooled meringue shell. Sprinkle the reserved ground nuts over the top of the pie filling.

6. Refrigerate the pie for a few hours before serving. Serve with an additional dollop of whipped cream, if desired.

Serves 6 to 8

Double-Chocolate Cream Pie

This is just a good ol' chocolate pie. Have whipped cream and toasted pecans ready to dress it up when it's served.

1 cup sugar

¼ cup cocoa

¼ cup cornstarch

   Pinch of salt

3 cups whole milk

3 egg yolks

1½ teaspoons vanilla extract

1 cup semisweet chocolate chips

   One 9-inch deep-dish piecrust, baked and cooled

   Sweetened whipped cream

   Chopped toasted pecans

In a heavy-bottomed 1-quart saucepan, combine the sugar, cocoa, cornstarch, and salt. Stir with a spoon to mix. Combine the milk and egg yolks and whisk until well blended. Slowly begin adding the milk and egg mixture to the chocolate mixture, blending well with a metal spoon. Cook the mixture over medium heat until it thickens, stirring constantly, about 5 minutes. When it is quite thick, add the vanilla and chocolate chips. Stir until completely blended. Pour into the piecrust. Allow to cool, then cover and refrigerate until ready to serve. Serve with plenty of whipped cream and chopped toasted pecans.

Serves 8

Fresh Fruit Tart

This is just about the most beautiful dessert you'll ever make. Martha often takes it to new neighbors when they move in. If you're feeling really generous, you can include the recipe and offer the tart pan as a gift.

A food processor makes short work of the crust, but you can also make it in a bowl with a spoon.

Crust

- ½ cup confectioners' sugar
- 1½ cups all-purpose flour
- ¾ cup (1½ sticks) butter, softened

Filling

- One 8-ounce package cream cheese, softened
- ½ cup granulated sugar
- 1 teaspoon vanilla extract

Topping

- Strawberries, kiwi slices, blueberries, raspberries

Glaze

- One 6-ounce can frozen limeade concentrate, thawed
- 1 tablespoon cornstarch
- 1 tablespoon fresh lime juice
- ¼ cup granulated sugar

- Whipped cream, for garnish

1. Preheat the oven to 350°F.

2. To make the crust: In a food processor, combine the confectioners' sugar, flour, and butter, and process until the mixture forms a ball. With your fingers, press the dough into a 12-inch tart pan with a removable bottom, taking care to push the crust into the indentations in the sides. Pat until the crust is even. Bake for 10 to 12 minutes, until very lightly browned. Set aside to cool.

3. To make the filling: Beat the cream cheese, sugar, and vanilla together until smooth. Spread over the cooled crust.

4. Cut the strawberries into ¼-inch slices and arrange around the edge of the crust. For the next circle, use kiwi slices. Add another circle of strawberries, and fill in any spaces with blueberries. Cluster the raspberries in the center of the tart.

5. To make the glaze: Combine the limeade, cornstarch, lime juice, and sugar in a small saucepan and cook over medium heat until clear and thick, about 2 minutes. Let cool. With a pastry brush, glaze the entire tart. You will not use all of the glaze.

6. Keep the tart in the refrigerator. Remove about 15 minutes before serving. Slice into 8 wedges and serve with a dollop of whipped cream.

Serves 8

Peach Cream Tart

This is so pretty and good. Make it a couple of hours before the party and leave it at room temperature. The crust is like a shortbread cookie: you don't have to roll it out, and it doesn't get soggy.

Crust

- 1¼ cups all-purpose flour
- ½ cup (1 stick) butter, softened
- 2 tablespoons sour cream

Filling

- About 6 medium peaches, peeled and sliced, or one 28-ounce can and one 16-ounce can sliced peaches in light syrup, well drained
- 3 large egg yolks
- ¾ cup sour cream
- ¾ cup sugar
- ¼ cup all-purpose flour

Glaze

- ½ cup peach preserves or jelly
- 1 tablespoon frozen lemonade concentrate

1. Preheat the oven to 375°F.

2. To make the crust: Place the flour, butter, and sour cream in a food processor and pulse to combine. When the dough has formed a ball, pat with lightly floured hands into the bottom and sides of an ungreased 10-inch tart pan with a removable bottom and ½-inch sides, or a round au gratin dish. Bake for about 15 minutes, until the crust is set but not browned. Let cool while preparing the filling. Lower the oven temperature to 350°F.

3. To make the filling: If using fresh peaches, peel and thickly slice the peaches. Arrange the fresh or canned peach slices in overlapping circles on top of the crust, until it's completely covered. Overfill the crust, as peaches will draw up during cooking.

4. Combine the egg yolks, sour cream, sugar, and flour and beat until smooth. Pour the mixture over the peaches. Place the tart pan on a baking sheet and bake for about 1 hour, until the custard sets and is pale golden in color. Cover with an aluminum foil tent if the crust gets too dark. Transfer the tart pan to a wire rack to cool. When cool, remove the side wall of the pan.

5. To make the glaze: Combine the preserves or jelly and lemonade. Spread with a pastry brush over the top of the warm tart. Serve the tart warm, at room temperature, or chilled.

Serves 6

Dutch-Oven Peach Cobbler

Campers from other sites come drifting over to see what's cooking when they smell this cinnamony peach cobbler. Sometimes, Robert English adds fresh blueberries. Be sure to share! It's the southern thing to do!

Two 16-ounce cans sliced peaches in heavy or light syrup, or in fruit juice, your choice

1 pint fresh blueberries (optional)

½ cup Bisquick baking mix

⅓ cup sugar

Ground cinnamon

Topping

2¼ cups Bisquick baking mix

¼ cup sugar

¼ cup (½ stick) butter, melted

½ cup milk

Cinnamon sugar (¼ cup sugar combined with 2 teaspoons ground cinnamon; store in an empty spice shaker jar; shake well before each use)

1. Spray a Dutch oven with vegetable oil cooking spray.

2. Drain 1 can of the peaches. Combine both cans of peaches, including the juice from the undrained can; the blueberries, if using; Bisquick; sugar; and a sprinkling of cinnamon. Place this mixture into the Dutch oven.

3. To make the topping: Combine the Bisquick, sugar, butter, and milk in a resealable plastic bag. Drop bits of dough, using your fingers, on top of the peaches. Sprinkle with cinnamon sugar.

4. Place the Dutch oven over about 12 coals, cover with the lid, and place about 12 coals on top. Check in about 10 minutes; if the dough is brown, there are too many coals on top. If it is not brown at all, add a few coals. The cobbler usually cooks in 30 minutes.

Serves about 10 hungry campers

Note: To prepare in the oven, preheat the oven to 350°F. Prepare following steps 2 and 3. Bake, covered, for 30 minutes. Remove the lid and bake for 10 to 15 minutes, until topping is golden.

Apple Strudel

Chef Walter Dasher and his wife, Alice, are known for their fabulous desserts. This is one of them.

¼ cup bourbon or apple juice

½ cup golden raisins

2 to 3 Granny Smith apples (about 1 pound), peeled, cored, halved, and thinly sliced

Juice of ½ lemon

1 tablespoon lemon zest, finely chopped

1 teaspoon ground cinnamon, plus more for sprinkling

½ cup packed light brown sugar

¼ cup crushed shortbread cookies

¼ cup chopped pecans

2 tablespoons butter, cut into pieces

6 sheets phyllo dough from a 1-pound package of frozen dough

2 tablespoons butter, melted, for brushing phyllo sheets; more if needed

1 tablespoon granulated sugar

Confectioners' sugar

Purchased caramel sauce

1. Preheat the oven to 350°F. Line a baking sheet with parchment paper.

2. Pour the bourbon or apple juice over the raisins in a small bowl and microwave on high for 25 seconds to plump the raisins. Let sit for 15 minutes.

3. Combine the raisins, apples, lemon juice, lemon zest, cinnamon, brown sugar, cookie crumbs, pecans, and butter in a large bowl.

4. Remove the phyllo dough from the box, unfold, and cover with a damp tea towel. Place 1 sheet of phyllo on the work surface and brush lightly with melted butter. Repeat with the remaining sheets, brushing each with melted butter, stacking when done, being sure to keep the unbuttered phyllo covered.

5. Place the apple mixture on the nearest third of the phyllo stack, being sure to leave a 2-inch border. Gently lift the bottom edge of the phyllo stack to cover the filling and fold the side edges over. Continue to roll the stack away from you until the filling is completely sealed in and the seam is on the bottom. Transfer to the prepared baking sheet. Brush the top with melted butter and sprinkle with the granulated sugar.

6. Bake for 30 minutes, until golden brown. Sprinkle with cinnamon and confectioners' sugar. Pass warm caramel sauce to drizzle over the strudel.

Serves 8

Raspberry and Sherry Trifle

This has to be prepared, refrigerated for several hours, and eaten the same day or the next day. It does not freeze, so don't try it. You could present it to your distressed friends in several ways: Buy an inexpensive trifle bowl and send it with a note attached to keep the bowl as a gift. Or you could layer the trifle in a 13-by-10-inch disposable aluminum foil pan. Either way, it's a terrific dessert for a crowd.

One 18½-ounce package Duncan Hines Moist Deluxe Butter Recipe Golden Cake mix

1½ cups dry sherry

7 egg yolks

¾ cup granulated sugar

2 cups whipping cream

2 tablespoons confectioners' sugar

Three 12-ounce packages frozen sweetened raspberries, thawed

Whipped cream, for garnish (optional)

Fresh raspberries, for garnish (optional)

Mint leaves, for garnish (optional)

1. Butter and flour a 13-by-9-inch baking pan. Prepare the cake according to package directions, but use ½ cup of the sherry in place of ½ cup water. When baked, let cool in the pan for about 10 minutes, then invert onto a wire rack to cool completely. Cut the cake into large chunks, about 1½ inches wide.

2. Place the egg yolks, granulated sugar, and remaining 1 cup sherry into the top of a double boiler. Whisk until completely combined. Place the top pan over simmering water (do not let water touch the bottom of the top pan). With a wooden spoon, stir over medium heat for about 8 minutes, until the custard is quite thick, about the consistency of mayonnaise. Let cool.

3. Whip the cream with the confectioners' sugar. Take half of the whipped cream and add it to the cooled custard, stirring well.

4. To assemble: In the bottom of a trifle bowl or a 13-by-9-inch disposable aluminum foil pan, layer one-third of the cake cubes, one-third of the raspberries, and one-third of the custard. Continue layering, ending with custard. Take the remaining whipped cream and completely cover the top of the custard. Refrigerate at least 4 hours before serving.

5. Serve with additional whipped cream and fresh raspberries and a sprig of mint, if desired.

Serves 12

Tassie Cups with Lemon Curd Filling

You can make dozens of these and freeze them in plastic bags. Defrost and recrisp for 5 minutes in a 350°F oven before filling.

One 3-ounce package cream cheese, softened

½ **cup (1 stick) butter or margarine, softened**

1 **cup all-purpose flour**

¼ **teaspoon salt**

1. Place all of the ingredients in a food processor and pulse until the mixture forms a ball. Wrap in plastic wrap and chill until firm, about 1 hour.

2. Preheat the oven to 350°F. Form the pastry into 24 small balls; press with fingers into the bottom and up the sides of ungreased miniature muffin tins.

3. Bake for 20 minutes, until lightly browned.

Makes 24 cups

Lemon Curd

This is delicious on toast, and to die for on toasted pound cake. Don't fill the tassie cups until just before the party, so they won't get soggy.

3 **large lemons**

1 **cup sugar**

4 **eggs**

½ **cup (1 stick) butter, melted**

1. Grate the zest from the lemons, then juice the lemons. Place the zest and sugar in a food processor and process until combined. Add the lemon juice and eggs and process until smooth. Slowly add the butter to the mixture, pulsing as you go.

2. Place the mixture in the top of a double boiler and cook over simmering water for about 5 minutes, until thick. The lemon curd will keep in a jar in the refrigerator for up to 3 weeks.

Makes enough filling for 24 tassie cups

Mini Chocolate Éclairs

I made these on my "House Tour" episode. They look beautiful on a silver tray, and can be frozen in an airtight container until party time.

Pastry

- ½ cup (1 stick) margarine or butter
- 1 cup sifted all-purpose flour
- 4 eggs

Filling

- 3 cups whole milk
- ¾ cup sugar
- ½ teaspoon salt
- 6 tablespoons flour
- 3 eggs, lightly beaten
- 2 teaspoons vanilla extract

Icing

- 2 squares (2 ounces) unsweetened chocolate
- 2 cups sugar
- 1 cup whipping cream

1. Preheat the oven to 400°F. Grease a cookie sheet or line with parchment paper.

2. To make the pastry: Bring 1 cup water and the margarine to a boil. Add the flour and stir constantly until the mixture is smooth and forms a ball. Remove from the heat and let cool. Beat in the eggs, one at a time. Drop the dough by teaspoonfuls onto the prepared cookie sheet. Bake for approximately 30 minutes, or until light brown. Set aside on a rack to cool.

3. To make the filling: Combine the milk, sugar, salt, and flour in a medium saucepan; cook slowly until mixture thickens, stirring constantly. Add the eggs and cook, stirring, until the mixture is even thicker, about the consistency of mayonnaise. Remove from the heat, let cool, and add the vanilla.

4. With a serrated knife, slice the pastry puffs lengthwise but not all the way through. Pipe the custard into the center.

5. To make the icing: Melt the chocolate in the microwave at full power for 30 seconds; place in a medium saucepan and stir, then add the sugar and cream. Cook over medium heat until soft ball stage, 240°F on a candy thermometer. Let cool and beat until smooth. Ice the tops of the éclairs.

Makes 24 medium or 60 mini éclairs

Tortilla Dessert Wraps

My son Bobby got a variation of this recipe from a pretty señorita friend of his, and he re-created the original recipe for my barbecue special. It's really easy; the kids can assemble them themselves. My website reviewers rate this recipe five stars!

½ cup almond paste
Four 8-inch flour tortillas
1 cup mini marshmallows
½ cup milk chocolate chips
⅓ cup coconut flakes
Canned whipped cream

1. Crumble 2 tablespoons of the almond paste evenly over each tortilla. Sprinkle one-fourth of the marshmallows, one-fourth of the chocolate chips, and one-fourth of the coconut on half of each tortilla. Roll up the tortillas, wrap each in heavy-duty aluminum foil, and seal tightly.

2. Cook in the coals for about 5 to 8 minutes, until the chocolate is melted. Remove the foil and place on a plate. Garnish with whipped cream.

Serves 4

Note: To prepare in the oven, prepare as above and place on baking sheet. Bake in preheated 375°F oven for 5 minutes.

S'mores

No camping trip is complete without this yummy treat. Roast marshmallows on green sticks or coat hangers that you bring from home already unfolded.

For each s'more:
1 marshmallow
2 graham cracker squares
Half a 1½-ounce chocolate bar

Roast the marshmallow until done to your liking. Remove and place on top of 1 graham cracker. Top with the chocolate. Place the other graham cracker on the chocolate and press together to make a "sandwich." Plan to have at least 2 per person.

Chocolate Bundles with Chocolate Sauce

Frozen puff pastry is really a cook's good friend; you can create so many wonderful dishes with so little effort! When I make these for Michael, I use miniature Snickers—his favorite candy bar—for the filling. Choose your sweetie's favorite candy; he (or she!) will appreciate the thought.

Bundles

1 sheet frozen puff pastry dough

2 eggs

1 teaspoon whipping cream

8 chocolate Kisses

8 miniature chocolate candy bars

Chocolate Sauce

½ cup whipping cream

4 ounces milk chocolate, broken into small pieces

Sweetened whipped cream (optional)

Sliced fresh strawberries, for garnish

Mint sprigs, for garnish

1. Preheat the oven to 350°F. Line a cookie sheet with parchment paper.

2. To make the bundles, allow the puff pastry to thaw, covered, for 30 minutes at room temperature. When it is pliable, unfold the pastry and cut the sheet into four 4-by-4-inch squares.

3. Beat the eggs and cream together to make an egg wash. Brush the entire surface of each pastry square with the egg wash. In the center of each pastry square, place 2 chocolate Kisses and 2 mini candy bars. Pull the corners of each square up around the chocolate, and twist the top of the dough clockwise to complete the "bundle." Brush the exteriors of the chocolate bundles with more egg wash.

4. Place the bundles on the cookie sheet. Bake about 35 minutes, until golden brown.

5. To make the chocolate sauce: In a small saucepan, bring the cream to a boil. Place the chocolate pieces in a bowl and pour the hot cream over the top. Whisk until the sauce is smooth.

6. Puddle the chocolate sauce on a plate and place a bundle on top. Top with whipped cream and additional chocolate sauce, if desired. Serve the bundles garnished with strawberry slices and mint sprigs.

Makes 4 chocolate bundles

Turtle Pizza

It is hard to think about movies without thinking about candy! For your next movie night, here's a "pizza" inspired by the flavors of the traditional Turtle.

Four 10-inch flour tortillas

One 12-ounce package caramel candies, unwrapped

½ **cup sweetened condensed milk**

1 **cup chocolate chips**

1 **cup toasted pecan pieces**

1. Preheat the oven to 350°F.

2. Cut each tortilla into 8 wedges. Bake the tortilla wedges for 7 to 9 minutes, until a light golden color. (If you try to cut the baked tortilla, it will break and crack.)

3. Combine the caramels and condensed milk in a microwave-safe glass dish. Microwave on high (100%) for 1 minute, stir, and microwave again for 1 minute. Stir again. When the caramels are melted, stir the mixture until it is smooth. Spread it evenly on the 32 tortilla wedges.

4. Melt the chocolate chips in a microwave-safe glass dish on high (100%) for 1 minute, stir, and micro-wave 10 seconds more. Stir until smooth. Spread the chocolate layer over the caramel layer. Sprinkle the pecans evenly over the chocolate. Refrigerate until serving time.

Makes 32 wedges

Magnolia Lace Trumpets

These are so pretty on a plate. When I serve them, everyone oohs and aahs.

½ cup sugar

½ cup (1 stick) butter

⅓ cup dark corn syrup

¾ cup all-purpose flour

½ teaspoon ground ginger

1 tablespoon Irish cream liqueur (optional)

Filling

1½ cups vegetable shortening

½ cup (1 stick) butter, softened

1½ cups sugar

1 egg white

2 teaspoons vanilla extract

½ cup hot milk

1. Preheat the oven to 350°F. Line a cookie sheet with aluminum foil or a nonstick baking mat. Lightly grease the foil. (If you don't grease the foil, the cookies will stick and be ruined.)

2. In a medium saucepan, combine the sugar, butter, and corn syrup. Cook the mixture over low heat until the butter melts, then remove from the heat. In a small bowl, stir together the flour and ginger and add to the butter mixture, mixing well. Stir in the liqueur, if desired.

3. Drop the batter by rounded teaspoonfuls 3 to 4 inches apart onto the prepared cookie sheet. Bake only 2 or 3 cookies at a time because they will spread, and you must work quickly to form the cones before they cool and become brittle. (If the cookies do become too brittle to roll, put them back in the oven for a minute to soften.)

4. Bake for 9 to 10 minutes, until bubbly and golden brown. Quickly invert the cookies onto another cookie sheet and wrap each cookie around the greased handle of a wooden spoon or a metal cone, available from specialty cookware stores. When the cookie is set, slide it off the spoon or cone; let cool on a wire rack.

5. While the cookies are cooling, make the filling: Using an electric mixer, cream together the shortening and butter. Add the sugar and beat well. Add the egg white and vanilla; beat thoroughly. Add the hot milk, 1 tablespoon at a time, and beat until creamy. Put the filling into a pastry tube fitted with the star tip and fill the cookies.

6. To store: Place unfilled cookies in a single layer in an airtight container. Store at room temperature in a cool, dry place for up to 3 days, or freeze unfilled cookies for up to 3 months. Thaw the cookies and fill.

Makes 2½ dozen

Lemon Blossoms

These little cakes are literally dunked in lemony glaze. The vegetable oil gives the glaze a little crispness. Betcha your guests can't eat just one!

This recipe makes 60 little "blossoms." If you don't have enough muffin tins or oven space to make all 60 at once (and I don't know anyone who does!), you can bake two or three tins at a time. While the first cakes are cooling, wash, dry, respray, and refill the tins, then bake.

One 18½-ounce package yellow cake mix

One 3½-ounce package instant lemon pudding mix

4 large eggs

¾ cup vegetable oil

Glaze

4 cups confectioners' sugar

⅓ cup fresh lemon juice

Grated zest of 1 lemon

3 tablespoons vegetable oil

1. Preheat the oven to 350°F. Spray miniature muffin tins with vegetable oil cooking spray.

2. Combine the cake mix, pudding mix, eggs, and oil and blend well with an electric mixer until smooth, about 2 minutes. Pour a small amount of batter (about a tablespoon) into each cup of the prepared tins. Bake for 12 minutes. Turn out onto a tea towel.

3. To make the glaze: Sift the sugar into a mixing bowl. Add the lemon juice, zest, oil, and 3 tablespoons water. Mix with a spoon until smooth. With fingers, dip the cupcakes into the glaze while they're still warm, covering as much of the cake as possible. Or spoon the glaze over the warm cupcakes, turning them to completely coat. Place on wire racks with waxed paper underneath to catch any drips. Let the glaze set thoroughly (this may take an hour) before storing in containers with tight-fitting lids.

Makes 5 dozen

Lemon Bars

Tart lemon bars on a shortbread crust look pretty and are a real crowd-pleaser.

Crust

- 1 **cup (2 sticks) butter, melted**
- 2 **cups all-purpose flour**
- 1 **cup confectioners' sugar**
- 1/8 **teaspoon salt**

Filling

- 6 **eggs**
- 3 **cups granulated sugar**
- 3 **tablespoons grated lemon zest**
- 1/2 **cup fresh lemon juice**
- 1 **cup all-purpose flour**

  Additional confectioners' sugar for dusting

1. Preheat the oven to 350°F. Spray a 9-by-13-inch pan with vegetable oil cooking spray.

2. To make the crust: Combine the butter, flour, confectioners' sugar, and salt in a glass bowl. Mix with spoon or fingers until well combined. Shape into a ball and pat into the prepared pan. Bake for 15 to 20 minutes, until set and just beginning to turn color.

3. To make the filling: While the crust is baking, using an electric mixer at medium speed, beat together the eggs, granulated sugar, lemon zest, lemon juice, and flour. Pour over the baked crust and bake for an additional 30 to 35 minutes, until golden brown. Let cool completely, then sift confectioners' sugar over the top. Cut, then cover with plastic wrap and refrigerate until serving.

Makes 24 large or 48 small bars

Lemon Cups

Crisp phyllo cups are filled with tangy lemon curd. They're so good with tea! Don't fill the cups until the last minute or they'll become soggy.

3 **large lemons**

1 **cup sugar**

4 **eggs**

½ **cup (1 stick) butter**

Two 15-count packages frozen mini phyllo (filo) shells, thawed

Slivers of fresh fruit— strawberries or kiwi—or blueberries, for garnish (optional)

1. Grate the zest from the lemons, then juice the lemons. Combine the zest and sugar in the bowl of a food processor fitted with the steel blade and process to mix. Add the lemon juice and eggs and process until blended.

2. Melt the butter in a double boiler. Add the egg mixture to the butter and stir until blended. Cook over medium-low heat until the mixture thickens, about 5 minutes.

3. Pour the lemon curd into a plastic container with a lid and allow to cool. Refrigerate until ready to use.

4. Spoon or pipe the cold lemon filling into the phyllo shells. Garnish with fresh fruit, if desired. Serve at once.

Makes 24 to 30 cups

Notes: Phyllo cups may be stored frozen, refrigerated, or at room temperature. If frozen, thaw at room temperature for 10 minutes. The cups may also be heated for extra crispness. Place the shells on a baking sheet and bake for 3 minutes at 350°F. Allow the shells to cool before filling.

Pecan Squares

This is an old-fashioned boiled cookie. I cut these into very tiny pieces, as they are very sweet, like a praline.

4 eggs

One 1-pound box light brown sugar

1½ cups all-purpose flour

½ teaspoon baking powder

1 teaspoon vanilla extract

1½ cups chopped pecans

1. Preheat the oven to 350°F. Spray a 13-by-9-inch pan with vegetable oil cooking spray and dust with flour.

2. In a medium bowl, beat the eggs with a whisk. Stir in the brown sugar until smooth. Pour into the top of a double boiler. Cook the mixture over simmering water for 20 minutes, stirring constantly, until it reaches the soft boil stage on a candy thermometer, 240°F. Let cool for 5 minutes.

3. Sift the flour and baking powder together. Stir into the cooked mixture. Add the vanilla and pecans and stir until combined. (The batter will be thin.) Pour the batter into the prepared pan and place the pan in the oven. Bake for 12 minutes.

4. Allow to cool completely in the pan before cutting into pieces. Store in the refrigerator in an airtight tin.

Makes 48 pieces

Brown Sugar Chewies

These are always a surprise, because people are expecting brownies. Instead, they get a chewy butterscotch treat!

¼ cup (½ stick) butter

1 cup packed light brown sugar

1 egg, beaten

¾ cup all-purpose flour

1 teaspoon baking powder

½ teaspoon vanilla extract

¼ cup chopped pecans

Confectioners' sugar for dusting

1. Preheat the oven to 350°F. Spray an 8-inch square pan with vegetable oil cooking spray.

2. In a small saucepan, melt the butter. Turn off the heat, add the brown sugar, and stir until smooth. Stir in the egg. Sift together the flour and baking powder and stir into the brown sugar mixture. Add the vanilla and pecans.

3. Pour the batter into the prepared pan and bake for 20 minutes.

4. When cool, dust the top with a sifting of confectioners' sugar. After cutting into squares, remove from the pan and store in a plastic container with a tight-fitting lid.

Makes 16 small squares

Pumpkin Bars

These are so moist and delicious! Because canned pumpkin is sometimes considered "seasonal" by grocery stores, it may be hard to come by. When it's available, stock up so you can always make these in a hurry. This recipe is from Patty Ronning's files.

4 eggs

1⅔ cups granulated sugar

1 cup vegetable oil

One 15-ounce can pumpkin

2 cups sifted all-purpose flour

2 teaspoons baking powder

2 teaspoons ground cinnamon

1 teaspoon salt

1 teaspoon baking soda

Icing

One 3-ounce package cream cheese, softened

½ cup (1 stick) butter or margarine, softened

2 cups sifted confectioners' sugar

1 teaspoon vanilla extract

1. Preheat the oven to 350°F.

2. Using an electric mixer at medium speed, combine the eggs, sugar, oil, and pumpkin until light and fluffy. Stir together the flour, baking powder, cinnamon, salt, and baking soda. Add the dry ingredients to the pumpkin mixture and mix at low speed until thoroughly combined and the batter is smooth.

3. Spread the batter in an ungreased nonstick 13-by-10-inch baking pan. Bake for 30 minutes. Let cool completely before frosting.

4. To make the icing: Combine the cream cheese and butter in a medium bowl with an electric mixer until smooth. Add the sugar and mix at low speed until combined. Stir in the vanilla and mix again. Spread on cooled pumpkin bars.

Makes 48 small bars or 24 larger ones

Crème de Menthe Brownies

These are a staple at Savannah St. Pat's parties. And no wonder. They look beautiful and taste delicious!

4 ounces (4 squares) unsweetened baking chocolate

1 cup (2 sticks) butter

4 large eggs

2 cups granulated sugar

½ teaspoon salt

1 teaspoon vanilla extract

1 cup all-purpose flour

Filling

½ cup (1 stick) butter, softened

2 cups sifted confectioners' sugar

4 tablespoons green crème de menthe

Icing

6 ounces (1 cup) semisweet chocolate chips

6 tablespoons (¾ stick) butter

1. Preheat the oven to 350°F. Spray a 13-by-9-inch baking pan with vegetable oil cooking spray.

2. In a double boiler, melt the chocolate and butter over simmering water. Cool slightly.

3. In a medium mixing bowl, beat the eggs with a whisk until blended, then add the sugar and continue whisking until the mixture is light and fluffy. Add the cooled chocolate mixture, the salt, vanilla, and flour. Beat with the whisk until all of the ingredients are thoroughly blended.

4. Pour the batter into the prepared pan. Bake for 25 minutes. Cool in the pan.

5. Make the filling: With an electric mixer, beat together the butter and sugar until well blended. Stir in the crème de menthe. Blend well. Spread over the cooled brownies. Refrigerate in the original baking pan until the filling is firm.

6. Make the icing: Melt the chocolate chips and butter in the top of a double boiler. Stir until smooth. Pour the warm glaze over the filling. Tilt the pan to ice the filling evenly. Refrigerate until the chocolate hardens.

7. To cut the brownies, remove the pan from the refrigerator and allow the brownies to come to room temperature so the chocolate will not crack. Cut into 48 brownies. Remove the brownies from the pan and store in the refrigerator in an airtight container.

Makes 48 brownies

Symphony Brownies

Symphony bars take brownies to a whole new level.

One 17.6-ounce package brownie mix with walnuts

Three 6-ounce Symphony candy bars with almonds and toffee chips

1. Prepare the brownie mix according to the package directions.

2. Line a 13-by-9-inch cake pan with aluminum foil and spray with vegetable oil cooking spray. Spoon in half of the brownie batter and smooth with a spatula or the back of a spoon. Place the candy bars side by side on top of the batter. Cover with the remaining batter.

3. Bake according to package directions. Let cool completely, then lift from the pan using the edges of the foil. This makes it easy to cut the brownies into squares.

Makes 24 large or 48 small brownies

These brownies make a spectacular party dessert. Slightly warm a 2-by-2-inch square for 10 seconds in the microwave. Serve with a scoop of French vanilla ice cream, fresh raspberries, and a sprig of mint. Beautiful and delicious!

Maggie's Decadent Brownies

These are so fudgy and rich, you can't have but a little taste. Then, a minute later, you want just one more taste. The next thing you know, the pan is empty!

4 ounces (4 squares) unsweetened chocolate

1 cup (2 sticks) butter—no substitute!

4 large eggs

2 cups sugar

1 teaspoon vanilla extract

1 cup all-purpose flour, sifted

Frosting

4 ounces (4 squares) unsweetened chocolate

1 cup (2 sticks) butter, softened

½ cup pasteurized egg substitute, such as Egg Beaters

1 teaspoon vanilla extract

One 1-pound box confectioners' sugar, sifted

4 cups mini marshmallows

1. Preheat the oven to 350°F. Grease a 12-by-9-inch baking pan.

2. Melt the chocolate and butter in a 2-quart bowl in the microwave on high for 2 minutes. Stir until the chocolate is completely melted. Add the eggs, sugar, and vanilla and mix well with a spatula. Add the flour and stir to combine. Spread the batter evenly in the prepared pan. Bake for 25 minutes.

3. While the brownies are baking, make the frosting: Melt the chocolate and butter in a medium bowl in the microwave on high for 3 minutes. Stir until the chocolate is completely melted. Add the egg substitute, vanilla, and sugar and stir with a spoon until smooth. Stir in the marshmallows; they will soften but not melt completely. Spread the frosting over the warm brownies. The frosting will set up when the brownies are completely cooled. When cool, cut into 1½-inch squares and store in the refrigerator in a plastic container with a snap-on lid.

Makes 4 dozen

Savannah Bow Ties

I call this "my ultimate cookie recipe." I just think it's the best.

1 sheet frozen puff pastry from a 17¼-ounce package

½ cup almond paste

1 egg, separated

¼ cup packed light brown sugar

2 teaspoons milk

Flour for dusting the work surface

Granulated or coarse sugar, for sprinkling

Chocolate Dipping Sauce

¾ cup granulated sugar

2 tablespoons cornstarch

¼ teaspoon salt

Six 1½-ounce milk chocolate bars

2 cups whipping cream

1 egg yolk, beaten

½ teaspoon vanilla extract

1. Let the puff pastry stand at room temperature for 20 minutes, or until easy to roll. Preheat the oven to 400°F. Line cookie sheets with aluminum foil, parchment paper, or nonstick baking mats.

2. Crumble the almond paste into a small mixing bowl. Add the egg yolk, brown sugar, and milk. Beat with an electric mixer at medium speed until well combined. The filling will be very stiff.

3. Unfold the pastry on a lightly floured surface. Roll out into a 14-inch square. Cut the square in half with a fluted pastry wheel.

4. Drop dollops of filling uniformly over one of the rectangles of dough. Spray a piece of waxed paper with vegetable oil cooking spray and use it to press the filling evenly over the dough. Spray the waxed paper as often as necessary to prevent the filling from sticking.

5. Place the remaining rectangle on top of the filling. Using a fluted pastry wheel, cut the dough crosswise into fourteen 1-inch-wide strips, then cut each strip in half to make 28 pieces. Twist each piece twice. Place the twists about 2 inches apart on the prepared cookie sheets. Brush the twists with lightly beaten egg white. Sprinkle with granulated sugar.

6. Bake for 12 to 15 minutes, until golden. Transfer to wire racks to cool.

7. While the cookies are cooling, make the Chocolate Dipping Sauce: In a saucepan, stir together the sugar, cornstarch, and salt. Crumble the chocolate bars in one at a time. Gradually stir in the cream. Cook, stirring, over low heat until the chocolate is melted. In a

small bowl, combine ½ cup of the hot chocolate sauce with the egg yolk. Add the yolk mixture to the pot and cook, stirring, until the sauce comes to a boil. Remove from the heat. Stir in the vanilla and pour into a serving bowl. Any remaining sauce can be poured into custard cups, refrigerated, and served as pudding.

8. Serve the cookies with Chocolate Dipping Sauce.

Makes 28 cookies

Lace Cookies

This is a lacy, crisp, buttery cookie. The batter spreads considerably due to the high butter content and the small amount of flour in the recipe. These are so good that one of our young friends, Cameron Curlee, has requested them in her Christmas stocking instead of candy! Now, that's a good cookie!

½ cup (1 stick) butter or margarine, softened

1 cup sugar

1 egg

1 teaspoon vanilla extract

3 tablespoons all-purpose flour

½ teaspoon salt

1 cup quick-cooking oatmeal (not instant!)

1. Preheat the oven to 350°F. Line cookie sheets with aluminum foil, parchment paper, or nonstick baking mats.

2. Using an electric mixer at low speed, cream the butter and sugar until thoroughly combined. Add the egg and vanilla and mix well. Stir in the flour, salt, and oatmeal, mixing well with a spoon. Drop by teaspoonfuls 2 inches apart onto the prepared cookie sheets. Bake for 5 to 8 minutes, until lightly browned. Let cool completely before removing from the sheets; peel cookies away from the lining.

Makes 2½ dozen

Paula's Ultimate Oatmeal Cookies

I created this recipe on my television show. I could have eaten the whole plateful myself—and I just about did!

½ cup (1 stick) butter, softened

½ cup vegetable shortening

1½ cups packed light brown sugar

2 eggs

½ cup buttermilk

1¾ cups all-purpose flour

1 teaspoon baking soda

½ teaspoon salt

1 teaspoon baking powder

1 teaspoon ground ginger

1 teaspoon freshly grated nutmeg

1 teaspoon ground cinnamon

¼ teaspoon ground cloves

½ teaspoon ground allspice

2½ cups quick-cooking oatmeal (not instant!)

1 cup raisins

1½ cups chopped walnuts

1 teaspoon vanilla extract

Brown Butter Icing

½ cup (1 stick) butter

3 cups sifted confectioners' sugar

1 teaspoon vanilla extract

1. Preheat the oven to 350°F. Line cookie sheets with parchment paper or nonstick baking mats.

2. Using an electric mixer, cream together the butter, shortening, and sugar at low speed until fluffy. Add the eggs and beat until the mixture is light in color. Add the buttermilk and mix to combine.

3. Sift together the flour, baking soda, salt, baking powder, ginger, nutmeg, cinnamon, cloves, and allspice. At low speed, gradually add the dry ingredients. Using a spatula, fold in the oatmeal, raisins, walnuts, and vanilla, blending well. Drop by rounded teaspoonfuls 1½ inches apart onto the prepared cookie sheets. Bake for 12 to 15 minutes.

4. While the cookies are baking, make the icing: In a small saucepan, heat the butter over medium heat until golden brown, stirring occasionally. Remove the saucepan from the heat; stir in the sugar and vanilla. Stir in enough water (3 to 4 tablespoons) to make an icing of drizzling consistency.

5. Remove the cookies to wire racks to cool. Drizzle with Brown Butter Icing while the cookies are still warm.

Makes about 5 dozen

Rolled Oatmeal Cookies

Martha's mother-in-law, Mona Nesbit, of Statesboro, Georgia, made this recipe regionally famous by serving these to bridge partners, neighbors, and grandchildren.

1 cup vegetable shortening

1 cup packed dark brown sugar

1 cup granulated sugar

2 eggs, beaten

1 teaspoon vanilla extract

1½ cups all-purpose flour

1 teaspoon salt

1 teaspoon baking soda

3 cups old-fashioned oatmeal (not instant!)

½ cup chopped pecans

1. Using an electric mixer at low speed, cream the shortening and sugars until thoroughly combined. Add the eggs and vanilla and mix well.

2. Sift together the flour, salt, and baking soda. Add to the sugar mixture and mix well at low speed. Add the oatmeal and chopped pecans and stir with a metal spoon or spatula until mixed.

3. Spoon about half of the dough onto a sheet of waxed paper and shape into a roll. Wrap securely in the waxed paper, twisting the ends to close. Repeat with the remaining dough. Chill overnight in the refrigerator.

4. When ready to bake, preheat the oven to 375°F. Line cookie sheets with parchment paper or nonstick baking mats. Cut the dough into ⅓-inch slices. Place 1 inch apart on the prepared cookie sheets and bake for 10 to 13 minutes. Transfer to wire racks to cool.

Makes about 4 dozen

Animal-Shaped Sugar Cookies

Just think of all the times you could make sugar cookies and change the shapes to match the occasion! I used to like mine thin and crisp, but after tasting a nice, thick sugar cookie made commercially, I've started worrying less about how thin I roll the dough. Put these in a cute basket for the kids. Grown-ups like them, too.

1 cup (2 sticks) butter at room temperature

⅔ cup sugar

1 egg

1 teaspoon vanilla extract

1 teaspoon almond extract

2½ cups sifted all-purpose flour, plus more for dusting work surface

½ teaspoon salt

Icing

1½ cups confectioners' sugar

1 tablespoon milk

Food coloring

1. Using an electric mixer at medium speed, cream the butter and sugar. Beat in the egg, vanilla, and almond extract. In a separate bowl, combine the flour and salt, then stir into the butter mixture with a wooden spoon. Cover the dough with plastic wrap and chill for 30 minutes.

2. Preheat the oven to 350°F. Grease a cookie sheet, or line with parchment paper or a nonstick baking mat.

3. On a floured board, roll out the dough to a ¼-inch thickness and cut into animal shapes with floured cookie cutters. Place the cookies on the prepared cookie sheet and bake for 8 to 9 minutes, until the edges are just beginning to brown. Transfer the cookies to a wire rack to cool while you make the icing.

4. To make the icing: Sift the sugar into a small glass bowl, add the milk, and stir. If the icing is too stiff to handle, add a teaspoon more milk. When the icing is smooth, divide into thirds. Tint each bowl of icing a different pastel with a drop of blue, green, or yellow food coloring. Spread onto the cooled cookies. The icing will set up when completely dry. Store the cookies in an airtight container until ready to serve.

Makes about 18 cookies,
depending on the size of the cookie cutters

Gingerbread Boys and Girls

Kids especially love these. Serve them plain, and allow the kids to decorate with icing piped from a plastic bag with a hole in one corner made with a toothpick. Red, green, and white icing usually suffices for the holidays. Add miniature chocolate chips, jelly beans, sprinkles, and redhots if you like.

¾ **cup packed dark brown sugar**

½ **cup (1 stick) butter or margarine, softened**

2 **large eggs**

¼ **cup molasses**

3¾ **cups all-purpose flour, plus more for dusting work surface**

2 **teaspoons ground ginger**

1½ **teaspoons baking soda**

½ **teaspoon ground cinnamon**

½ **teaspoon freshly grated nutmeg**

½ **teaspoon salt**

Icing

1 **cup confectioners' sugar, sifted**

1 **tablespoon milk**

Food coloring as desired

1. Using an electric mixer at low speed, cream the sugar and butter until thoroughly combined. Add the eggs and molasses and mix until combined. Sift together the flour, ginger, baking soda, cinnamon, nutmeg, and salt. Add the dry ingredients to the butter mixture and combine with a spoon or spatula. Remove the dough from the bowl and wrap in plastic wrap; place in the refrigerator until firm, about 1 hour.

2. Preheat the oven to 350°F. Line cookie sheets with parchment paper. Allow the dough to sit at room temperature for about 15 minutes, until pliable. Take about ½ cup of dough at a time and roll onto a floured board until about ⅛ inch thick. Cut out with gingerbread boy and girl cookie cutters. You can reroll the scraps.

3. Using a spatula, transfer the cookies from the board to the prepared cookie sheets. Bake for 10 minutes, until just beginning to brown at the edges. Transfer to wire racks to cool.

4. To make the icing: Combine the confectioners' sugar and milk. Divide the mixture into thirds; leave one-third white, and color one-third green and the final third red. Decorate by piping eyes, mouths, buttons, and bow ties.

Makes 18 to 24 cookies,
depending on the size of your cookie cutters

Chocolate Sandwich Cookies

Okay, so this recipe is originally from Ohio. It was clipped from a newspaper cooking column by Judy Poad, Martha's husband Gary's cousin. Judy brought these cookies to a family reunion, and they were a big hit. They are appreciated on church youth group road trips.

Two 18½-ounce packages devil's food cake mix

4 eggs, lightly beaten

⅔ cup vegetable oil

One 8-ounce package cream cheese, softened

½ cup (1 stick) butter, at room temperature

3 cups sifted confectioners' sugar

½ teaspoon vanilla extract

1. Preheat the oven to 350°F. Line cookie sheets with parchment paper.

2. In a large mixing bowl, combine the cake mix, eggs, and oil. Beat with an electric mixer at low speed until completely combined. The batter will be very stiff. Pinch off pieces of batter and roll into 1-inch balls. Place 1 inch apart on the prepared cookie sheets and flatten slightly with fingertips. Bake for 8 to 10 minutes, until a slight indentation remains when lightly touched. Remove immediately from the cookie sheets with a spatula and cool on wire racks.

3. In a small glass mixing bowl, combine the cream cheese and butter until completely blended. Gradually add the sugar and vanilla and mix at low speed until the icing is smooth. Spread icing on half the cookies and top with the remaining cookies. Store in the refrigerator in large resealable plastic bags.

Makes about 4 dozen

Monster Cookies

Donna Haney, Gary Nesbit's cousin-in-law, brought these cookies to the Pennsylvania family reunion. She always made them before camping trips for her kids. You're reading the ingredients list right: there is no flour in the recipe.

6 eggs

One 1-pound box light brown sugar (2½ cups, packed)

2 cups granulated sugar

½ teaspoon salt

½ teaspoon vanilla extract

1 24-ounce jar creamy peanut butter

1 cup (2 sticks) butter, softened

8 ounces M&M's

8 ounces chocolate chips

½ cup raisins (optional)

4 teaspoons baking soda

9 cups quick-cooking oatmeal (not instant!)

1. Preheat the oven to 350°F. Line cookie sheets with parchment paper or nonstick baking mats.

2. In a very large mixing bowl, combine the eggs and sugars. Mix well. Add the salt, vanilla, peanut butter, and butter. Mix well. Stir in the M&M's, chocolate chips, raisins (if using), baking soda, and oatmeal.

3. Drop by tablespoonfuls 2 inches apart onto the prepared cookie sheets. Bake for 8 to 10 minutes. Do not overbake. Let stand for about 3 minutes before transferring to wire racks to cool. When cool, store in large resealable plastic bags.

Make about 6 dozen

Raisin Puffs

These are Martha's son Zack's favorite cookie. They've been sent along on many a church choir tour. Aunt Mary Lou Haney, of Reynoldsville, Pennsylvania, provided the recipe.

2 cups raisins

1½ cups sugar

1 cup (2 sticks) butter, softened

1 teaspoon vanilla extract

3 cups all-purpose flour

1 teaspoon baking soda

½ teaspoon salt

Additional sugar for rolling cookies

1. Preheat the oven to 350°F. Line cookie sheets with parchment paper or nonstick baking mats.

2. Place the raisins and ¾ cup water in a small saucepan and simmer gently until the raisins have absorbed most of the water and are soft, about 5 minutes. Drain.

3. Using an electric mixer at low speed, cream the sugar, butter, and vanilla until thoroughly combined. Sift together the flour, baking soda, and salt. Stir the dry ingredients and raisins into the butter mixture with a spoon. The batter will be crumbly.

4. Gather about a tablespoon of dough in your fingers and squeeze so dough holds together. Roll into a walnut-sized ball. Roll the balls in granulated sugar and place 1½ inches apart on the prepared cookie sheets. Bake for 12 to 15 minutes, until lightly browned and puffed. Transfer to wire racks to cool. Store in airtight tins, as these are quite fragile and have a tendency to fall apart if jostled.

Makes about 4 dozen

Benne Seed Cookies

Benne seed is another name for sesame seed. This is an old favorite Low-Country recipe given to Martha by a Savannah caterer, the late Sally Sullivan. It makes dozens of tiny, crisp brown-sugar cookies about the size of a quarter. Buy sesame seeds in bulk from a health-food store or Asian market; they are much cheaper than those little bitty jars from the grocery! If you can find toasted sesame seeds, you don't have to toast them yourself.

1½ **cups sesame seeds**

   One 1-pound box light brown sugar (2½ cups, packed)

1½ **cups (3 sticks) butter, room temperature**

  2 **large eggs**

  2 **cups all-purpose flour**

  1 **teaspoon baking powder**

¼ **teaspoon salt**

  2 **teaspoons vanilla extract**

1. Preheat the oven to 350°F.

2. If you're using raw sesame seeds, place the seeds in a single layer on a baking sheet. Place in the oven for about 3 minutes, watching carefully. They should just begin to brown lightly. Set aside to cool completely.

3. Lower the oven temperature to 300°F. Line cookie sheets with parchment paper.

4. Using an electric mixer, cream the sugar, butter, and eggs until very light, about 5 minutes. Sift the flour, baking powder, and salt. Add to the butter mixture and stir with a spatula until combined. Add the vanilla. Stir in the cooled sesame seeds. Drop the batter by ½ teaspoonfuls onto the prepared cookie sheets, 1 inch apart. It takes just a dab of batter to produce quarter-size cookies. They will spread into perfect circles during baking.

5. Bake until very brown but not burned at the edges, about 14 to 15 minutes. Important: Let the cookies cool completely on the parchment paper, then peel them away from the paper. Store between layers of waxed paper in an airtight container. These cookies freeze well in tins. They will crumble in a plastic freezer bag.

Makes about 12 dozen

Ginger Cookies

This recipe is the specialty of Gary Nesbit's aunt, Mary Lou Haney, of Reynoldsville, Pennsylvania. "I've been baking these cookies fifty years," says Aunt Mary Lou. "They're one of my family's favorites."

¾ cup vegetable shortening

1 cup sugar

1 egg

¼ cup molasses

2 cups sifted all-purpose flour

2 teaspoons baking soda

1 teaspoon ground cinnamon

1 teaspoon ground ginger

½ teaspoon ground cloves

½ teaspoon salt

Additional sugar, for rolling cookies

1. Preheat the oven to 350°F. Line cookie sheets with parchment paper or nonstick baking mats.

2. Using an electric mixer at low speed, cream the shortening and sugar until thoroughly combined. Add the egg and molasses and beat until completely incorporated.

3. Sift together the flour, baking soda, cinnamon, ginger, cloves, and salt and add to the mixture. Stir until combined.

4. Roll the dough into balls about 1 inch in diameter. Roll the balls in sugar. Place 1½ inches apart on the prepared cookie sheets. Flatten the balls slightly with fingertips. Bake for 12 minutes. Cool on wire racks. Store in resealable plastic bags.

Makes about 3 dozen

Petticoat Tails

This shortbread cookie is made with only three ingredients. How simple is that!

2½ cups all-purpose flour

½ cup confectioners' sugar

1 cup (2 sticks) butter, cut into chunks, at room temperature

1. Combine all of the ingredients in a food processor and process until the mixture just holds together. Dump the dough onto a lightly floured board and knead about ten turns, until it is smooth. Roll into a log and wrap in waxed paper. Place in the refrigerator for 2 hours.

2. Preheat the oven to 325°F.

3. Slice the roll thin, about ¼ inch thick, and place slices on an ungreased cookie sheet. Bake for 15 minutes, until very lightly browned.

4. Cool on wire racks. Store in airtight tins.

Makes about 36 cookies, depending on the diameter of the roll

Mexican Wedding Cookies

This recipe came from a wonderful cook, Catherine Taylor, of Savannah, who always made these for her daughters and grandson.

1 cup (2 sticks) butter, at room temperature

½ cup confectioners' sugar, plus more for coating baked cookies

1 teaspoon vanilla extract

1¾ cups all-purpose flour, plus more for dusting hands

1 cup pecans, chopped into very small pieces

1. Preheat the oven to 275°F. Line cookie sheets with parchment paper.

2. Using an electric mixer at low speed, cream the butter and confectioners' sugar until smooth. Beat in the vanilla. At low speed, gradually add the flour. Mix in the pecans with a spatula.

3. With floured hands, take out about 1 tablespoon of dough and shape it into a crescent. Continue to dust hands with flour as you make more cookies. Place them 1 inch apart from one another on prepared cookie sheets. Bake for 45 minutes. Roll in additional confectioners' sugar while still warm. Cool completely on wire racks and store in airtight tins.

Makes 2½ dozen

Margarita Mousse

Michael really doesn't like for me to cook with liqueurs. If you prefer, you can substitute tequila for the limeade and triple sec for the orange juice. This tastes like an old-fashioned lime fluff.

¾ cup sugar

1 envelope unflavored gelatin

¼ teaspoon salt

¼ cup fresh lemon juice

¼ cup fresh lime juice

¼ cup frozen limeade concentrate (thawed) or tequila

¼ cup fresh orange juice or triple sec

4 eggs, separated

1 teaspoon grated lime zest

⅔ teaspoon cream of tartar

1 cup whipping cream, whipped until stiff

Lime slices, for garnish

1. In a medium saucepan, combine ¼ cup of the sugar, the gelatin, and the salt. Stir in the lemon juice, lime juice, limeade, and orange juice. Stir well. In a medium glass dish, whip the egg yolks until they are light. Stir them into the saucepan and cook over low heat, stirring constantly, until the gelatin is dissolved, about 3 minutes. Remove from the heat.

2. Stir in the lime zest. Transfer to a plastic container and allow to come to room temperature. Cover and refrigerate, stirring occasionally, until the mixture has begun to gel, about 30 minutes.

3. In a large bowl, beat the egg whites and cream of tartar until foamy. Add the remaining ½ cup sugar gradually, beating constantly, until the sugar has dissolved and the egg whites are stiff and glossy. Thoroughly fold together the gelled mixture, the egg whites, and the whipped cream.

4. Place in a glass soufflé dish and chill until firm. Garnish with lime slices.

Serves 10 to 12

Mom's Banana Dessert

When preparing for "A Teenager's Slumber Party" (page 32), serve this yummy dessert after the flip-flops and purses are made, the hair is styled, the toenails are painted. It's a winner anytime. It is another recipe from Patty Ronning's files.

2 cups whipping cream

2 tablespoons sugar, or a little more if you like it sweeter

15 Oreo cookies, crushed in a food processor or by hand in a plastic bag using a rolling pin

4 bananas, sliced

2 tablespoons chocolate syrup

2 tablespoons chopped pecans, toasted

1. Whip the cream with the sugar until peaks form.

2. Fill a large glass bowl with half of the cookie crumbs. Cover with half of the banana slices and half of the whipped cream. Repeat layers with remaining ingredients. Drizzle chocolate syrup over the top layer of whipped cream. Scatter the toasted pecans over all and serve.

Serves 6 to 8

Strawberry Delight

No need to make your own; store-bought angel food cake is fine. If you don't have a trifle bowl, any large glass bowl will do.

1 large angel food cake

One 8-ounce package cream cheese, softened

One 14-ounce can sweetened condensed milk, regular or fat free

2 cups whipping cream

2 tablespoons sugar

Two 10-ounce packages frozen sweetened, halved strawberries, thawed

1. Cut the angel food cake into cubes about the size of a walnut. In a small mixing bowl, combine the cream cheese and sweetened condensed milk, mixing until smooth and completely blended. In a separate medium bowl, whip the cream with the sugar until stiff.

2. To assemble: In a trifle bowl, layer half the angel food cake cubes, cream cheese mixture, whipped cream, and strawberries. Repeat, layering the remaining ingredients, ending with whipped cream and strawberries.

Serves about 16

Chocolate Delight

One 18½-ounce package devil's food chocolate cake mix

Three 3½-ounce packages instant chocolate pudding mix, regular or sugar free

2 cups milk, for making pudding

2 cups whipping cream

2 tablespoons sugar

1 cup chopped pecans, lightly toasted

Chocolate sauce or syrup, any variety, for garnish

1. Prepare the cake mix and bake in a 13-by-9-inch pan according to package directions. Let cool thoroughly, then cut into cubes about the size of a walnut.

2. Prepare the chocolate pudding according to package directions.

3. In a medium bowl, whip the cream with the sugar until stiff.

4. To assemble: In a trifle bowl, layer half the chocolate cake cubes, pudding, whipped cream, and nuts. Repeat, layering the remaining ingredients, ending with whipped cream and nuts.

5. Drizzle decoratively with chocolate sauce or syrup.

Serves about 20

Banana Sherbet

This recipe from Glena Harlan, of Savannah, has been in the Harlan family for more than fifty years. The recipe uses only ½ cup of condensed milk, so I guess you'll just have to make another batch to use up the rest of the can!

¾ cup sugar

2 tablespoons frozen orange juice concentrate

2 tablespoons frozen lemonade concentrate

½ cup sweetened condensed milk

2 ripe bananas, mashed

3 cups whole milk

In an 8-cup glass measuring cup with a spout, combine all of the ingredients. Whisk until the sugar is dissolved. Pour the mixture into an ice cream maker and freeze according to manufacturer's instructions. Serve immediately or store in the freezer in a plastic container with a snap-on lid.

Makes about ten ½-cup servings

Fresh Strawberry Sorbet

Serve this recipe for sorbet at your next ice cream social. Why? Because some people can't tolerate milk products, bless their hearts. This is a great little recipe to have on hand at all times. Kids love it, but it also makes a good palate cleanser during a fancy dinner party.

2 cups sugar

4 pints strawberries, hulled and sliced

¼ cup fresh lime juice

½ cup light corn syrup

1. Bring the sugar and 2 cups water to a boil in a medium saucepan over medium-high heat. Reduce the heat and allow the mixture to simmer, without stirring, until the sugar dissolves, about 3 minutes. Set aside to cool completely.

2. Place the strawberries and lime juice in a food processor and puree. Press the strawberry puree through a strainer to remove the seeds. When the sugar syrup has cooled completely, combine with the strawberry puree. Add the corn syrup and stir well.

3. Pour the mixture into an ice cream maker and freeze according to manufacturer's instructions. Sorbet is particularly soft after churning but firms up after freezing.

Makes about six ½-cup servings

Peach Ice Cream

Peggy Grimsley, of Macon, Georgia, got this recipe from her mother. It tastes like frozen peaches and cream.

1 cup sugar

1 pound ripe peaches, peeled and mashed with a fork or potato masher

1¼ cups half-and-half

1¼ cups whipping cream

1¼ cups whole milk

⅛ teaspoon salt

½ teaspoon almond extract

½ teaspoon vanilla extract

1. Sprinkle ¼ cup of the sugar over the peaches and set aside.

2. Bring the remaining ¾ cup sugar, half-and-half, cream, milk, and salt to a boil in a medium saucepan over medium heat. Let cool until the mixture reaches room temperature, then add the almond and vanilla extracts. Pour the mixture into an ice cream maker and freeze according to manufacturer's instructions, adding the peaches during the final 10 minutes of freezing. Serve immediately or store in the freezer in a plastic container with a snap-on lid.

Makes about ten ½-cup servings

Buttermilk Ice Cream

I know what you're thinking: This can't be good! But it is! Sally Scott brought this tangy surprise to an ice cream social several years back. She got the recipe from Kimi Hoffman, who contributed it to the church cookbook published in 1996. It's so easy and so good!

2½ cups buttermilk

1½ cups whipping cream

1⅓ cups sugar

1 tablespoon vanilla extract

In an 8-cup glass measuring cup with a spout, combine all of the ingredients. Whisk until the sugar is dissolved. Pour the mixture into an ice cream maker and freeze according to manufacturer's instructions. Serve immediately or store in the freezer in a plastic container with a snap-on lid.

Makes about ten ½-cup servings

Butter Pecan Ice Cream

This recipe was made famous by Libby Lindsey, of the Isle of Hope, in Savannah. The buttery pecans are just delicious!

1 tablespoon unsalted butter

⅔ cup chopped pecans

One 13-ounce can evaporated milk

One 3¾-ounce package instant French vanilla pudding mix

¾ cup sugar

1 teaspoon vanilla extract

3 cups whole milk

1. Melt the butter in a small saucepan. Cook the pecans over low heat until they are browned, about 3 minutes. Place on paper towels to drain and cool.

2. In an 8-cup glass measuring cup with a spout, combine the remaining ingredients. Whisk until the sugar is dissolved. Pour the mixture into an ice cream maker and freeze according to manufacturer's instructions, adding the pecans during the final 10 minutes of freezing. Serve immediately or store in the freezer in a plastic container with a snap-on lid.

Makes about ten ½-cup servings

Lemon Ice Cream

Karen Pannell, of Savannah, wows all her guests with this one.

1½ cups sugar

Juice of 3 lemons

1 tablespoon grated lemon zest

4 cups half-and-half

In an 8-cup glass measuring cup with spout, combine all of the ingredients. Whisk until the sugar is dissolved. Pour the mixture into an ice cream maker and freeze according to manufacturer's instructions. Serve immediately or store in the freezer in a plastic container with a snap-on lid.

Makes about ten ½-cup servings

Vanilla Bean Custard Ice Cream

David Slagel created this recipe for a Fourth of July potluck picnic. David and his wife, Katherine, were honored to have been asked to the home of Gary and Deanne Butch, along with the staff and families of Savannah's famed Elizabeth's on 37th restaurant. Gary and his brother, Greg, prepared delicious tuna steaks, and the rest of the guests were in charge of the sides. Needless to say, the cooking was competitive! David and others churned many quarts of ice cream, and his received the highest accolades. Michael and Elizabeth Terry proclaimed that his was the best ice cream they had ever tasted. "David has never quite recovered from this compliment," says Katherine. "Believe me, it is worth the effort!" We adapted David's proportions to use in our countertop machine.

$1\frac{1}{2}$ **cups whole milk**

$1\frac{1}{2}$ **cups whipping cream**

1 **vanilla bean, split in half lengthwise**

3 **egg yolks**

$\frac{7}{8}$ **cup sugar**

Pinch of salt

1. Combine the milk and cream in the top of a double boiler. Scrape the soft seeds from the vanilla bean and add half the seeds and half the pod to the milk mixture. Heat the mixture over simmering water until it is hot and steaming, stirring constantly to prevent scorching, for 15 minutes. Let cool, covered, for 15 minutes.

2. Beat the egg yolks, sugar, and salt with an electric mixer until fluffy and a light yellow color, about 3 minutes.

3. Strain the cooled milk mixture into the egg mixture and mix at low speed until combined, about 2 minutes. Return the mixture to the double boiler and cook over medium-low heat for 10 to 15 minutes, until thick enough to coat the back of a spoon. Strain into a container with a tight-fitting lid. Cool overnight in the refrigerator, or cool the mixture in an ice bath.

4. Pour the cooled mixture into an ice cream maker and freeze according to manufacturer's instructions.

Makes about eight ½-cup servings

Strawberries Dipped in White Chocolate

If you want to be extra-fancy, you can decorate the finished berries with drizzles of melted dark chocolate.

1 pint strawberries

Three 1-ounce squares white baking chocolate

Rinse, but do not hull, the strawberries. Drain and pat completely dry. Melt the chocolate in a glass dish in the microwave on high (100%) power for 60 seconds. Remove, stir, and microwave for 10 seconds more until the chocolate has melted. Allow the chocolate to cool slightly to thicken. Dip the bottom half of each strawberry in the melted chocolate. Twist the strawberry so that the chocolate forms a "tail" at the end. Place on waxed paper to harden.

Makes about 24 strawberries

Chocolate-Dipped Strawberries

Strawberries dipped in chocolate . . . yum-my. You can also make a Cream Cheese Pound Cake (page 220) and cut it into cubes for dipping. The sauce will taste different depending on the type of liqueur you use: a coffee-flavored liqueur gives you a mocha sauce; try an orange or raspberry liqueur, or even dark rum.

One 12-ounce package semisweet chocolate chips

One 14-ounce can sweetened condensed milk

1 **teaspoon vanilla extract or liqueur (optional)**

2 **pints strawberries, washed but left unstemmed**

1. Place the chocolate chips and milk in a 3-cup glass dish. Microwave on high for 1 minute and stir. If not completely melted, microwave for 15 seconds more; stir. Repeat if necessary. When completely melted, stir in the sweetened condensed milk or vanilla extract or liqueur, if using.

2. When ready to serve, reheat in the microwave over low power until warm. Place in a fondue pot over a very low flame and surround with strawberries and pound cake, if using. Have someone stir the pot as needed to keep the sauce from scorching.

Makes about 2 cups

Fruit Kebabs

Kids love fruit, especially when it's cleverly presented. You can buy wooden skewers at the supermarket and let the kids make these themselves.

1 **pint ripe strawberries, hulled**

1 **pineapple, peeled, cored, and cut into chunks**

Green and red grapes

Alternate pieces of fruit on skewers.

Makes 6 to 8 skewers

Watermelon Fruit Basket

This can be the centerpiece on your table.

1 large seedless watermelon,
  about 12 pounds
1 cantaloupe
1 honeydew
1 pint strawberries, hulled
2 cups seedless red grapes
2 cups seedless green grapes
½ cup sugar
½ cup fresh lime juice
1 teaspoon vanilla extract

1. To carve the watermelon, lay a towel underneath it to keep it from rolling. With a water-soluble marker, draw an outline of a basket onto the melon, using a zigzag pattern. Leave a "handle" about 1¼ inches wide across the top. Using a large sharp knife, cut along the marker line. With a melon baller, cut the watermelon into balls and place in a large glass bowl. Refrigerate the melon basket.

2. Make melon balls with both the cantaloupe and honeydew. Add to the watermelon in the bowl. Add the strawberries and grapes.

3. Combine the sugar, lime juice, and vanilla. Pour over the fruit and toss to coat. Cover the bowl with plastic wrap and chill in the refrigerator until ready to serve. Just before serving, transfer the fruit to the watermelon basket.

Serves 18

Ginger~Poppy Seed Fruit Dressing

Serve this in a small bowl next to the fruit for dipping.

½ cup whipping cream
  One 6-ounce can frozen
  orange juice concentrate,
  thawed
1 teaspoon poppy seeds
½ teaspoon ground ginger

Place all of the ingredients in a jar with a tight-fitting lid and shake well. Pour into a serving bowl and use as a dipping sauce for fruit.

Makes 1½ cups of dressing

Puttin' It All Together

The Cookie Swap

Peope may claim to be counting calories and carbs, but few people in their right mind will turn down a homemade cookie, and you can always find people willing to chuck their diets to attend a Cookie Swap!

The Cookie Swap is typically a holiday event, held early enough in the season so that cooks still have time to use their new recipes for their friends and family. But this party also makes a nice wedding shower (every new bride needs good cookie recipes to try out on her new husband and neighbors) or baby shower (every mother needs a stash of recipes to take to preschool parties, swim meets, and ballet recitals). And if you happen to be hosting a neighborhood coffee for a political candidate, a Cookie Swap is a good way to draw constituents.

Here's how this very easy party works: The guests bring a plate of their best cookies, along with copies of the recipe. Guests sample the cookies and take home the recipes they like the most. Of course, polite guests take home one of every recipe so as not to hurt anybody's feelings.

All the hostess has to do is provide a lovely tablecloth and a big centerpiece—showy flowers (hydrangeas, tulips, roses, or sunflowers), perhaps with recipes stuck among the flowers on metal holders. Guests bring their cookies artfully arranged on pretty plates, and the plates are placed on the table. For serving, you can provide small glass or china plates (best) or pretty paper plates (acceptable). Serve lemonade, iced or hot tea, and coffee, although ice-cold milk would certainly be appreciated!

Here's a tip when baking cookies: You will find that lining your cookie sheets will help your cookies brown more evenly and will keep the cookies from sticking. Silpat, a reusable nonstick liner available in kitchen stores, is fab-u-lous, but parchment paper works well, too. The parchment can be used for several batches of cookies, until it gets sticky. Do wipe the crumbs off between batches, however, so the crumbs don't burn.

We've tried dozens of cookies over the years but have whittled the list down to these favorites. Some are preferred by children, some by adults, but there's something for everyone!

An Ice Cream Social

Each June, the parishioners at the Isle of Hope United Methodist Church, in Savannah, welcome the new ministers, whether they are really new or just returning for another year, with an ice cream social. Tables are set up in the social hall and folks are invited to bring in their best homemade ice cream.

Talented parishioners like Matra Jordon are responsible for decorating, which is always casual, sometimes with a red-white-and-blue all-American theme. "Sometimes, I'll just use summer flowers and surround them with items that represent the interests of the ministers, like when I did tennis rackets, balls, and hats for one of our preacher's wives who taught tennis."

The children all head for the sundae table, where they load up on store-bought ice cream, chocolate syrup, and sprinkles. But older and wiser folks make a beeline for their favorite homemade ice cream in flavors like lemon, banana, peach, butter pecan, and buttermilk.

In testing these recipes, we decided to take the easy way out and use one of the tabletop ice cream makers—the kind with the bowl you keep in the freezer. Boy, do those machines make homemade ice cream easy! Most of these machines make 1½ quarts of ice cream, so if you decide to use the old electric or hand-cranked kind, triple these recipes. If the ingredients came straight from the fridge, there is no need to chill the mixture before churning. When you make the vanilla custard ice cream, however, you need to chill the mixture overnight. All of the ice creams we tested had a soft-serve texture right after churning and a more solid consistency after freezing.

Menu

Banana Sherbet
264

Fresh Strawberry Sorbet
264

Peach Ice Cream
265

Buttermilk Ice Cream
265

Butter Pecan Ice Cream
266

Lemon Ice Cream
266

Vanilla Bean Custard Ice Cream
267

SPECIAL OCCASIONS

Valentine's Day

Valentine's Day is a night for lovers and the one day at the restaurant that I take reservations for tables for two.

This celebration is just for me and Michael. Michael's job is to make sure that I have a big bouquet of flowers, and my job is to make him a delicious meal. Some of his favorite foods are shrimp, lobster, steak, and chocolate, so I'll make my version of surf-'n'-turf and something rich and decadent for dessert. 'Course, his very favorite food is oxtail, but that's not a very romantical (that's Michael's word) meal and it's messy to eat. This Valentine's Day, I'll probably set us a table in our private garden and have a fireplace going—real romantic and intimate. After dinner we'll head to the hot tub with some motion lotion!

Some of these recipes appeared in the January/February 2006 issue of *Cooking with Paula Deen* and they are just wonderful! Save any of the leftovers for a delicious lunch.

If I was short on time, I would not be above buying a really high-quality dessert. But the rich chocolate treat—especially if you serve it warm with vanilla ice cream—will end your meal with a bang!

Menu

The Lady & Sons Crab-Stuffed Shrimp
84

Stuffed Beef Tenderloin
121

Garlic Mashed Potatoes
176

Phyllo-Wrapped Asparagus
177

Chocolate Bundles with Chocolate Sauce
236

St. Patrick's Day

Growing up in Albany, Georgia, the only thing I knew about St. Patrick's Day was that if you didn't wear green to school, you'd get pinched. When I moved to Savannah in 1987, I discovered that St. Patrick's Day was a much bigger deal; because Savannah has such a large Irish Catholic population, everybody celebrates this holiday. In fact, the Savannah celebration is second in size only to New York City's.

At one time, I lived on the parade route. I opened my home to family and friends and would feed them a St. Patrick's–style breakfast—link sausage, scrambled eggs, and green grits. My little house would be filled with guests—the balcony would be loaded, and others would be setting up their chairs on the sidewalk outside of the house to get a front-row seat for the parade. Each St. Patrick's Day brings back so many good memories!

Well, after the parade, it would be time to start on the rest of our eating frenzy, and that could be anything from lamb stew to corned beef and cabbage to Reuben sandwiches. So, whether you prefer to celebrate your St. Patrick's Day with a breakfast, a lunch, or a dinner, I think you'll really like these recipes. They certainly are very, very big in our community!

Menu

Lamb Stew
130

Butterhorns
22

Green Grits Pie
224

Crème de Menthe Brownies
245

Easter Dinner

When I was growing up, I went to regular church services with my family. For Easter I always had a new bonnet and a fancy new outfit. Mama would be rushing around, trying to finish the Easter meal, which always featured ham.

After I married and had children, my favorite way to spend Easter was to attend sunrise services, take the children to breakfast, and come back home so that they could see if the Easter bunny had come. They could enjoy their baskets and I could take the opportunity to slip back into bed!

Now that I'm in the restaurant business, I'm back to cooking the traditional Easter meal for my restaurant guests, and it still stars ham!

Like having a big turkey at Thanksgiving, one of the best things about ham is the leftovers. I do love ham salad, and I've included one of my favorite recipes.

Menu

Peanut Butter–Glazed Ham
129

Succotash
189

Spinach-Swiss Casserole
186

Squash Boats
188

Butterhorns
22

Carrot Cake
215

The Next Day

Ham Salad
44

Cinco de Mayo Fiesta

My kids love Mexican food. Savannah has quite a large Mexican population, and we've got some pretty good Mexican restaurants here. The limit to my Mexican cooking has been tacos and beans, but I'm branching out! People think I'm "just a southern cook," and while I take that as a supreme compliment, I do like to try new things.

Cinco de Mayo literally means "Fifth of May," and the holiday commemorates the victory of the Mexican army over the French at the Battle of Puebla in 1862. It is celebrated regionally in Mexico and in some parts of the United States with large Mexican populations. For my family, it's an excuse to cook up some of that delicious south-of-the-border food!

Menu

MARGARITAS
108

GREEN CHILI SQUARES
95

MACHO NACHOS
92

ENCHILADAS DE POLLO (CREAM CHEESE AND CHICKEN ENCHILADAS)
139

ARROZ CON TOMATE (RED RICE)
172

MARGARITA MOUSSE
261

Mother's Day Tea

When I was twenty-three years old, my mother passed away, leaving an incredible void in my life. But I was so blessed that there were other women to nurture and love me as my mother would—my Grandmother Paul, my Grandmother Hiers, my Aunt Peggy, my Aunt Trina, my Aunt Jesse—you know these women have been there for me all of my life.

A woman doesn't have to give birth to you for you to celebrate her on Mother's Day. A perfect example is my niece, Corrie Hiers. The day that her mother, Jill, put her in my arms, I was hopelessly and totally lost in my love for her, and I know the feeling has been mutual over the span of her life.

So if you're like me and have many women in your life whom you would like to make feel special, here's a great idea for an old-fashioned tea. You'll want to plan to have this the Saturday before Mother's Day so that you'll be able to be with your own family that Sunday. You may want to invite some little girls, too, because very few of them have probably ever been to a real tea.

This is an occasion to get out your silver tea service if you have one, or your prettiest china teapot if you don't. Give each guest of honor a personalized Mother's Day card that explains why she was invited. Oh, and be sure to have plenty of tissues handy!

Afternoon tea is an English tradition, and since Savannah was founded by the English, it is the perfect choice for our gathering. Tea is usually an elegant meal served between 2 and 5 P.M., and often includes small sandwiches, cakes, and cookies. There are wonderful teas available now in the grocery store, and tea bags are perfectly acceptable.

For the recipes, we turned to a facsimile edition of a handwritten Victorian recipe book, published by The Downtown Garden Club of Savannah in 1981. You'll see from these recipes that our forefathers loved to eat nuts, even with cheese, and our foremothers loved to use 'em!

Menu

PETTICOAT TAILS
259

PECAN SQUARES
242

LEMON CUPS
241

CHEESE SANDWICHES
42

CUCUMBER SANDWICHES
42

HAM SALAD SANDWICHES
44

GINGER-NUT SANDWICHES
43

ASSORTED TEAS

SUGAR CUBES, LEMON AND ORANGE SLICES,
MILK, MINT

Fourth of July Outdoor Grill Party and Low-Country Boil

The Fourth of July just has to be spent outdoors. I am lucky enough to live in a perfect spot for outdoor celebrating—my house sits right on a creek, and we might see several shrimp boats a day go by. I just love it when all of my family gathers, and the dogs are running around, and everyone—including the dogs—cools off in the creek. When we built our new house, we made a covered outdoor kitchen that we call Michael's smokehouse. We put in an ice maker, a sink, a refrigerator—everything we need to make outdoor cooking convenient. It sits twenty feet from the water, so Michael can tend the brisket while he's enjoying the festivities!

I've included our recipe for Low-Country Boil because that's probably the number one favorite at our house for summer entertaining. You can put all kinds of things in a Low-Country boil, but I really like mine with just sausage, new potatoes, corn (if you can get it fresh), and, finally, big old wild Georgia shrimp. Our Low-Country boils are so good because we don't skimp on the quality of the shrimp—we use those big, juicy 16 to 20 count shrimp—and we take care not to overcook 'em. I don't eat many because I just love the sausage, but there's always somebody else to eat my share! We might throw in some crab legs or blue crab if Bobby's caught some off his dock. We season our pot with Old Bay. And if we have potatoes, my family insists on my serving my potato sauce. You just throw it all out on the table and everybody gets to diggin' in! Then, after everybody's cooled off in the creek, serve a flag cake. So, hang the flag and let's get to celebrating!

Menu

CRABBIES
88

TEXAS BRISKET
118

SLOW COOKER PINTO BEANS
181

HOT SLAW
56

LOW-COUNTRY BOIL
146

TARTAR SAUCE
147

COCKTAIL SAUCE
147

POTATO SAUCE
147

FLAG CAKE
213

A Week at the Lake with the Kids

There is nothing quite like an extended family vacation. You know, not just an "extended" vacation, but one with all the extended family—aunts and uncles and cousins and grandparents! So many of our girlfriends are lucky to have families who have vacationed together for twenty-five years or more, with the number of "guests" ranging from thirteen to thirty and the settings anywhere from the hot sands of a beach to the cool porches of a mountain retreat. We know the old saying about family and fish—don't keep either longer than three days, 'cause they both start to stink. But these families disagree. They claim that some of the best times of their lives have occurred while vacationing together—fishing, crabbing, playing horseshoes, volleyball, cards, Pictionary, Clue, or poker! Food plays a big part in those memories, of course.

When it comes to cooking for a crowd, which is something I know all about, I can tell you one thing: Do as much of the cooking as you can before the vacation or it's no vacation! Nobody wants to be stuck in a kitchen cooking for thirty people if she can help it! Almost everyone has a favorite casserole that can be doubled or tripled and frozen. I do like to serve fresh vegetables—green beans, pole beans, squash or zucchini, sliced tomatoes or fried green tomatoes—to round out the meal. To keep things easy, take along some boxed mixes to make corn or blueberry muffins, or buy frozen biscuits or yeast rolls. Come on, girls, you're on vacation, not competing in the Pillsbury Bake-Off!

We've gathered the best ideas from a variety of friends to present this smorgasbord of winning recipes, primarily casseroles, appetizers, and desserts. Pick and choose the ones that make the most sense to you. Our girlfriends suggest that you divide the cooking responsibilities among the families who will be vacationing, with each family taking a night to cook. This means you'll always have a variety of styles of cooking, and no one person will have to do all the work.

Here are some suggestions for recipes that travel well and hold up for several days: Cream Cheese Pound Cake, page 220; any of the cookies, pages 248–260; Lemon Blossoms, page 239; Symphony Brownies, page 246; Good Seasons Salsa, page 93; and Pimiento Cheese, page 101.

Menu

ALL-PURPOSE CHEESE SPREAD
100

BLT APPETIZER
97

SHRIMP AND SCALLOP LASAGNA
144

PATTY'S SHRIMP CREOLE
151

CUBAN SANDWICHES
45

TOMATO PIE
39

TACO SALAD
53

ALICE JO'S SPAGHETTI SAUCE
192

PUMPKIN BARS
244

A Family Shabbat Dinner

Being invited to a bar or bat mitzvah is a very special honor. When we originally thought of adding a bar or bat mitzvah menu to this book, we spoke with several Jewish friends, all of whom responded, "We had our party catered!"

However, when we asked good cooks Robbie Hollander, a schoolteacher, and her husband, Sandy, a restaurateur whose establishments include The Pirates' House, 45 South, and 45 South Bistro, Robbie had this response: "When asked to plan a menu for a bar or bat mitzvah, my thoughts immediately focused on the traditional Shabbat, or Friday night, dinner. Typically, the large events of this festive weekend are catered. However, we were fortunate to have friends who hosted Shabbat dinners for our son and daughter. This dinner is often held in someone's home for family and guests from out of town. It is an intimate way to greet one another and to welcome the Sabbath together, enjoying a home-cooked meal served on the 'company stuff,' as our children referred to our fine china."

These are the Hollanders' friends' treasured recipes. When Robbie makes the Friday night dinner, she prepares the main meal herself. "However, I do cheat on dessert," she admits, and asks chef Walter Dasher and his wife, Alice, to make the dessert. Walter and Alice provided the apple strudel recipe.

Menu

Chopped Liver
91

Mama's Brisket
119

Sweet Noodle Kugel
11

Asparagus with Shallot Vinaigrette
179

Squash Casserole
187

Sandee's Challah
18

Apple Strudel
231

Thanksgiving

Thanksgiving is my favorite holiday. The whole family gathers together, but you don't have the pressure of gift giving, which to me is so very stressful when you have to really think, "What does this person need that they don't have?," because we've got everything we need. In fact, we're all stinking spoiled. So I adore Thanksgiving because it's all about family, it's all about food, and it's all about just being together.

After my mama and daddy died, we spent every Thanksgiving over in Statesboro, Georgia, where my daddy's brother, Uncle Burney, and my Aunt Glynnis lived. I was like a kid waiting on it; I could not hardly wait. We would have the most wonderful time. There were almost thirty people and Uncle Burney would have to go borrow campers from friends 'cause there wasn't enough room in the house. Aunt Jesse was a very good cook, plus we all would bring our favorite dishes. Bubba's wife would bring lasagna and cheesecakes. Our aunt, Beth Hiers, would bring sweet potato pies and fresh vegetables from Uncle Bob's garden. I would always make chicken potpies, some kind of dessert, and the dressing. I've always used the same dressing recipe through the years—I just don't think it can be improved upon.

If you've got a small family, and you don't want to go the turkey route, a roasted hen is wonderful, or a roasted chicken if you're talking about a really small family. Another way to stay in keeping with the Thanksgiving meal, but really downsize, is to go with Cornish game hens.

But no matter what the bird is, for it to be Thanksgiving, I've got to have gravy, I've got to have the dressing, I've got to have fresh green beans, and I've got to have cranberry sauce. I've got to have some kind of dessert with pumpkin in it, whether it's pumpkin trifle or pumpkin gooey butter cakes or pumpkin cheesecake or pumpkin pie.

In 2005, I tried something new: a turducken—a boneless turkey, duck, and chicken tied together and baked with my famous oyster dressing. With Michael, Jamie, and

Bobby assisting me, and the rest of my family looking on, that show became one of the Food Network's top-rated shows of all time. And now the whole world knows that while our meal is cooking and my home is taking on all those delicious smells, my family sits around and plays poker! Anyway, I'm giving you some of my treasured recipes in this menu so that your Thanksgiving meal can be as wonderful as ours was that day. I feel so blessed every day. I hope you do, too.

Menu

TURDUCKEN 141	BAKED SWEET POTATOES WITH BUTTER AND BROWN SUGAR 173
BROWN GRAVY 141	AMBROSIA 193
SOUTHERN CORN BREAD DRESSING 170	FRESH APPLE CAKE 219
CREAMY MACARONI AND CHEESE 171	DOUBLE-CHOCOLATE CREAM PIE 227
SOUTHERN POLE BEANS 182	PUMPKIN CHEESECAKE 218

Christmas Dinner

My family and I just love Christmas. It's all about family, food, and fun to us. Christmas 2005 had to be one of the most exciting Christmases in recent history. That was because my niece, Corrie Hiers, helped me select the perfect gift to give her daddy, my brother, Bubba Hiers, and we managed to pull off this surprise together, with the help of Bubba's fiancée, Dawn. Bubba wanted a dog, and I was able to find a chocolate Lab puppy in Atlanta. We met the people halfway, picked up the puppy, and managed to hide him from Bubba until Christmas morning. I put a note on his collar that said, "Hi, I'm not sure what my name is, but I know my daddy's name is Bubba. Would you please help me find him?" Well, Bubba was in a state of shock; he couldn't believe that beautiful puppy was his. You couldn't slap the grin off Bubba's face all day long. Well, he named his puppy UB, after Uncle Bubba's, and UB is now Uncle Bubba's very best friend. Do you know how exciting it is to give somebody a gift that they want so badly? For Corrie, Dawn, and me, giving Bubba that dog was giving ourselves the greatest gift by bringing pleasure to him.

I don't do a lot of variations on my Christmas Day meal. At my house, we are full up with turkey and ham from Thanksgiving, and at the restaurant, we have to cook so many turkeys and hams for Thanksgiving, and throw so many parties with turkey and dressing, that I am just sick to death of turkey by the time Christmas rolls around. All I want is beef. My favorite is the standing rib roast, but let me tell you something: I won't throw away a beef tenderloin, either. And naturally, you have to have a tater—a tater's got to be invited to the table in some shape, form, or fashion.

Menu

CRANBERRY HOLIDAY BRIE
98

STANDING RIB ROAST
122

TWICE-BAKED POTATO CASSEROLE
174

BRUSSELS SPROUTS WITH ONION AND BACON
183

DINNER ROLLS

COCONUT POUND CAKE WITH 7-MINUTE FROSTING
208

Index

Underscored page references indicate boxed text. An asterisk (*) indicates that photos are shown in the insert pages.